How the Talmud
Can Change
Your Life

*Aliya: Three Generations of American-Jewish
Immigration to Israel*

Lili Marlene: The Soldiers' Song of World War II
(with Matthew Miller)

*The Chosen Peoples: America, Israel, and
the Ordeals of Divine Election* (with Todd Gitlin)

*Fortunate Sons: The 120 Chinese Boys Who
Came to America, Went to School, and Revolutionized
an Ancient Civilization* (with Matthew Miller)

Conspiracy of Letters (Kindle Single)

God in the Machine: Video Games as Spiritual Pursuit

*A Broken Hallelujah: Rock and Roll, Redemption,
and the Life of Leonard Cohen*

*The Newish Jewish Encyclopedia:
From Abraham to Zabar's and Everything in Between*
(with Stephanie Butnick and Mark Oppenheimer)

Stan Lee: A Life in Comics
(Yale Jewish Lives series)

How the Talmud Can Change Your Life

*Surprisingly Modern Advice
from a Very Old Book*

Liel Leibovitz

W. W. NORTON & COMPANY
Celebrating a Century of Independent Publishing

For information about permission to reproduce selections from this book,
write to Permissions, W. W. Norton & Company, Inc.,
500 Fifth Avenue, New York, NY 10110

For information about special discounts for bulk purchases, please contact
W. W. Norton Special Sales at specialsales@wwnorton.com or 800-233-4830

Manufacturing by LSC Harrisonburg
Book design by Brooke Koven
Production manager: Louise Mattarelliano

ISBN: 978-1-324-02082-0

W. W. Norton & Company, Inc.
500 Fifth Avenue, New York, N.Y. 10110
www.wwnorton.com

W. W. Norton & Company Ltd.
15 Carlisle Street, London W1D 3BS

1 2 3 4 5 6 7 8 9 0

To Lisa, Lily, and Hudson

Each blade of grass has an angel
bending over it, whispering "grow."
—Rabbi Simon, Midrash Rabba, Bereshit 10:6

CONTENTS

How the Talmud
Can Change
Your Life

Introduction

or

How and Why to Read the Talmud

ONCE UPON A TIME, it was told, there was a rabbi who really loved prostitutes.

There wasn't a working girl anywhere in town with whom he wasn't intimately familiar. Every free moment and every spare shekel he had went to seeking out and frequenting harlots, a pursuit so pervasive that the rabbi became known as Elazar ben Durdayya, which, loosely translated, means Elazar, Man of the Dregs of Society.[1]

Imagine, then, how great this seasoned fornicator's excitement must have been when his friends rushed in with a bit of news: there was an ascendant working girl in the game, better than any who'd ever practiced the world's most ancient craft. There were, Elazar's friends added sheepishly, only two problems: This magical new hooker lived far, far away—in fact, Elazar would have to cross no less than seven major rivers if he fancied a visit. And, second, she charged a small fortune for her services, a purse thick with silver coins.

But a man like Rabbi Elazar would not let financial and geographic inconveniences deter him from his mission, and so he toiled day and night, raising the funds he needed and preparing for what he believed would be the trip of a lifetime. Finally, the big moment arrived, and Elazar, his weariness undone by his arousal, knocked on the prostitute's door. He presented himself and his pay, undressed, and began doing what he'd come so far to do.

And then, mid coitus, the woman let out a mighty fart.

Rabbi Elazar froze. The prostitute smiled, and, looking the rabbi right in the eye, said, "Know, Elazar, that just as this fart of mine could never return to where it came from, so, too, can you never repent for your many sins."

Terrified and naked, Elazar ran out, realizing the profound and horrible truth of the prostitute's statement: his life, he now understood, was an uninterrupted stream of debauchery, an existence so base and so vile that no hope of redemption remained. The realization must have driven him mad, because he ran to the mountains, prostrated himself on the ground, and begged for forgiveness.

"Mountains and hills!" he bellowed, "pray for mercy on my behalf, so that my repentance will be accepted."

The mountains and the hills, however, were unmoved. "Before we pray for mercy on your behalf," they told Rabbi Elazar, "we must pray for mercy on our own behalf." Growing more despondent, the rabbi looked up and asked the sky itself to pray that a poor and sorry man might be forgiven. But the sky, too, was indifferent, so Elazar decided to give it one last shot.

"Sun and moon!" he howled, nearly insane, "pray for mercy on my behalf!" "Pardon," said the moon and the sun, "but if we'd be praying for mercy, we'd be praying for ourselves, not for you."

Suddenly, Rabbi Elazar ben Durdayya felt a sense of calm. "Clearly," he said to no one in particular, "the matter depends on nothing other than myself." He sat down, placed his head between his knees, and cried loudly, letting himself feel the real and immense weight of his remorse. Within a moment or two, he was dead.

The story of Rabbi Elazar, however, doesn't end there. As he lay dying, a voice emanated from heaven, informing everyone and no one in particular that Elazar ben Durdayya had just won himself a spot in the World to Come, the future paradise to which only the most righteous are admitted, not as animated carbon-based life-forms but as pure, angelic souls.

Hearing this, Elazar's friends were baffled. "Really?" they asked. "That guy? Rewarded with the sweetest, most exalted prize imaginable, a promise of eternal life? A prize purportedly reserved only for the best and the purest? After being the most debauched dude on the scene?" They were all confused, except for the wisest among them, Rabbi Yehuda HaNasi, who was weeping softly. "There is one who acquires his share in the World to Come only after many years of toil," he said, "and there is one who acquires his share in the World to Come in one moment." That, and more: "Not only are penitents accepted," Rabbi Yehuda HaNasi added, "but they are even called rabbi."

The story of Rabbi Elazar comes to us not from some dimly lit collection of folklore or from a compendium of bawdy tales entertained late at night by inebriated men. It appears, more or less verbatim, in the Talmud, the central text of Jewish theology, ethics, and laws, a mass of volumes compiled over the centuries and studied closely until this very day. And the tale's inclusion is a testament to the Talmud's unparalleled essence as a literary work. The Talmud is concerned both with divine will and with human desire. It is filled with sweeping accounts and competing commentaries. It excavates layer upon layer of meaning in an effort to unearth the intricacies of life and explore the larger question of what, if anything, this life is all about.

The rabbis who cobbled together the Talmud over the course of hundreds of years were the first to point out the enormity of their project, an attempt not only to capture all of God's heavenly laws but also to think through every imaginable human response to each stricture and commandment in the Torah, the Five Books of Moses. The Talmud, they explained, is like a very stormy sea: "Just as in the sea there are small waves between a large wave and the next, so between any two commandments there are the details and the letters of the Torah."[2]

How does one go about floating, to say nothing of swimming, with so many waves crashing into each other? And why should you bother? Ben Bag Bag, a rabbi who lived sometime in the first century, addressed these very questions: "Turn it, and turn it, for everything is in it. Reflect on it and grow old and gray with it. Don't turn from it, for nothing is better than it."[3] His advice on how to read the Talmud is recorded in . . . the Talmud.

Today, we may be forgiven for calling this sort of self-reflection postmodern. And it's precisely this rich and strange weave of attitudes and approaches that makes the Talmud feel so compelling for those of us who spend hours each day clicking on hyperlinks that take us from news of the latest celebrity breakup to a thousand-word screed about global warming. Despite being finally redacted more than fifteen hundred years ago, the Talmud, the writer Jonathan Rosen observed in a masterful meditation, feels a lot like the Internet, that other thicket of interlaced conversations. Even the terminology, Rosen noted, was eerily similar: The Talmud is divided into different tractates; the Hebrew word for each of those is *masechta*, literally, "a web."

"The Talmud," Rosen writes, "is a book and is not a book, and the Rabbi's phrase flexibly found its way into it because, oral and written both, the Talmud reached out and drew into itself the world around it, even as it declared itself the unchanging word of God."[4]

To hear the Talmud tell it, God himself would agree. He,[5] too, we learn in tractate Gittin, spends a few hours each day studying the Talmud; the glorious book that contains all of His laws is so intricate that even the Creator of all things must buckle down and read it.

In fact, imagining the Talmud as the sort of book God reads

in His spare time isn't a bad way to approach reading the Talmud, because to read the Talmud isn't really to read at all. Reading gives us the nearly alchemical satisfaction of forging meaning where none was before. Slowly and deliberately, one sentence at a time, we cobble together some coherence until something like closure, or at least a deeper understanding, appears and quiets our minds. The Talmud issues a very different invitation. It wants us to grapple—with it, with the wise men and women it cites, with tradition, with ourselves, with God. It leaves a lot, if not most, of the story blank and urges us to write the rest.

Consider, for example, that story about Rabbi Elazar. The Tosafists, medieval commentators on the Talmud whose insights the Talmud, too, captures, argued that Rabbi Elazar wasn't really screaming at the skies, but that the conversation was instead taking place largely inside his head, a monologue suggesting just how tortured his soul had become.[6] Writing in Vienna centuries later in the 1920s, Rabbi Aaron Lewin—taking a page, perhaps, from his neighbor, Sigmund Freud—put rabbi Elazar on the therapist's couch and suggested that the mountains represented the sinner's parents and the heavens the superego of society.[7] Nonsense, claimed the Hasidic master Rabbi Yisroel Shapira nearly two decades later, shortly before the Nazis murdered him in Treblinka; the exchange between man and nature was to be taken literally, as a person committed to real repentance is able to unlock the deepest secrets of the universe, bridging the gap between the animate and inanimate and conversing with all of God's creations.[8] Attention, too, was paid to the prostitute. The Ben Ish Hai, a sage who lived in Baghdad in the late nineteenth century, noted that a professional of her caliber surely would've taken precautions to prevent such embarrassing instances of flatulence from occurring, which meant that she, too, was experiencing a moment of transformation. Sensing her own body fail her in this unusual way, she understood the passing of wind as a sign from above, a call back to righteousness for her as well as her client.[9] And Rabbi Aharon Leib Shteinman, an Israeli Orthodox eminence who passed away in 2017, noted that the prostitute represented not just the temptations of carnality but, more acutely, the far more ruinous temptations of despair: it was her insistence that repentance was impossible that woke Rabbi Elazar up, urging him to finally take charge of his life and take responsibility for his actions.[10]

That these commentaries are rarely complementary, often conflicting, and sometimes mutually exclusive is precisely the point. If the Talmud is any one thing, it is a record of centuries of arguments and an invitation to millennia more. These arguments aren't incidental. They are the scars of a civilization again and again facing the possibility of extinction, frantically searching for ways to stay alive when all the odds point in the other direction. The Talmud captures roughly seven hundred years of disputations—from about 180 BCE to 500 CE. This period brought a torrent of calamities upon the Jews, including attempted genocide by the Greeks, the destruction of the Temple and the sacking of Jerusalem by the Romans, a failed revolt that left more than half a million dead, persecution by the Persians, and the rise of a new religion, Christianity, which announced that it had arrived to supplant the more ancient faith from which it had sprung. These weren't mere hurdles; each posed an existential threat to a tiny nation tucked away in a dusty corner of the Mediterranean, squeezed by a succession of ravenous empires, and desperate to protect its monotheistic observance in a world dedicated to competing practices. And yet, the Talmud isn't a record of how the Jews managed to survive. It's *why* they survived—the book itself becoming a shelter to which Jews could safely retreat as their more earthly dwellings were torched.

"The Talmud," Rosen writes, "offered a virtual home for an uprooted culture, and grew out of the Jewish need to pack civilization into words and wander out into the world. The Talmud became essential for Jewish survival once the Temple—God's pre-Talmud home—was destroyed, and the Temple practices, those bodily rituals of blood and fire and physical atonement, could no longer be performed." It was then that "Jews became the people of the book. . . . They became the people of the book because they had no place else to live."[11]

But how to live in a book? How to go from a life rich with corporeal practices to one of contemplation? Jews fulfilling the religious obligation of pilgrimage to the ancient Temple in Jerusalem before Titus burned it down in 70 CE would have been treated, as Jews had for the 423 years during which the Temple stood, to a heady swirl of sights, sounds, and smells. They would've witnessed oxen, sheep, goats, doves, and pigeons being burned at the altar along with wheat, olive oil, and frankincense—the deep aroma of roasted meat laced lightly with perfume. They would've seen the High Priest clad in golden garments and wearing a breastplate of onyx, agate, sapphire, amethyst, and diamonds. They would have heard the Levites singing and blowing the shofar—the ram's horn—in God's praise. What consolation might scrolls and words offer for the loss of such visceral bounties? And why would anyone remain faithful to the old ideas now that the way of life that they prescribed was vanquished?

The sages of the Talmud took these observations and reservations as their points of departure. They understood, as the story of Rabbi Elazar so starkly shows, that humans are blessedly fallible creatures under the best of circumstances and that faced with moral and mortal reckonings, they run the risk of losing their courage and their minds. They understood, too, that guiding the flock forward, through uncertainty and violence, involved much more than merely writing down laws and praying that future generations continued to obey them. Instead, the rabbis chose to record their arguments because they understood a few profound truths about human nature: that change was as terrifying as it was inevitable; that people have a tendency to think of history as a positive linear progression and are therefore likely to view the latest development as necessarily optimal; that the human urge to break rules is just as mighty and eternal as the need for boundaries; and that when all that we know and love and believe comes tumbling down, our first and most disastrous instinct is often to abandon all hope. Give desperate people an order and they'll dismiss it as yet another yoke; invite them into a spirited conversation, and they may just find some way to save themselves.

This may be why so many people still study the Talmud today, including those who do not adhere to Judaism's observances or aren't even Jewish. On the first day of 2020, for example, more than ninety thousand people crammed into New Jersey's MetLife Stadium, home of the Giants and the Jets, to celebrate *Siyum HaShas*, a commemoration of finishing a seven-and-a-half-year cycle of reading Daf Yomi, or one of the Talmud's 2,711 pages each day. Present were bearded men in black hats and robes and young tattooed Brooklynites in denim and flannel, old rabbis who perched each morning over large leather-bound volumes and young women who tuned into one of the many Talmud podcasts, Jews and non-Jews alike who came to share the comfort they found in the world's most confounding, maddening, inspiring, energizing, and demanding book. If marketers sought to slap a tagline on the Talmud—not an urgent need, given the book's surging popularity—they could hardly do better than to borrow a line from the late singer and songwriter Leonard Cohen, himself a Talmud enthusiast: the Talmud is "a manual for living with defeat," a book about what to do when everything seems broken and how to think about life when little about it makes sense.

What, then, is the Talmud?

By now, you won't be surprised to learn that even this seemingly simple question contains multitudes. For one thing, there isn't a single Talmud but two, the Bavli, or Babylonian, and the Yerushalmi, or Jerusalemite, one compiled by Jews who went into exile in the land we now know as Iraq and the other by those who remained behind in the Land of Israel.[12] For another, the Talmud page, as anyone who has ever seen its unique typographical shape knows, is really a collection of sources, with text and commentary presented in parallel columns and inviting readers to skip from one box to another in search of clarity and context. Before we ask ourselves why the Talmud matters, then, and what it has to teach us today, a brief history of it is in order.

The story begins, if it begins anywhere, at the foothills of Mount Sinai. There, circa 1313 BCE, Moses, a stuttering disgraced Egyptian royal thrust into a position of leadership by circumstances familiar to anyone who has ever celebrated Passover or watched *The Ten Commandments*, receives from the Almighty not one gift but two. The first is the Torah, the core—along with later entries—of the Hebrew Bible, which Christians, having later added some new stories of their own about their lord and savior, call the Old Testament. But alongside the Torah, God also bequeathed unto his servant another gift: *Torah Shebe'al Peh*, or the Oral Torah, a long list of laws and statutes not recorded in the Torah but nonetheless binding. The Torah and the Oral Torah alike have been passed down from generation to generation, from Moses to his brother Aaron and from there on down to the elders and rabbis of each generation, a transmission recorded in the Talmud and largely confirmed by archaeologists, historians, and other scholars.

There are many reasons to study the Torah and the Oral Torah—moral instruction, historical record, literary pleasure— but religious Jews continue to grapple with these twin pillars of their faith for a more practical reason: to understand the halacha, the collection of Jewish religious laws that governs everything from what Jews may eat to what they must do should their ox gore another ox. The halacha isn't written down in any one dedicated book, though later rabbis have produced many volumes attempting to make it more accessible. Instead, it is a work of creative interpretation, requiring Jews to study the Torah and the Oral Torah, single out the commandments prescribed therein, and argue over how, precisely, these commandments should be observed.

This the Jews have done even as they rushed forth out of Egypt, wandered in the wilderness, entered Canaan, established a sovereign nation led by King David and his heirs, built the Temple in Jerusalem, split into two bickering kingdoms, fell to the Babylonians, watched the Temple burn, dispersed into exile, returned to the Land of Israel, and rebuilt the Temple. All throughout this dramatic millennium, they continued to study, teach, and debate the stories and the laws they passed down from one generation to the next. Like checking out a library book and tracing the volume's journey from reader to reader, anyone who opens the Talmud can easily follow this precise lineage.

And then the plot thickens.

Maybe it was the arrival of Alexander III of Macedon, nicknamed the Great, the ancient Greek king whose empire, one of the largest in recorded history, spread all the way to northwestern India, carrying with it Greek customs and culture that were anathema to Jewish observance. Or maybe it was *Yeridat HaDorot*, a rabbinic theory that holds that while Adam and Eve pranced around Eden as God's carefree children, each successive generation that followed grew just a bit more alienated from their maker; "If the early generations are characterized as sons of angels, we are the sons of men," Rabbi Zeira informs us in one of the Talmud's earlier tractates. "And if the early generations are characterized as the sons of men, we are akin to donkeys."[13] The rabbis now felt that the plain retellings that passed Moses's laws down from one generation to the next were no longer enough. If tradition was to survive, it needed to be protected by a more rigid system of teaching, one that made sure that Jews—now dispersed across different regions and living largely in mixed communities with non-Jews—continued to study and practice the same laws and ordinances in the same way.

And so began the period of the Tannaim, which literally means those who repeat what they had heard. From roughly 180 BCE to the end of the second or beginning of the third century CE, hundreds of scholars engaged in setting up houses of study, teaching the young, and adjudicating religious disputes. And because religious disputes were many and fiery, especially among those who made study their life's work, the Tannaim often chose a pair among their best and brightest, with one rabbi serving as the *Nasi*—communal leader—and the other as *Av Beit Din*—supreme justice. With each sage checking and balancing his friend's ambitions and convictions, the Tannaim perfected the art of what they called disputes for the sake of heaven, which allowed ample room for interpretation without skidding into schisms.

But disputes, purehearted as they may be, can only carry a people hell-bent on survival so far. Within the span of sixty years, the Jews experienced two tragedies so enormous that each can count as an extinction event. Both involved failed uprisings against Rome. The first, amplified by a bitter civil war, ended with sixty-five thousand Roman soldiers laying siege to Jerusalem and eventually setting fire to the Temple in 70 AD. Sixty years later, Jewish history again took a grim turn when the Roman emperor Hadrian, retracting an earlier intimation that he might rebuild the Temple, instead erected the garrison town Aelia Capitolina over the ruins of Jewish Jerusalem. Within two years, what started as occasional anti-Roman outbursts matured into a second full-court rebellion, led by a brilliant and charismatic Jewish warrior named Shimon Bar Kochva. Fervently supported by Rabbi Akiva, the most prominent religious figure of the day, Bar Kochva was seen as something very close to the Messiah, a redeemer who would cast off Rome's onerous yoke and restore freedom and dignity to the Jews. Three years and hundreds of thousands of dead later, however, all hopes were dashed, and Hadrian, after insisting on personally holding Bar Kochva's severed head, set out to punish the insurrectionists with all his imperial might. Any form of Jewish life or practice—studying Torah, circumcising children, observing the Sabbath, eating matzah—were banned, and transgressors were often punished horrifically; the Talmud notes that one favorite Roman form of punishment involved placing red-hot iron balls under victims' armpits until they succumbed to their burns.

With such threats hanging over their heads, many Jews chose to acquiesce and abandon their religion. Many more struggled to keep it alive, often opting to martyr themselves rather than transgress. The Talmud tells us that Rabbi Yishmael, for example, was skinned alive and that Hadrian's daughter, who found Yishmael attractive, preserved his remains and forced one of her subjects to wear Yishamel's skin like a mask. Luckily, then, when Hadrian died at the age of sixty-two in 138 CE, he was replaced by his adoptive son, Antoninus Pius, largely acknowledged as the most peaceful sovereign of the early Roman Empire. Whereas the father built fortifications—such as the 73-mile-long mammoth in northern England known as Hadrian's Wall—the son built theaters, cultivated relationships with teachers and philosophers, and pardoned many of the men his predecessor had sentenced to death. He also did away with Hadrian's decrees against practicing Judaism, perhaps under the influence of his Jewish childhood friend, the prominent Rabbi Yehuda HaNasi.

How close were the wealthy rabbi and the enlightened emperor? The Talmud regales us with stories, most of which portray the Roman as a bumbling simp eternally grateful for the wisdom of his superior Jewish chum. Here's one example: "Every day Antoninus would minister to Rabbi Yehuda HaNasi; he would feed him and give him [something] to drink." Grateful for the attention, Rabbi Yehuda HaNasi still had the good sense to treat the sovereign with deference and respect. But Antonius wouldn't budge. When the rabbi wanted to retire to bed, the emperor, the Talmud continues, would bend down in front of the bed and say to him, "Ascend upon me to your bed." When Rabbi Yehuda HaNasi refused, Antoninus said, "Oh, that I were set as a mattress under you in the World-to-Come!"[14]

The same keen mind that helped Rabbi Yehuda HaNasi navigate his friendship with the royal also led him to realize that a nation recovering from years of religious persecution needed strong measures to help it regain some of the erudition and confidence it had lost under duress. It was with this insight that he set out to deliver the work that would become the cornerstone of the Talmud: the Mishnah.

Hebrew for study by repetition, the Mishnah is a monumental

codification of the laws and traditions passed down and recited from Moses to the last of the Tannaim. The project of condensing so much information into sixty-three tractates arranged according to six thematic units—known as *sedarim*, or orders, and addressing agriculture laws, Sabbath and festival laws, marriage and divorce, criminal justice, sacrificial rites, and purity and impurity—is so mind-bogglingly vast that scholars have spent centuries commenting on each and every choice made by Rabbi Yehuda HaNasi and his associates. Here, for example, is how the Mishnah begins:

> From when does one recite *Shema* in the evening? From the time when the priests enter to partake of their *teruma*, until the end of the first watch. That is the statement of Rabbi Eliezer. The Rabbis say: until midnight. Rabban Gamliel says: until dawn. There was an incident where Rabban Gamliel's sons returned from a wedding hall. They said to him: We did not recite *Shema*. He said to them: If the dawn has not yet arrived, you are obligated to recite *Shema*. And not only that, but rather, wherever the Rabbis say until midnight, the mitzvah may be performed until dawn. The burning of fats and limbs, the mitzvah may be performed until dawn. And all that are eaten for one day, the mitzvah may be performed until dawn. If so, why did the Sages say until midnight? In order to distance a person from transgression.[15]

What can we learn from this dense and inscrutable paragraph? Unless we are steeped in rabbinic law, probably very little about the actual question at hand, which deals with when Jews must recite the Shema, the central prayer of both morning and evening services. But even to the uninitiated, the passage is telling. Why is the question of timing so central? Why not kick things off with an explanation of the meaning of the Shema, say, or its centrality to Jewish theology, or what we're supposed to be thinking about when we pray, or why we believe that prayers even matter? Why not, in other words, lure readers in with ideas or feelings before saddling them with what appears to be a rather trivial technical question?

And then there's the prose. The Mishnah, still a product of oral culture, repeats itself in clear and easy to memorize sentences—"the mitzvah," or commandment, "may be performed until dawn"—and often transmits snippets of direct dialogue. What it doesn't do is bother to fill in the gaps: What is the *teruma*? It is the portion of produce that is offered to the priests as a sacrifice. What's that about the burning of fat and limbs? It's Rabban Gamliel explaining that the priests, often overwhelmed by the volume of offerings, burned them on the altar all night and into the morning. He uses it to make the analogy that prayers, another kind of offering, may be concluded before sunrise.

But why go on for so long about priests and sacrifices? We say the Shema in private; the priests perform their duties publicly, in the Temple. The contemporary scholar Rabbi Avraham Walfish explains that this probably holds a coded message.[16] The Mishnah tethers the times of reciting the Shema to the priestly schedule because now that the Temple is gone, each of us should see ourselves as a priest and every synagogue as a tiny shard of the Temple. Everything we do should be understood as "a stand-in for the Temple rituals."[17] This turns the Jewish people's central calamity, the loss of God's earthly home, into an opportunity for empowerment, elevating each one of us to an exalted rank.

How might we pull off such a mystical transformation? The Mishnah saves the best for last, setting off one last bit of insight like a depth charge. Think about the central question at hand here: If we go by the priests in the Temple, and the priests attend their altar all night long, why cap the saying of Shema at midnight? The answer the Mishnah gives is brief—"in order to distance a person from transgression"—but it contains multitudes. To understand it, imagine returning home after a long day at the office. You know you're still obligated to pray, but if tradition permits you to conclude your business before the night's over, you may be forgiven for not exactly rushing to the task. First, you may have a martini to dull the day's edge, and then dinner and some time with the spouse and the kids. Then maybe an hour or two of TV and a little stretch on the couch. Hours pass, and you startle yourself awake, realizing that it's already morning. You may no longer recite the night's Shema. You have abdicated your responsibility. Better, then, the Mishnah argues, to set an earlier, artificial deadline, just to make sure well-intentioned but hurried and tired and preoccupied people don't fall behind and needlessly stumble into sin. It's a Talmudic principle known as making a fence around the Torah; it teaches even those of us who aren't believers to identify the things we hold most dear and then take every precaution necessary to make sure we don't mess them up.

This is why each page of the Talmud begins with a snippet of Mishnah and includes sidebars of interpretation and elucidation; the text itself is just an invitation to inquire. The confluence of the sacred and the mundane, the ephemeral and the practical, quickly transformed the Mishnah into a text seen as holding transformational powers.

Still, the Mishnah was too radiant and too elusive to satisfy a people facing life in a still-hostile world. Snippets of rabbinic rulings and allusions to biblical verses; commandments and contemplations; intricate legalistic reasoning wrapped around deep psychological illuminations—no sooner was the Mishnah handed down than the faithful felt that it, too, left too much unexplored and unexplained. It was time for in-depth analysis of what was now the Golden Standard, which called for a new class of scholars: the Amoraim, or those who speak. For eight generations, roughly from 230 CE to 500 CE, these rabbis, many of them living in Babylonia, tore into the Mishnah, fiercely debating its every word or, sometimes, letter. But they were no longer itinerant scholars presiding over disparate houses of study and free to teach in whatever manner they chose; they were now beholden to a uniform written work, which meant that they had to find a different way of engaging in teaching and learning, one that focused intensely on the Mishnah.

How did they do it? Once again, a bit of the real thing is illuminating. Here the Amoraim debate Brachot, Hebrew for "blessings," the first tractate of the Mishnah. "How," the Mishnah asks, "does one recite a blessing over fruit?" A short and uncomplicated list ensues—over fruit growing from the earth, we bless He "who creates fruit of the ground" and over various herbs we thank He "who creates various kinds of herbs"—but the Amoraim aren't satisfied. Why, they inquire, bless at all? What is the deeper meaning of a blessing?

Rabbi Hanina bar Pappa comes in strong. "Anyone who derives benefit from this world without a blessing," he says, "it is as if he stole from God,"[18] the real source of all sustenance. He goes on to offer some biblical passages in support of his ideas, but then remembers that elsewhere, the Bible also says "and you shall gather your grain, your wine and your oil."[19] The first verse suggests that all earthly bounty belongs exclusively to the Creator; the second says that it belongs to the people who cultivate the fields and the vineyards. Which is it?

"This is not difficult," Hanina's fellow Amoraim reply. The grain—and the fruit, and the vegetables, and everything else on earth—belongs to God. When people follow His commandments, God gives them His bounty. When people sin, God takes it all away.

And with that, the Amoraim are off to the races. If God gives us grain when we do his will and withholds it when we don't, should we even, they ask, bother working at all? Why not simply study Torah—presumably, God wants us to know His teachings—and trust the Almighty to furnish us with all our earthly needs? And if He wants us to work as well as to study Torah, how much time should we devote to each? Here the Amoraim, as they so often do, reach back to their predecessors, the giants cited in the Mishnah: "Rabba bar bar Hana said that Rabbi Yohanan said in the name of the *tanna* Rabbi Yehuda, son of Rabbi El'ai: Come and see that the latter generations are not like the earlier generations; rather they are their inferiors. The earlier generations made their Torah permanent and their work occasional, and this, Torah study, and that, their work, were successful for them. However, the latter generations who made their work permanent and their Torah occasional, neither this nor that was successful for them."[20]

Not much more is offered by way of resolution, but not much more is needed. The Amoraic methodology is itself the point. How do you show deference to earlier generations but also take their work apart in order to better understand it and make it your own? How do you pass down religious laws while making sure that your students actually understand the reason for each ordinance and accept each ancient commandment as contemporary and relevant? A new literary approach was needed, one that evolved beyond the Mishnah's condensed and definitive statements and focused instead on a different challenge: how to approach difficult questions, particularly metaphysical ones, especially when humankind's ability to systematically order the world around it was still in its infancy.

The Amoraim attempted to answer this question by creating the concept of the *sugiya*, or issue. A *sugiya* is a question that arises as the Amoraim study the words of their predecessors and stumble upon some difficulty in understanding, which is a pretty good description of the entire purpose of their pursuit. When this happens—and it does more or less on every page of the Talmud—a clear system is set in motion. First, and logically, we hear from earlier generations, those great teachers, the Tannaim, with a handful of them mentioned by name as they opine on the issue. Then the Amoraim have their say, too, and are also named. Finally, an anonymous editorial voice emerges to offer, if not a resolution, then at least a summary of where the issue stands.

These three voices—Tannaim, Amoraim, anonymous—are in constant dialogue, which cracks three important and usually insurmountable barriers. The first two are time and space: If you didn't know that Shmuel, say, lived by the Euphrates in the third century CE while Yohanan Ben Zakai was born in the Galilee nearly two hundred years earlier, you could be forgiven for reading a *sugiya* and thinking that the debate it captures happened in real time and a real setting and that both men had physically met somewhere more corporeal than on a page of the Talmud. Every page is an exercise in literary imagination, the same sort of what-if game that excites children when they clutch their comic books and heatedly debate whether Thor, say, could ever overcome the Incredible Hulk in a fight.

Even more intricate, however, is the third broken barrier, between the sages of the Talmud and us, the readers. That anonymous voice following the words of the great rabbis is an invitation for us all to join in on the fun, a reminder that a *sugiya* is not there to be definitively resolved by the ancient and the wise and the deceased, but there for us, the living, to engage with it, whether we're believers or nonbelievers, Jewish or otherwise.

How does anything get decided then? Sometimes, the *sugiya* is simple enough: one rabbi asks for clarification, another provides information, and the conversation moves on. More often, however, the anonymous voice delivers a delightful Aramaic word, *Kashya*, or difficult, letting us know that there's trouble ahead. Perhaps two previous teachings in the Mishnah appear to be contradicting one another. Or perhaps two statements are cited that seem so similar as to be redundant. When that happens, the Amoraim—with the Mishnah, the Torah, and a strong grasp of logic at their disposal—jump in and argue their way until they're satisfied that they fully understand what the halacha should be. Or not; sometimes we're treated to exhaustive discussions about a particularly thorny *sugiya* only to meet at its end another delightful Aramaic word: *Teiku*, or let the difficulty stand, an admission that even erudition and reason have their limits.

The scholars living in the Land of Israel, mainly in Tiberias and Caesarea, finished collecting their analysis around 400 CE. Their kin in Babylonia, home to a more robust spiritual and intellectual life, concluded their work a hundred years later. Each work was different, sometimes very much so, but both were called by the same name—the Gemara, Aramaic for "to finish" or "to complete." Together, the Mishnah and the Gemara are often referred to as the Talmud, and the Talmud most people speak of and study—and the one that will be cited and discussed in this book unless noted otherwise—is the Babylonian one.

But understanding what the Talmud is or how it constructs its arguments tells us very little about why it would attract anyone but the most fervently Orthodox Jews. Why is a secular young woman's stream of daily reactions to the Talmud—always hilarious, often profane—a viral hit on TikTok? Why did a translation of the Talmud into Italian take only three days to sell out its first print run, and not much longer to run through thousands of copies more? Why do South Koreans turn to the Talmud en masse, gobbling up everything from the Mishnah to illustrated children's books about the Talmud's sages?

There are many plausible theories, but mine is decidedly un-Talmudic in its bluntness: The Talmud grows increasingly popular because the Talmud is good for you.

In an age of screen-assisted loneliness—the rate of teenagers hanging out with their friends in person dropped 40 percent from 2000 to 2015, for example, and continues to decline the more prevalent smart phones, laptops, and tablets become—the Talmud is a call to community, not only inducting readers into a brotherhood of ancient arguers but also encouraging them to seek study partners, online or in real life, and join the rumble themselves.[21] In a society plagued by deaths of despair—we lose approximately 158,000 Americans annually to suicide, overdoses, and alcohol-related diseases, the equivalent, to borrow a stark phrase from Princeton economists Anne Case and Angus Deaton, of "three fully loaded Boeing 737 MAX jets falling out of the sky every day for a year"[22]—the conversations of people who faced conquests, exiles, and oppression and wrote their way out of despair constitute a useful manual. In a country haunted by its past and left with few, if any, common goals for its future, a book devoted to scrutinizing the judgment of your elders without discarding the traditions and teachings that had kept them united as a people goes a long way.

The Talmud doesn't offer facile self-affirmations or treacly simplifications. It can't be reduced to pithy maxims, like love yourself or be kind or spark joy. No sooner has it raised a piercing question than it proceeds to complicate it further, often leaving readers confounded. And yet, the Talmud is every bit a self-help book, maybe even the best one ever written. It is certainly unparalleled in the scope of topics it addresses, which include, to give a very partial list, how to love, how to grieve, how to fight, how to be a better spouse, how to be a grown-up, how to fix the government, how to come to terms with your body, how to let go, how to build a community, how to be a good friend, and how to prepare for death.

None of these how-tos, however, make any sense unless the reader is willing to grow. Change and its relentless sidekick, doubt, are the Talmud's true heroes. The rabbis recognized, long before organizational psychologists did, how truly terrified we are when our circumstances are altered. Even mild aberrations— arriving at the supermarket and not finding our favorite cheese in its usual spot on the shelf, or driving to the office and finding our favorite parking spot occupied—aggravate us. Because we know, deep down inside, how little we know about our existence, and because we know that on some day we can't predict, and for reasons we can't control or even understand, this existence will come to an end, we rush to take comfort in the patterns we do recognize. Children invent games and fret about their rules because it's the only way they can begin to make sense of, and assert agency in, a universe that strikes them, justly, as chaotic and unknowable and vaguely menacing. Adults cultivate routines—taco Tuesdays, Sunday mornings with coffee and pancakes—for the same reason, even if it means staying in jobs they hate or in relationships that have grown cold. Anything, we often tell ourselves, is better than change, and when change is foisted upon us, doubt, too, comes apace: Are we certain we're doing the right thing? Are there better options? Are we sure?

It's ironic, then, that "Talmudic" is commonly used as a term of mild derision, connoting exhaustive, even excessive, analysis. It ought, if the Talmud is properly studied and understood, to mean something very different: a method of answering doubt's questions seriously and respectfully, of quieting our minds and our hearts while realizing that certainty and stability are luxuries no human can afford for very long. Instead, the Talmud offers us three more modest yet more sustainable gifts. First, it teaches us how to think, giving us a crash course in reasoning that, as we'll see, is blissfully free from the clever curlicues that too often distracted the ancient Greeks. The Talmud is simultaneously remarkably disinterested in logic as a discipline and deeply invested in applying it toward purely practical ends. The what-ifs the rabbis generate on nearly every page of the Talmud aren't exercises in entertaining slouching minds, but attempts to figure out everything we can about human nature for the explicit purpose of making life here on earth a little bit better for all.

Second, the Talmud teaches us what to think about, directing our attention to questions that may appear remote—why should I, idling on my iPhone, care much about the precise manner in which the High Priest approached his duties on Yom Kippur two millennia ago?—but that, on closer inspection, reveal raw and relevant insights that will resonate for as long as our species persists.

Ultimately, the Talmud teaches us that we are all in this life together. We can't learn anything on our own, let alone practice what we believe or attempt anything like a good life unless we do it with other people, which means that we must take not only our own hazy hearts and muddled minds into account but also the even more impenetrable minds and hearts of our loved ones and neighbors and strangers we meet. Long before the philosopher Ludwig Wittgenstein, the rabbis decreed that none of us were at liberty to obey a rule privately. The rules are the rules because they were designed to amplify what we cherish, to help us forge a shared vision, and to bring us together.

In the coming pages, I will do my best to honor the spirit of the Talmud. What follows isn't a history of the Talmud, though it will proceed in chronological order and stop to introduce those who gave us this remarkable work of literature, thought, and moral imagination. Nor is it a work of scholarship or analysis, though attention will be paid to more than a few key passages, showing the Talmud at work. Instead, I will examine a handful of thorny topics, like love and loss and friendship, and show how the Talmud addresses them and how the wisdom of the rabbis continues to illuminate these complicated matters today. My aim here is humble: to open the door for those who, like me, look around them and feel sad and scared and broken and wish they had some sort of guide to nudge them closer to hope.

That, after all, is the point of one of the Talmud's best-known stories. It tells of a non-Jewish gentleman who wished to test the two great rabbis of his time, Shammai and Hillel. He came before the former, known as a stickler who believed only the sharpest and most able students were worthy of attention. "Convert me," the man said to Shammai, "on condition that you teach me the entire Torah while I am standing on one foot." Shammai, a builder by trade, was so incensed by this insolent request that he pulled out his measuring stick and started beating the stranger. And yet, the man was undeterred; he went to see Hillel and asked him the very same question. Hillel, who believed in embracing anyone who wished to commit themselves to a life of learning and introspection, was only too happy to comply. The Talmud tells us what happened next: "[Hillel] converted him and said to him: That which is hateful to you do not do to another; that is the entire Torah, and the rest is commentary. Now go study."[23]

Let us now go and do the same.

CHAPTER ONE

Our Bodies, Our Selves

or

How Having a Snack, Taking a Bath,
and Pooping Can Save Your Soul

JEAN NIDTECH, nee Slutsky, was born in Brooklyn, New York, on October 12, 1923, to Mae, a manicurist, and David, a cab driver. She weighed 7 pounds, 3 ounces. Whenever she cried, or laughed, or complained, or interacted with the world in any way, her mother treated her to a piece of candy. "Somehow," she recalled later in life, "I learned that food would fix any hurt. And that it would celebrate any joy."[1]

It was an easy conclusion to reach in a household whose rhythms emanated from the kitchen. Sundays, David's day off, were a countdown to a dinner of steak and fries. Most other days, it was lamb stew cooked in huge vats, and Thursdays were designated healthy-eating night, which, for the Slutskys, meant potatoes and corn followed by cake and Jean's favorite, chocolate pudding. She took a quarter with her every day to school, but rather than settling for milk and a sandwich like most of her peers, she'd buy five ice cream pops for a nickel each and have herself a sweet lunch.

At first, she looked down at her expanding waist and dismissed it with a shrug. She was just chubby, she told herself, roly-poly and adorable. But by the time Jean made it to high school, she realized that her girth was becoming her single defining feature and that most of her classmates saw it—and her—as undesirable. She masked her hurt with a torrent of jokes and a good-humored attitude that bought her some social clout, but when she was being honest with herself, she knew she couldn't trust her friends, or at least not the skinny ones. "Occasionally," she wrote decades later, "I would truly like a thin girl, but I didn't want to become too friendly with her because she could never understand me."[2]

Still, Jean was too cheerful to let anything drive her to despair, so with the help of her mother, she tried a few fad diets, got herself down to a size 18, and started college with high hopes. If she got the right education, she told herself, she could become someone important, someone people saw as more than just rotund. Four months into her first semester, however, her father fell ill; after three days of coughing and wheezing, he finally agreed to see a doctor. He was advised to check into the hospital right away, and when he got there he was told his lung had collapsed. He died four days later.

Mae, Jean's mother, was thirty-six, and she had one daughter barely out of her adolescence and another, Helen, just hitting puberty. Both girls had to quit school and find jobs to help make ends meet. Jean first tried the Mullin Furniture Company in Jamaica, New York, which paid her $10 a week for secretarial work. She then went to work for Man O'War, publishers of a shady horse racing tip sheet. They were eventually shut down by the police. Distraught, Jean found a job with the Internal Revenue Service and distracted herself with snacks. She loved these pretty little cakes that came two to a pack and could never refrain from immediately scarfing both down. Then there were these chocolate-covered marshmallows, which were easy to squish and swallow. Ice cream, too, was a constant comfort. Before too long,

Jean was a size 20, 22, 24. And then, one day, she went to her favorite luncheonette for some coffee and a Danish and met the love of her life.

His name was Marty Nidtech. He was 5 feet, 10 inches tall and weighed 265 pounds. He made her laugh by telling her stories about the war he'd just fought in Europe. He didn't understand, he told Jean, why so many folks complained about the food in the army, which he thought was pretty much universally terrific. He also regaled her with stories about how he'd always carry an onion or two in his pocket, which he'd then dice up and add to whatever he was eating to make it taste even better. He'd often joke about his weight, too, pointing down to his bulging stomach and saying things like "I got this when meat was cheap!" The two fell in love, got married, and moved around in search of employment, the only constant in their lives being the nightly visit to the ice cream parlor.

This would've likely remained the cadence of Jean's life if it wasn't for a visit to a supermarket in Little Neck, Long Island, where she was living at the time, in September 1961. An acquaintance spotted her shopping for produce and zipped over, giddily, inquiring about Jean's summer. "You look so marvelous!" the woman exclaimed. "When are you due?"³

Jean was crestfallen. She resolved to lose weight, a lot of it, and quickly. She went on a diet eating only eggs and grapefruit, then on another limited to cottage cheese, peaches, and bananas. A neighbor recommended sticking to black coffee and watermelon, which worked for a while until Jean could no longer stand it. Another friend told her to eat sunflower seeds, which keeps the hands too busy removing shells to worry about them reaching for something more substantial. None of these diets worked. The weight wasn't coming off. It was time for stronger stuff. A doctor in a far corner of New Jersey charged her a small fortune and told her to eat anything she liked as long as she made sure to end each meal with a long, tall glass of whole milk. A hypnotist told her to place her hands on her stomach and simply tell herself she was full. She lost a few pounds, then gained a bunch more. She was 5 feet, 7 inches tall and weighed 214 pounds. She needed real help.

Someone told her that the city of New York ran a clinic for the morbidly obese. She applied and was admitted, and on her first day she wore a big coat with a bold print and spent longer than usual on her hair and makeup, hoping that no one looked at anything but her clothes and her face. She arrived at a large, drab building and struggled to find the right room. Not wanting to call any attention to herself by asking for directions to the fat person's bootcamp, she instead approached the receptionist and asked for directions to the nutrition clinic.

"You want the obesity clinic!" the young woman said, loudly enough for everyone in the waiting room to hear. "It's down the hall, third door on your right."

The clinic turned out to be a small room packed with large women. After a few minutes of nervous chatter, the instructor walked in. She was precisely the sort of slender person Jean had come to distrust.

"Ladies," the instructor asked, "how do you feel when you look at a smorgasbord table?"

Looking amused, the woman sitting next to Jean was quick to answer. "I feel like diving in," she said. "Don't you?"

"When I look at a smorgasbord," the instructor replied with a clear look of disgust, "I get sick to my stomach."[4]

Jean was baffled by the woman's vitriol, but she hadn't long to ponder her feelings. Soon she was taken to an even smaller room, weighed, measured, and told that she needed to get down to precisely 142 pounds. She was then handed a menu that struck her as ridiculously strict and was sent home with a heavy heart. For weeks she did her best to follow the diet as closely as she could. For weeks she faced the skinny instructor with shame, not daring to admit that she hadn't lost as much weight as she was supposed to because, after following the rigid regimen all day long, she waited for her husband and children to fall asleep, snuck into the bathroom, locked the door, and quickly devoured an entire box of cookies, hiding the empty packaging in the hamper so that no one would discover her secret. Within a few months, she was out of the program, no thinner than she had hoped to be. She was also out of options. That's when she had her big idea.

The people who had tried to help her before, she realized, might have been well meaning. Some even had the right credentials and a firm understanding of the science. But all had exactly the wrong approach. They assumed that a human being was an amorphous mess of appetites and desires and hang-ups, perpetually at war with the fleshy cage, the body, into which it had been thrust. And their methods all involved somehow trying to break out of that cage, either by forcing it into submission or by tricking it into feeling satiated. It was, Jean thought, not only a terrible way to lose weight, but also a terrible way to go through life. She wanted something different. She wanted a way to lose weight by bringing body and self together, by understanding why she felt compelled to sneak around to eat sweets, by talking her way into better habits with other people who faced the same predicament. Not sure what else to do, she picked up the phone and invited six friends over for a chat.

The women came, and they talked, and they shared stories about hiding treats behind cans of asparagus in the cupboard and about lying motionless until everyone else was asleep so that the nightly binge might begin. And when the meeting was over, one woman asked Jean if they could come back the following week as well. Jean said yes. More women joined, invited by friends or informed by word of mouth. Within two months, there were forty women cramming into Jean's kitchen, then even more, and then people who couldn't attend started asking Jean if she'd come teach them at their homes because her method was working. She now realized she had a business on her hands. She called it Weight Watchers.

If you're one of the million and a half people who are currently Weight Watchers members, or the millions more who have applied its methodology to lose weight and stay fit, you might have caught a bit of the spirit of Jean Nidtech's original soul-searching just by attending a meeting. Weight Watchers officials love talking about "hedonic hunger"—eating when you are not physiologically hungry—which is why it's so important to learn how to bring body and mind into alignment, recognize food-related cues, and forge a healthier approach to eating. Do that, and whether you realize it or not, you'll be partaking in one of humanity's most ancient philosophical debates, one that the Talmud heavily influenced, the debate about how we are to understand—and live with and live in—the human body.

To the ancient Egyptians, the body was, at best, an inconvenience. Here, for example, is a passage from the *Book of the Dead*, which began life as inscriptions on the walls of tombs as early as the Third Dynasty, 2670–2613 BCE, and roughly a millennium later was committed to papyrus and placed in graves to prepare the deceased for their journey to the afterlife:

> *The place of bondage is opened,*
> *That which was shut is opened,*
> *And the place of bondage is open to my soul*
> *[According to the bidding of] the eye of Horus.*

You hardly have to know much about Horus, the falcon-headed god, or his mother, Isis, or the Egyptian belief in a complex cosmology of deities to understand the passage's key idea: our body is a prison, and when we die, our soul is finally released from captivity and permitted to reunite with the cosmos. Plato, no stranger to the writings of antiquity, expressed a similar idea nearly two thousand years after the Third Dynasty, in the *Phaedrus*. "Being permitted as initiates to the sight of perfect and simple and calm and happy apparitions," he wrote, "which we saw in the pure light, being ourselves pure and not entombed in this which we carry about with us and call the body, in which we are imprisoned like an oyster in its shell."[5] The expression is more mellifluous in its original Greek: *Soma Sema*, the body is a tomb.

With this central understanding of the self and the flesh in mind, Plato went on to create his best-known contribution, the Theory of Forms, which, roughly speaking, posits the existence of nonphysical essences to all things of which the material objects we see here on earth are merely pale facsimiles. Why can we call both a Louis XIV–period masterwork by André-Charles Boulle, made by hand from wood, pewter, brass, copper, horn, and tortoiseshell, and the Sandsberg, made by Ikea from particle board, melamine foil, and plastic edging, by the same name, "table"? The latter costs $59.99, the former many magnitudes more, if you can convince the museum that probably holds it to sell. We understand these two distinct creations to be the same, Plato argued, because they both correspond to some ur-table that we know innately and intimately, the perfect ideal of a table that helps us understand what we're looking at every time we see something with four legs and a flat surface. The same, Plato argued, was true for the human soul, of which the body was just a restrictive casing; the soul was immaterial and eternal, supreme and self-moving. This is why all learning, Plato believed, is merely recalling what we already knew before birth, before the unhappy occurrence of the perfect, all-seeing soul being trapped in its earthly, degradable packaging.

This was the sort of stuff taught daily at Plato's famous Academy, at whose gate hung a sign warning "Let no one ignorant of geometry enter," a tribute to the branch of human knowledge Plato believed was most closely aligned with his Theory of Forms. To know geometry isn't to worry about this triangle or that trapezoid, but rather about the universal, theoretical rules that applied to all these shapes without exception.

Presumably, then, the seventeen-year-old orphan seeking admission in 367 BCE had at least some passing knowledge of geometry, because he was not only let in but soon promoted to Plato's assistant and invited to take long walks and argue with the famous philosopher about everything. And argue he did, because the young man, Aristotle, saw the world in radically different terms than his celebrated teacher. Aristotle's father, Nicomachus, had been the personal physician to King Amyntas III of Macedon, and the young boy grew up among endless talk of bodies, healthy and ailing and fading away. He was also a keen observer of the natural world around him, if not always the most accurate: redstarts, he believed, somehow transformed themselves into robins come winter, and garden warblers into blackcaps. He played around in the mud and concluded that while most fish reproduced sexually, some simply arose "from mud, or from sand and from decayed matter that rises thence as scum."[6] Even when his theories about the natural world were incorrect, though, his inclination to observe things as they were stood in direct contrast to his teacher's approach. Whereas Plato looked for intangible Forms, Aristotle examined the real, the present, the perceptible. Whereas the teacher believed that each embodied thing vaguely corresponded to some ethereal ideal, the student believed that each embodied thing already contained a bit of that ideal within it; to him, even if we're not sure what this bird or that one might be, we recognize them all as birds because each contains something of the ideal of a bird in it, which makes each individual bird worthy of our attention and admiration. The poet Louis MacNeice captured this seminal disagreement between the two ancient Greek giants, but placed his bet with Aristotle, who, watching nature evolve, was attuned to the blossoming of the natural world, "Stressing the function, scrapping the Form in Itself, / Taking the horse from the shelf and letting it gallop."[7]

Plato and Aristotle, however, were arguing about much more than lofty philosophical abstractions. If you followed the former, you believed that living "is a function of the soul,"[8] which gave you permission to pay little attention to that embarrassing mound of meat in which the soul just happened to reside. This lack of curiosity about all things corporeal opened the door to competition; Plato's contemporary, Aristippus, took pleasure not only in insulting the great thinker's sexual mores, but also in proposing a radically different theory, hedonism, which argued that our ultimate goal ought to be the pursuit of whatever felt good.

Aristotle offered a more elegant way of being in the world. In his *Nicomachean Ethics*, he introduced the intricate concept of eudaimonia, *eu* meaning good and *daimonia* referring to the divine spirit or power. Eudaimonia, to Aristotle, meant happiness, but a much deeper and more profound and more impactful sort than the fleeting satisfaction you get from polishing off a delicious slice of pizza, say, or taking a long nap. In a recent book on Aristotle's ongoing centrality to our modern way of thinking, the classicist Edith Hall explained eudaimonia nicely. According to Aristotle, she wrote, "life itself consists of having an *active mind*. Aristotle was convinced that most people get most of their pleasure from learning things and wondering about and at the world. Indeed, he regarded the attainment of an understanding of the world—not just academic knowledge, but understanding of any aspect of experience—as the actual goal of life itself."[9] As long as you were learning—which meant not only applying your intellect but also paying attention to the sensory experiences that revealed themselves with every touch and sight and smell—you were happy.

Where did Aristotle come up with such a radical idea? Explanations abound, beginning with his childhood as the son of a physician. But from at least the end of the first century CE, and with some regularity—not always backed up by facts—a different explanation emerged: he got it from the Jews.

Writing sometime around 94 CE, Flavius Josephus, the Jewish general turned Roman historian who remains our best primary source of the era, penned a defense of Judaism as a worthy philosophical tradition. It was titled *Against Apion*, after the Hellenized Egyptian sophist who accused Judaism of being irrelevant, and it offers us the earliest account of Aristotle's possible Jewish influence. Josephus quotes at length from the *De Somno* ("On Sleep"), a since-lost essay by Aristotle's contemporary Clearchus, which describes a meeting between the great Greek thinker and a Jewish traveler.

"Now this man," Josephus quotes Clearchus as writing, "when he was hospitably treated by a great many, came down from the upper country to the places near the sea, and became a Grecian, not only in his language, but in his soul also. . . . He conversed with us, and with other philosophical persons, and made a trial of our skill in philosophy; and as he had lived with many learned men, he communicated to us more information than he received from us."[10] Josephus then goes on to note that "Aristotle discoursed also particularly of the great and wonderful fortitude of this Jew in his diet, and continent way of living."[11] The same meeting is described by several early Christian theologians, though some contemporary scholars doubt that it had actually taken place. And in the tenth century, a book known as *Liber de Pomo*, or the *Book of the Apple*, circulated in Latin, Greek, Arabic, and Hebrew. It was attributed to Aristotle, although that is almost certainly apocryphal. In it, the dying philosopher, holding an apple in his hand and kept alive by its refreshing smell, delivers a soliloquy on body and soul. As it draws to an end, the Greek philosopher more or less declares himself to be a believer in Judaism's eternal teachings; "now it came to pass," the book concludes, "when the Philosopher had ceased speaking these words, that his hands grew weak, the apple dropped from his hand, his face changed color, and he died." Aristotle's disciples then mourn him in what sounds suspiciously like Jewish prayer.[12] The historical veracity of this account, too, is questionable.

None, however, doubt that in 343 BCE, Aristotle was summoned by King Philip II of Macedon and ordered to tutor the young prince Alexander, soon to be known to history as Alexander the Great. He held this position for eight years before returning to Athens, establishing an academy of his own and, in all likelihood, writing most of the works for which he is known today before passing away in 322 BCE.

Was he there by his student's side when Alexander entered

Jerusalem on his way to conquer much of the known world? Probably not, but Alexander's arrival nonetheless had a profound impact on both Jewish and Hellenic thought, forcing both to contemplate the essential questions of being, starting with how, exactly, are we to see our bodies and our selves. And it began with a meeting between the dashing king and a Jewish High Priest named Shimon HaTzadik, or Shimon the Righteous.

The Talmud captures it in detail, as it does many of Shimon's teachings and adventures. The Samaritans, it tells us, frequent foes of the Jews, go to Alexander and ask him to destroy the Jewish Temple in Jerusalem. The Greek, not knowing or caring much for such things, tells the Samaritans to go ahead and do as they please, and news of the impending catastrophe travels back to Shimon. Without wasting a moment, he wraps himself in his finest robes, assembles an entourage of fellow priests and dignitaries, and instructs each one to hold a torch in his hand. This strange procession marches all night long, until, at dawn, it finally meets Alexander and his Samaritan allies.

"Who," Alexander asks, "are these people coming to meet us?" And the Samaritans answer, "These are the Jews who rebelled against you." But when Alexander saw Shimon, something strange happened. The mighty monarch, the Talmud continues, leapt off his chariot and bowed before the priest. "His escorts," goes the story, "said to him: Should an important king such as you bow to this Jew? He said to them: I do so because the image of this man's face is victorious before me on my battlefields, i.e., when I fight I see his image going before me as a sign of victory, and therefore I know that he has supreme sanctity."[13]

Who was this mysterious priest, all clad in white, who appeared in Alexander's daydreams and offered him mystical guidance? The Talmud, which offers us many insights into Shimon's thought and teachings, gives us little by way of biography. According to the Talmud, Shimon was most likely a student of Ezra the Scribe, who, the Bible tells us, led a small band of Jews from Babylon back to Jerusalem around 400 BCE to help rebuild the Temple after it was destroyed by King Nebuchadnezzar the Great a century earlier. Ezra's order might've been tall, but Shimon's was taller: in many ways, he was responsible for transforming Jewish practice—and the Jewish people—from just another of antiquity's tribes into a people geared for survival, ushering in the centuries of rabbinic flourishing that gave us the Talmud.

And it was because of Alexander that Shimon had his historical mission. Until the Macedonian's arrival, empires rose and collapsed with some regularity, and while some had an impact on Jewish life—the Babylonians, for example, forced the Jews into a decades-long exile—none propelled Jewish leaders to rethink the fundamentals of faith. Religious life was organized around sacrifices, which were intricately detailed and clearly prescribed, performed by a priestly class that served as intermediaries between God and the Jewish people. In this, Judaism, at the time, was not so different from its peer belief systems, all of which revolved around appeasing the deity or deities with various burnt offerings.

Alexander changed all that. Heeding the advice of his wise teacher, he often showed respect to the people he conquered, acknowledging their gods and sometimes adopting their ways of government. But he made sure the military officials in charge were always Macedonian, and he took with gusto to building Greek-style cities in all corners of his new, vast empire. The officials who governed these cities spoke only Greek, and Greek settlers soon flocked to these remote corners in search of new opportunities. In cities like Alexandria they could find marketplaces and theaters, academies and gymnasiums, broad avenues humming with commerce and agoras welcoming anyone in the mood for a good philosophical argument.

And this new and robust cosmopolitanism, Alexander's Jewish contemporaries realized, was a massive threat. Some before had tried to force the Jews to abandon their ancient religion and were met by spirited resistance. Alexander took a very different approach. He offered an alternative, an appealing way of life that seemed modern and inviting and infinitely more attractive than the old ideas of the Torah. Who would continue to pray to the unseen God who forbids graven images when right there in the center of town was a gorgeous marble tribute to the chiseled Olympians?

This was the question facing Shimon HaTzadik and his colleagues, and the answer they gave was a radical one. Greek religion, they understood, featured many of the same characteristics as Judaism—temples, animal sacrifices, intricate ceremonies performed by a priestly class—and now, thanks to Alexander, these rites were readily available everywhere you went, performed on a grander scale for all to admire and join. To survive, Shimon and his colleagues realized, Judaism had to double down on what made it truly special.

The Greeks believed that the body was either a playground to be enjoyed or, at best, the corporeal manifestation of some vague ideal of human physical perfection. And they believed that the soul was the distillation of reason and wisdom, of the capacity for thinking that made humans greater than animals. You don't have to read very far in Genesis, the first book of the Torah, to stumble on a very different account of body and soul. Human beings, it tells us, were created in God's image, which means that any attempt to draw nearer to the Creator would necessarily involve rejecting the dualism so fundamental to nearly all of Greek thought and instead embracing the radical notion that body and soul were one cohesive, coherent unit, both partaking in and seminal to the religious experience.

So if you wanted to keep people engaged with religious life, Shimon realized, you had to rethink what it meant to be religious and, for that matter, what it meant to be a person. You had to uproot the religious experience from the Temple's altar and replant it in a more intimate setting. You had, in other words, to introduce the body to religion, and religion to the body. That such ideas were comprehensible to the rabbis, trained theologians, is not surprising. But if Judaism was going to succeed in resisting Hellenic influences, it had to make sure they were clear to those too troubled by work and family and other obligations to stop and ponder deep philosophical questions like the relationship between the body and the soul. Previously, when such ordinary Jews wanted clarity, they turned to priests, who knew the procedures of ritual sacrifice, and to prophets, who were said to receive instructions directly from God and who spoke with inspiring certainty. To empower ordinary believers to take charge of their own spiritual lives, Shimon and his colleagues took a number of bold steps.

Some, like translating the Bible into Aramaic, the language spoken by most uneducated Jews, were fairly obvious. Others, like mandating personal daily prayers, were inspired; and others were cryptic, like the habit, mentioned in the Talmud, of fasting and pleading with God to keep Torah scribes from growing too wealthy lest they stop feeling motivated to pursue their holy craft.

But these measures, Shimon understood, were merely a strong skeleton on which to build a religious practice, not a beating heart. If Judaism were to have any real appeal, it had to become more personal, more relevant, more basic. And nothing, Shimon knew, was more basic or more relevant than one's own body. It was time, then, to give his followers a new way of understanding what it meant to be Jewish, to be human, to be alive. And it began with a simple story.

Once upon a time, Shimon told his followers, I was sitting in the Temple when a shepherd came to offer his sacrifice. He was a strikingly handsome young man, with piercing eyes and gorgeous hair, but he had taken an ascetic vow, which meant that once his sacrifice was accepted, he would have to shave his head. Why, I asked him, would you ever willingly consent to having your beautiful hair shorn? The young shepherd told me that he was drinking from the river one day when he caught a glimpse of his own handsome face. The sight made him swoon and think impure thoughts about all the earthly pleasures he could pursue with such fine features. A few heady moments later, the shepherd came back to himself, and, feeling enormously guilty for thinking such lustful thoughts, took a vow to shave his head. "Wicked one!" the shepherd said to his own reflection, "this beauty is not yours, and it will one day soon crumble into dust and worms!" I was so moved, Shimon concluded, that I lowered his head, kissed it, and told him, "my son, may there be many more like you who do God's bidding."[14]

We've no way of knowing if Shimon knew the Greek myth of Narcissus, but his tale flips the story of the handsome hunter from Thespiae on its head. Narcissus falls in love with his own reflection, falls into the pool, drowns, and turns into a flower. Shimon's shepherd feels a pang of pride followed by a bout of remorse that propels him to action. But the story doesn't end there; its punch line is subtle, as Talmudic punch lines so often are, but mighty. At no other time, Shimon informs his listeners, did he accept a sacrificial offering from anyone who had taken a similar vow. Why, then, make an exception for the young shepherd?

Ordinarily, Shimon taught his followers, ascetic vows spelled trouble. Too often, they were the easy way out: you let yourself get carried away, you feel immensely guilty for having been so weak, you pledge to make things right by depriving yourself of a host of earthly pleasures, a pattern familiar, say, to anyone who has ever tried a no-carb diet. This, Shimon believed, was a very bad way to go through life; if your emotional and spiritual pursuit is nothing more than a series of very low lows followed by very high highs, you are eventually going to wear yourself out. Furthermore, life wasn't about succumbing to these urges, both destructive and pious, but about working through them, about understanding the bad and the good, about reconciling body and soul. And that's why Shimon kissed the shepherd and accepted his offering: the young man may have taken the extreme and easy way out, but before he did, he stopped and acknowledged that his beauty wasn't his, that it was God's gift, and that, therefore, it shouldn't be dismissed as altogether undesirable but merely a distraction that had to be mastered. Just as Jean Nidetch struggled to learn how to eat with gusto and remain healthy, the shepherd was struggling to learn how to appreciate his beauty and remain committed to a virtuous life.

At the heart of this insight stood a simple yet radical commitment to including body and soul alike in the devotional process. No sooner had the rabbis decreed praying daily, for example, than they also advised their followers to rock gently back and forth while uttering the sacred words, a practice known today as "shukling," from the Yiddish word for "shaking." They did so because they knew that real trancelike devotion couldn't be had simply by sitting or standing and reciting text; to truly talk to God—or, for that matter, to yourself—you need to bring your whole body into the conversation. This, too, is why religious Jews wear tefillin, the small leather boxes containing verses from the Torah that are affixed to the head and the arm with leather straps, while praying. If something is truly sacred, Judaism tells us, you should feel it in your limbs just as tightly as you do in your heart.

During his four decades as High Priest, Shimon HaTzadik toiled to forge a new way of being in the world. He never spoke of happiness, but he believed that understanding every aspect of our experience, sacred and profane alike, spiritual as well as physical, was at the heart of the religious pursuit, which was the supreme form of human existence. And his death, too, was a pas de deux between body and soul. One year, the Talmud tells us, Shimon HaTzadik came out of the Holy of Holies—the inner sanctum in the Temple in which Jews believe the *shekhina*, or God's spirit, resided and into which only the High Priest was allowed and only on one day of the year, Yom Kippur, the Day of Atonement—and informed his followers that he would soon be dead. Each year, he told them, as he entered the Holy of Holies, he would see an old man dressed all in white walking behind him, waiting patiently for Shimon to conclude his prayers, and then escorting him out. And this year, he continued, the man, most likely the embodiment of the *shekhina* itself, was dressed all in black, and when Shimon left, the man did not follow. The moral of the story was simple: When body and soul are aligned, even death, the ultimate mystery, becomes knowable, predictable, almost comforting. Shimon prepared for his passing, and a week later he was dead. It was up to his followers to carry on his tradition.

Sadly, they weren't always up to the task.

The rabbis who followed Shimon were all learned, passionate, and committed to do their best to lead the Jews in turbulent times. Over the next four hundred years, they endured the death of Alexander; a long period of instability brought about by his string of unworthy heirs; a bloody and victorious war against the Greeks, commemorated in the holiday of Hanukkah; the rise of a troubled Jewish ruling dynasty, the Hasmoneans; and finally, the ascent of Herod, a ruthless despot committed to turning his kingdom into a regional Hellenic powerhouse.

Some of Shimon's successors, like Antigonus of Socho, reversed course and believed that the best way to survive such tumult was to turn your back on all worldly affairs and serve God, expecting no reward and paying no attention to worldly pleasures and suffering. Others, like the mystic Honi HaMe'agel, saw themselves as God's spoiled children, making demands and expecting the Creator to satisfy their every whim: Honi, the Talmud tells us, addressed a severe drought by drawing a circle on the ground, hopping into it, and vowing not to leave until God made it rain. He lucked out: it soon rained. Hanina ben Dosa delivered his own variation by living simply and seeing extreme humility as the key to redemption. And Yossi ben Yoezer did his best to pass laws that made it much more difficult for Jews to mingle with non-Jews, only to see his son turn his back on Judaism and seek his thrills with the Greek gods instead. Not surprisingly, each of these different approaches, all of them removed from the direct simplicity of Shimon's teachings, had minor advantages and major drawbacks. Judaism was waiting for another giant to come and continue Shimon's work.

He arrived sometime in the year 113 BCE. Hillel was born in Babylon to a wealthy family. We know little about his early life and not much about why he decided, at the age of forty, to move to the Land of Israel. We do know that once he arrived there, he worked as a lumberjack, earning half a dinar each day and giving half of that meager sum to the guard at the study hall in order to gain entrance and study some Torah. The Talmud introduces his arrival, as it does that of several of its greatest sages, in a mystical fashion. One day, the story goes, Hillel was unable to find work, and the guard refused him entry. Eager not to miss even a day of study, Hillel climbed onto the roof and sat at the edge of the skylight to hear the two great teachers of the time, Shemaya and Avtalyon, speak.

"That day," the Talmud continues, "was Shabbat eve and it was the winter season of Tevet, and snow fell upon him from the sky. When it was dawn, Shemaya said to Avtalyon: Avtalyon, my brother, every day at this hour the study hall is already bright from the sunlight streaming through the skylight, and today it is dark; is it perhaps a cloudy day?"[15] The two rabbis, squinting just so, looked up and saw what appeared to be the shape of a man lying on the roof. Running up, they found Hillel shivering, covered by 5 feet of snow. They pulled him out of it, goes the story, "and they washed him and smeared oil on him, and they sat him opposite the bonfire to warm him. They said: This man is worthy for us to desecrate Shabbat for him."[16]

According to the Torah, one is permitted, indeed obligated, to desecrate Shabbat, the holiest of days, in order to save a life. That last comment in the story, about Hillel's worthiness, teaches us that he wasn't redeemed merely because Shemaya and Avtalyon considered it their basic duty to aid him. Instead, they recognized the stranger as someone who was willing to put his body on the line, who considered studying Torah just as essential to his survival as keeping warm. When Hillel recovered, they began teaching him. It didn't take him long to ascend to the position of Nasi, the communal leader.

But the community in those days was led by pairs of scholars, and Hillel's counterpart—serving as the Av Beit Din, or supreme justice—was a man named Shammai. The best way to make sure the Torah was preserved, Shammai believed, was to teach it precisely as it had been taught by previous generations, which meant that anytime a question arose, it was probably more prudent to err on the side of stricture. A humble man who did his best to be kind and cheerful, especially with his students, he was nonetheless a stern interpreter of the tradition, insisting that even the young and the helpless were obligated to obey the Torah's commandments. When his son was still a toddler, for example, he argued that the child wasn't too young to fast on Yom Kippur. It took a host of his colleagues quite a while to convince him otherwise. And when his daughter-in-law gave birth on the festival of Sukkot, during which Jews are commanded to sleep in an outdoor hut, he punched a hole in the roof of the room where she was nursing her baby so that his newborn grandchild could fulfill the holiday's religious obligations.

Hillel had radically different ideas. Unlike Shammai, he was an outsider, an immigrant, and as such had no ancient traditions to which he could cling. Instead, he had to stop and ponder what the Torah meant to him and how best to teach it to others. We've already encountered the pure distillation of his ideas, delivered to a gentile who came seeking to be converted—that which is hateful to you do not do to another. But Hillel's ideas were much more complex than this short and shiny adage suggests. And like Shimon HaTzadik's teachings, they stemmed from an insistence that life could only be lived to the fullest if the intricacies of human experience were all stitched together into one elegant quilt.

Right at the start of the Mishnah, for example, we find Hillel and Shammai arguing over a question that may seem trivial but that captures their different approaches: What is the proper way to recite the seminal Shema prayer? The Shema, argued Shammai, is basically an admission of God's glory as Master of the Universe; it's a supplication before a king and, as such, ought to be recited in ceremonious ways. Just as you wouldn't stand before a king in your ratty pajamas, Shammai argued, so, too, you mustn't ever address God in any way that isn't decorous. In the morning, Shammai explained, a man must stand erect as he recites the Shema, indicating he is about to rise and worship the Lord. And in the evening, he must recline, showing the Creator gratitude for another day.

Not so, said Hillel. Let every person recite the Shema as they wish. Are you a lumberjack that just happens to be atop a tree when it's time to pray? Are you walking around downtown? Riding your mule to the next town over? It doesn't matter: prayer oughtn't to be stuffy and cumbersome nor an invitation to interrupt normal life and gum it up with pomp and circumstance. Prayer has to be as natural and as comfortable as everything else people do or else they will never make it an integral part of their lives.

This insight would have been enough had it applied merely to lofty matters like prayer. But Hillel, the supreme rationalist, didn't stop there. No unified theory of religious worship, he knew, was complete until it accounted for our lowliest urges as well. One day, the Talmud tells us in one of its most amusing stories, Hillel rose from his studies and announced to his students that he was about to perform a mitzvah, or righteous deed. His disciples, most likely, were riveted; it wasn't every day that the greatest teacher of his generation, usually an understated man, got up and advertised an upcoming feat of piety. And so, the students followed Hillel, and were shocked to learn that he had entered the restroom to defecate. Silent and stunned, they waited outside, and when the great rabbi emerged, they asked, "Was this a mitzvah?" Hillel beamed at them. "Yes," he said, "so that my body doesn't break down."[17] A body that isn't able to function properly by removing its waste, in other words, is a body that is also unable to assist the soul in other, more spiritual matters.

Another, nearly identical Talmudic story better explains Hillel's approach. It begins in just the same way, but instead of the restroom, Hillel rushed to the bathhouse. When his students inquired why washing yourself should count as a righteous deed, he told them a little parable. Think, he told them, of the statues of great kings, imperiously towering over theaters and arenas for all to adore. And consider the person appointed to wash them and keep them clean and glistening. That person is not only fed and cared for by the kings, but also revered as someone important, as he is the custodian of their icons. And if that man is respected, Hillel concluded, "I, who was created in the [Divine] Image and Form, as it is written 'For in the Image of God He Made Man' (Genesis 9:6) even more so!"[18]

The contemporary Israeli scholar Rabbi Binyamin Lau argued that the story folds within it a complex theological understanding of humankind's true essence. Hillel's understanding of the human body, he noted, was layered. For the ancient sage, a person was both the statue and its custodian, both an object created by God and a subject entrusted with keeping the creation alive and well. By washing, then, the person cares for his own divine likeness. "It's impossible to divide a living human being into an exalted, divine part and a lower, bodily part," Lau wrote. "Because Man was created in the Image of God, everything about him is holy."[19]

But what does it mean to live as if everything about you was holy? If you asked Shammai, he would tell you that it meant taking great care in everything you did and standing on ceremony, remembering always that you hang in the balance between hungry beast and celestial being, and that if you're not extremely cautious in everything you say or do or think, you'd soon end up in a sty rather than in the heavens. Shammai was so eager to make sure he celebrated Shabbat with the festive respect it deserved that he spent all week searching for the perfect thing to eat come Friday night. "If he found a choice animal," the Talmud tells us, "he would say: This is for Shabbat. If he subsequently found another one choicer than it, he would set aside the second for Shabbat and eat the first."[20] Hillel had other ideas. "All his actions," the Talmud continues, "including those on a weekday, were for the sake of Heaven, as it is stated: 'Blessed by the Lord, day by day; He bears our burden, our God who is our salvation;

Selah' (Psalms 68:20), meaning that God gives a blessing for each and every day."[21]

Hillel seized each day because he understood that you didn't need the weight of ritual to know that life was sacred, every moment of it. Sure, a Thanksgiving meal served on the finest china and enjoyed around a table decorated with gourds and lit by a crackling fireplace might feel special. But if you stop to consider just how fortunate we are to be here right now, able to enjoy a delicious bite and a meaty conversation with people we love, then a pizza and a cheap bottle of wine shared by a few good friends around the kitchen table feel just as magical. Everything we do is sacred, because we can never separate our basest appetites from our loftiest aspirations. If we can't poop, we can't pray, which makes both actions holy and wholly worthy of our consideration.

Live life this way, and you'll soon arrive at something very close to Aristotle's idea of eudaimonia, that deep sense of happiness that can be felt only when we actively engage with the world, reflecting on our own behavior. One final story about Hillel shows him in his most eudaimonic state and delivers a master class in what life looks like when you consider even its irritants as part of the sacred fabric. Two rowdy gentlemen, the Talmud tells us, bet each other 400 zuz, a small fortune, on the question of whether Hillel could be driven to anger. And so, one of them waited until it was almost Shabbat. He went to Hillel's house, and when he saw the old rabbi enter the shower to wash his hair, he knocked on Hillel's door.

"Who here is Hillel?" cried the man. "Who here is Hillel?"

The sage wrapped himself in some clothes and went out to greet the stranger. "My son," Hillel said to the man, "what do you seek?" The man said he had a question and then proceeded to ask it. It was a profoundly idiotic one: Why, he wanted to know, were the heads of Babylonians oval?

Hillel could have been forgiven for fuming at the bumbling intruder and his silly query. Instead, he answered with kindness. "My son," Hillel said, "you have asked a significant question. The reason is because they do not have clever midwives. They do not know how to shape the child's head at birth."

The man thanked Hillel and left. An hour later, however, he returned.

"Who here is Hillel?" he cried, again, even though he'd already spoken to the sage. "Who here is Hillel?"

Again, Hillel identified himself, and, again, the man asked another dumb question: "Why," he wanted to know, "are the eyes of the residents of Tadmor bleary?"

Hillel smiled. "My son," he said, "you have asked a significant question. The reason is because they live among the sands and the sand gets into their eyes."

The man left, waited another hour, returned for the third time, and shouted out his lunatic mantra: "Who here is Hillel? Who here is Hillel?"

Hillel materialized, calm as always. "Why," asked the man, "do Africans have wide feet?" After telling him again that his question was significant, Hillel answered that it was because they lived in marshlands, and their feet widened to enable them to walk through those swampy areas.

At that point, just as the story is about to slide into the ridiculous, leaving the reader to wonder if Hillel was making up his answers or if they had any actual validity, the meddlesome stranger broke down. "I have many more questions to ask," he said, "but I am afraid lest you get angry." Hillel never flinched. He wrapped himself in a towel, sat down, and calmly told the man to ask away. "The man," the Talmud continues, "got angry and said to him: Are you Hillel whom they call the *Nasi* of Israel? He said to him: Yes. He said to him: If it is you, then may there not be many like you in Israel." And why, Hillel inquired, does the man say such a hurtful thing? "Because," replied the man, "I lost four hundred *zuz* because of you. Hillel said to him: Be vigilant of your spirit and avoid situations of this sort. Hillel is worthy of having you lose four hundred *zuz* and another four hundred *zuz* on his account, and Hillel will not get upset."[22]

Hillel's wisdom earned him the ultimate compliment: He was nearly the only one of the Talmud's sages who wasn't referred to as rabbi; his name itself, the Talmud explains, was greater than any title or honorific. The Talmud also recorded many of his aphorisms; unlike his fellow sages, who often communicated exclusively by issuing rabbinic decrees and interpretations too complex to understand without rigorous study and analysis, Hillel spoke in plain, heartfelt language. "Do not judge your fellow until you are in his place,"[23] he warns us, and then reminds us that "whosoever destroys one soul, it is as though he had destroyed the entire world; and whosoever saves a life, it is as though he had saved the entire world."[24] And while the Talmud chronicles many of Hillel's quibbles with Shammai—a deep ideological divide that was cultivated by their students after them—it also teaches us that Jewish law was almost always in accordance with the teachings of Hillel.

In their first five hundred or so years on the scene, then, the Tannaim, the earliest sages of the Talmud, resisted assimilation, transformed their religion from one focused on collective sacrifices to one interested in individual study and prayer, fashioned a radically new approach to body and self, inspired Greek kings and sages, and figured out a way to be happy in a world that gave them plenty of reasons to be anything but. They needed every bit of their hard-earned wisdom. Sixty-two years after Hillel's passing, and following an event so cataclysmic that many believed it to be the end of Jewish history, the rabbis had to grapple with an even thornier question than how to live happily in one's body: namely, what to do when the body—and the people, and the Temple, and the faith—is faced with the specter of death.

CHAPTER TWO

All Together Now

or

How to Play Well with Others

T HANKSGIVING WEEKEND, 1942, was a big one in Massachusetts. The Eagles of Boston College, undefeated, had
one more game to complete on their way to the Sugar Bowl
and a shot at the national college football championship. They
felt fortunate to play it against the Holy Cross Crusaders, who
were sputtering their way through a middling season with a 4-4-1
record. It would be, Boston fans reassured each other, just like
it had been two years earlier, when the Eagles met holy Cross
at Fenway Park and walked out with a brisk 7–0 victory before
crushing Tennessee and securing the coveted title. But when
Holy Cross's quarterback, the unimprovably named Ray Ball,
kicked things off with a 48-yard drive that was soon converted
to a touchdown, Boston fans were feeling jittery. They spent the
next few hours watching what is largely still acknowledged as the
biggest upset in college sports history. Final score: Holy Cross 55,
Boston 12.

To shake off the bitterness—of the defeat, of the world war still raging, of the frigid evening—many in the sellout crowd of 41,300 headed over to the Cocoanut Grove nightclub, about 2 miles up the road from Fenway. It was a Boston institution. Established during Prohibition by two musicians with warm ties to the mob, it ran as one of the city's most successful speakeasies and was soon taken over by Charlie "King" Solomon, a Russian-born racketeer who already controlled most of the city's gambling, prostitution, and narcotics trade. But in 1933, after Solomon was gunned down in the restroom of Boston's Cotton Club and Prohibition was repealed, the Grove was taken over by Solomon's lawyer, Barney Walensky, who did his best to class up the joint. He opened an upscale piano lounge on the floor above, connecting the formerly seedy saloon—located, conveniently for the purposes of a clan-destine institution, in a former parking garage with low ceilings and few access points—with what was now a 10,000-square-foot complex featuring four bars all stitched together by tight spiral staircases and windy corridors.

But anyone who came to the Grove, Walensky realized, was likely there to soak in a bit of the lore of the original iconic den of iniquity. So while he had the upstairs rooms done in a modern fashion—the bars covered with leatherette, the dirty window that looked out on Broadway removed and replaced with an opaque glass block, and the walls lined with bright, humming neon—he knew he had to keep the bar down in the basement true to its tacky self. The architect who was hired was told he couldn't do anything about the enormous imitation palm trees, each sporting laminated coconut husks that held little 7.5-watt light bulbs, and the room's minuscule dimensions, 35 by 55 square feet, which left no space for any other features or innovations. And so, to further thicken the dimly lit atmosphere that made the Grove so dear to so many connoisseurs of vice, the architect draped 1,966 square feet of dark blue satin across the entire lounge, making the 10-foot ceiling lower by an additional 18 inches. Walensky was pleased; it made the ceiling look like a starry night's sky, he thought, the kind conducive to romance.

And romance was afoot on Saturday, November 28. Even though the Grove was approved by the city's regulators to entertain a maximum of 460 patrons, by 10 p.m. the club was already teeming with more than twice as many revelers. In addition to football fans, some drowning their sorrows and some celebrating, there were the soldiers who, the previous weekend, partook in a successful air-raid drill, as well as others who passed through town on leave or en route to join the war. The cowboy movie star Buck Jones was there, too, relaxing after headlining a big parade supporting the troops.

Around 10:15 p.m., the head bartender, John Bradley, stopped for a second to survey his domain. It was hard to see much of anything—there were about 400 people in the basement bar alone, many of them smoking—but over in the far corner, Bradley could see a soldier in uniform making out with his lady friend. He smiled to himself and looked away, but a few moments later, when his gaze again turned to the same corner of the bar, he noticed it was pitch black.

It didn't take a genius to realize what was going on. The soldier, Bradley thought to himself, wanted a bit of privacy with his sweetheart and unscrewed one of the light bulbs to make sure that whatever he attempted next went unnoticed. The young singer and pianist Goody Goodelle, who was performing at the lounge that night, had just started crooning "White Christmas," one of Bradley's favorite tunes, and so he dispatched his bar boy, sixteen-year-old Stanley Tomaszewski, to go screw the bulb back in. Stanley wasn't going to bother asking the soldier for help; he walked over to the corner, climbed on a little stool, and lit a match. It didn't take him long to find what he was looking for, and, placing the match in his right hand, he tightened the bulb with his left. He climbed down, blew out the match, tossed it on the floor, and stepped on it. He was walking back to Bradley at the bar when he heard someone shout, "Hey, there's a fire in the palm tree!"[1]

By the time Deputy Chief Louis C. Stickel, one of the first

responders to arrive at the scene, pulled up to the Grove, he saw a man's head and arm poking through a small hole in the fancy glass block up front. Stickel and his men tried to break the glass and help the man escape, but the smoke and the heat made it impossible to come anywhere near it. They brought out the hose, but it was too late. The man inside looked at Stickel; "And then," the deputy chief later told investigators, "a flame took him up."[2]

By the time the smoke cleared and rescue operations were over, 492 people were dead, some burned alive and others succumbing to their wounds days later, the cowboy Buck Jones included. For weeks and weeks after the disaster, still one of the worst on record, nurses and doctors at Massachusetts General Hospital continued to care for the victims, joined by volunteers from Harvard Medical School's faculty. But as 1943 dawned and the war in Europe and the Pacific intensified, the Cocoanut Grove disaster faded from memory.

Over at Mass General, however, one doctor was facing an entirely new set of problems. Some patients, observed Erich Lindemann, the chief of psychiatry, were exhibiting strange symptoms. Lindemann wrote them down in a report: "Sensations of somatic distress occurring in waves lasting from twenty minutes to an hour at a time, a feeling of tightness in the throat, choking with shortness of breath, need for sighing, and an empty feeling in the abdomen." These distraught patients also repeated phrases like "It is almost impossible to climb up a stairway" or "everything I lift seems so heavy,"[3] even though their physical scans showed no reason for fatigue. Most lost their appetites; some their will to live.

These patients, Lindemann soon learned, had one thing in common: they'd all lost loved ones at the Grove. And their erratic behavior, he theorized, was simply an acute form of grieving. But how to treat it? Psychiatry, at the time, did not consider grief a condition worth studying. If anything, physicians believed they ought to interfere only if a patient *failed* to grieve, as feeling despondent after losing a loved one was seen as the emotionally desirable response. Making matters worse, the patients he was now seeing were behaving in ways that were difficult to categorize, analyze, or predict. One survivor, for example, returned to the hospital in January, nearly two months after the fire. He spoke of nothing else but his wife, who perished that night. "I should have saved her or I should have died too," the man said, over and over again, to no one in particular. "Nobody can help me. When is it going to happen? I am doomed, am I not?" Lindemann and his colleagues prescribed the usual medications, and within four days, the man grew calm. The doctors were pleased, noting in their patient's chart that a full recovery was forthcoming. On the sixth day of his hospital stay, the man sprinted through his room's closed window and jumped to his death.[4]

Grappling to make sense of such behavior, Lindemann had an idea. He'd seen patients acting similarly once before, he recalled, when he treated women who had undergone hysterectomies. Having lost a part of their body, they experienced what Lindemann, at the time, referred to as a "partial death." Without a uterus, these women felt themselves to be entirely different people, people who now had to relearn everything about being in the world. And teaching a person how to be in the world in the wake of tragic loss wasn't really a task that could ever be limited to the physician's clinic or toolbox—it would take a thicket of loving, supportive friends and family members and care providers and neighbors. It would take, in other words, a community.

This new insight struck most of Lindemann's colleagues as amateurish at best. The great doctor, they grumbled, was drifting away from the foundations of science and toward some sentimental and nonsensical sphere more suited for philosophers or, worse, members of the clergy. "And when he involved non-medical people" in his research, recalled one of his students at the time, "the medical people were just outraged—letting all those non-medical people into our citadel, and polluting the purity of medicine."[5]

But Lindemann wouldn't budge, and before too long, he found his collaborator. Gerald Caplan was born in Liverpool, the son of a prominent rabbi. He shared his father's passion for metaphysical inquiries, if not exactly his commitment to religious observance, so as soon as he graduated medical school he sought out Anna Freud, another scion of a prominent rabbinic family who was teaching a much more thrilling religion. Being an ardent Zionist, he then moved to Jerusalem to help the nascent Jewish state establish its psychiatric services. He had no shortage of patients. A stream of Holocaust survivors trickled in, and Caplan, working mostly with children who had lost their entire families to the Nazis' murderous machine, came to the same exact conclusion as Lindemann: grief was a communal challenge, not an individual crisis.

The textbook Caplan eventually wrote, *Principles of Preventive Psychiatry*, inspired President John F. Kennedy to sign the Community Mental Health Act, which provided government funding to community relief centers and research. It informed generations of psychiatrists, psychologists, and social workers and remains one of the most influential documents in shaping our approach to grief and mental health care to this day. And its ideas, still strikingly original and evocative, bear more than a passing resemblance to the principles detailed in another book, one with which Caplan, the rabbi's son, would have been intimately familiar—the Talmud.

To the extent that the Talmud is a literary work—it's better understood, perhaps, as a "drift net for catching God,"[6] to borrow Jonathan Rosen's perfect phrase—its major theme might be loss. The Talmud's very creation owes much to destruction—of the Temple, of Jerusalem, of Judaism's ancient way of life—and to the fear that the divine wisdom passed from generation to generation for millennia will somehow, someday, be lost and forgotten. What, then, can the Talmud teach us about loss and grief and how to cope with both? To answer this question, we must return to one of history's most disastrous dinner parties, held in Jerusalem sometime in the year 66 CE.

One of the town's dandies, the Talmud tells us, was throwing a lavish soiree. He invited all of the swells, but he was particularly keen to make sure his good pal Kamtza was in attendance, and so he dispatched his servant with a special invitation to Mr. Kamtza's house. The servant must've been preoccupied, or dim, or both, because he delivered the invite to a man named Bar Kamtza instead. And Bar Kamtza, it so happened, was his boss's sworn enemy.

Receiving the note, Bar Kamtza was delighted. Finally, he thought, his nemesis had come to his senses and was extending an olive branch. Bar Kamtza RSVPed right away and was looking forward to the climactic reconciliation that would ensue over some good wine, some rice, and delicious lamb. Imagine, then, his surprise when he showed up at the feast, only to be blocked by the host.

"You are my enemy," the rich man said bluntly. "What then do you want here? Arise and leave."[7]

Bar Kamtza was shocked. Realizing he must have been invited by mistake, he quickly looked around and saw all of his friends and acquaintances already reclining, looking at the unfolding drama. He was determined to save face. "Since I have already come," he told the host, speaking as calmly as he could, "let me stay and I will give you money for whatever I eat and drink. Just do not embarrass me by sending me out."

The host stared at him blankly. "No," he said finally. "You must leave."

"I will give you money for half the feast," said Bar Kamtza, growing agitated.

"No," the host repeated. "You must leave."

Bar Kamtza had one more card to play. "I will give you money for the entire feast," he told his host. "Just let me stay."

"No, you must leave," the host said a third time, and before Bar Kamtza could reply, the host grabbed his arm and dragged him out of the house and into the street as all of Jerusalem's elite looked on in stunned silence.

"These celebrated men, including many of the rabbis, were

sitting there and did not protest the actions of the host," a stung and steaming Bar Kamtza said to himself as he hurried home. "They saw how he humiliated me. I can only understand from their behavior that they were content with what he did. I will go to the king and inform against them."

Being a wealthy and well-connected gentleman, Bar Kamtza was soon standing before the emperor in Rome, telling tales of a secret Jewish plot to revolt against the crown. The emperor was skeptical; none of his officers had reported any new or troubling signs of unrest. But, his curiosity piqued, he asked Bar Kamtza for proof. Simple, said the scorned Jerusalemite: "Go and test them. Send them an offering to be brought in honor of the government, and see whether they will sacrifice it." The emperor agreed and selected one of the finest beasts in his cowshed, a gorgeous three-year-old calf, for Bar Kamtza to take to the priests in the Temple.

Bar Kamtza thanked the emperor, took the animal, and began the long march back east. On his way, he made a small cut on the calf's upper lip. Being well versed in the rules of halacha, he knew that any blemish made the calf unfit as an offering. With a wry smile, he delivered the calf to the priests. They, in turn, inspected the beast, found the blemish, realized what had happened, and convened an urgent meeting. Most present agreed that for the sake of peace, it was imperative to go ahead, slaughter the cow, and appease Rome. But Rabbi Zekharya ben Avkolas disagreed. "If the priests do that," he said, softly but firmly, "people will say that blemished animals may be sacrificed as offerings on the altar." That, the sages conceded, was a fair point. Was there an alternative? Yes, said one of the rabbis present: kill Bar Kamtza, thus making sure he never reports back to the emperor.

"If you kill him," Zekharya ben Avkolas opined again, "people will say that one who makes a blemish on a sacrificial animal is to be killed." Stumped, the rabbis decided that the best thing to do was nothing. Bar Kamtza wrote to the emperor with the news. War broke out. Four years later, the Temple was in flames and

Jerusalem destroyed. Judaism, as it was lived and practiced for centuries, was dead. So were scores of Jews.

The story of Kamtza and Bar Kamtza is one of the Talmud's most celebrated. Religious Jews tell it every year on the ninth day of the Hebrew month of Av, which falls in the middle of summer and commemorates this historical catastrophe. Seldom, however, do they—we—stop and ponder the profound strangeness of this tale.

Questions abound: Why would the Talmud, not a book known for being enamored with plot, deliver an uncharacteristically detailed drama in three acts, complete with inner monologues, scene settings, and other literary devices it otherwise applied rarely, if ever? And why make this story the prism through which to look at the greatest Jewish tragedy of antiquity?

If it is meant as an honest historical account, the story of Kamtza and Bar Kamtza is comically inept: the Roman emperor, for example, is never mentioned by name, nor do we learn anything about the identity of the dinner party's implacable host. The Talmud also has very little to say about what happens in the four years leading up to the cataclysm, about the bitter ideological and theological divides among the Jews or about the eventual armed resistance to Rome and its ultimate collapse. Is the story merely a morality tale, then? If so, it's a strange choice. Why would the victims of a terrible catastrophe choose to tell a story that blames themselves for the destruction? It wasn't Bar Kamtza, after all, who set fire to the Holy of Holies or slaughtered scores of Jewish defenders; it was Roman soldiers. How, then, are we to understand the meaning of this particular tale and its centrality to the Talmud?

By considering its sequel.

No sooner has the Talmud finished telling us about Kamtza and Bar Kamtza than it launches into another account of the destruction, this one starring a man named Rabbi Yohanan ben Zakkai.

What do we know about this controversial giant, accused

by some of failing to stop the Romans and celebrated by others for saving Judaism in perpetuity? The Talmud gives us another uncharacteristically long introduction. Rabbi Yohanan, we learn, never engaged in idle conversation; he never walked 4 cubits, or about 6 feet, without engaging in Torah study and without donning tefillin; no person ever preceded him into the study hall; he never slept in the study hall, neither substantial sleep nor a brief nap; and he never left anyone in the study hall and exited. He never contemplated matters of Torah in alleyways filthy with human excrement, as doing so is a display of contempt for the Torah. The account goes on: "no person ever found him sitting and silent, i.e., inactive; rather, he was always sitting and studying; and only he opened the door for his students, disregarding his own eminent standing; and he never said anything that he did not hear from his teacher."[8]

He was, in short, no one's idea of a natural-born leader. He hadn't Shimon HaTzadik's effortless charisma or Hillel's acrobatically active mind. He was a quiet and reserved reader and thinker who was much more comfortable poring over some passage in a book than he was thinking about big political, to say nothing of existential, questions. And yet he alone rose to the occasion.

At the time, Jerusalem's Jewish community was deeply divided between various warring sects. Some, socialists *avant la lettre*, railed at the prominence of the city's rich; one of their ranks even burned down the town's grain depot, arguing that collective hunger was precisely the sort of equalizing catalyst the Jews needed to come together and defeat their Roman foes. Others were murderous thugs interested in nothing but power, and still others timid priests who mistook inaction for caution and wisdom. All, however, were united by the belief that the war against Rome was still winnable.

Not ben Zakkai. It's unfair to call him pragmatic—the term had little meaning in a premodern society that still organized itself around intricate rituals and believed firmly in direct divine intervention. But as a keen observer of the human soul, he realized that the first thing it does when confronted with something as unthinkable as loss is to cling, wildly and madly and in all defiance of observable reality, to the belief that everything is going to be alright. Denial forever precedes acceptance, which at first appears as indistinguishable from surrender. We tell ourselves that it's nobler to fight, even as we don't bother thinking enough about the odds in suiting up for battle. And we tell ourselves that anything but a fight is a sad form of surrender.

Precisely because he was a deeply religious man, ben Zakkai knew that allowing yourself these heady pleasures of hope was a dangerous proposition: wish for something too fervently, and, when hope is ultimately dashed, you have no path remaining but down, toward despair, a one-way street. So wary was ben Zakkai of people losing themselves in glorious daydreams that he taught his students the following lesson: If you are holding a sapling in your hand and are about to plant it in the ground, and someone comes and tells you that the Messiah has just arrived and the end-times are upon us and heaven on earth is about to begin, ignore them and finish planting that sapling first. Otherwise, life becomes an intolerable seesaw, teetering between feeling uncritically optimistic about the future and stumbling into it with a heavy sense of dread. Hope and despair alike, to ben Zakkai, were beyond our capacity to fully grasp as human beings; only God could understand such complex emotions. We here on earth had no choice but to greet good news and bad alike with actions, preferably the sort of actions that left behind something timeless, like a tree.

Or a community: Seeing the Romans close in on Jerusalem, ben Zakkai, that most placid of men, concocted a plan. He summoned his two brightest students, Rabbi Eliezer and Rabbi Yehoshua, and had them help him into a plain wooden coffin. Inside the coffin, he placed something putrid, probably a bit of rotting bark, so that a strong smell of decomposition greeted anyone who came near. The two disciples walked the coffin to the city's gates and announced that Rabbi Yohanan ben Zakkai had died and had to be buried posthaste. The Jewish extremists guarding the gate were suspicious: Was the rabbi really dead, or was he trying to escape the sieged city? To settle matters, one guard removed his dagger and was about to stab the coffin. "Don't," said his colleague, a relative of ben Zakkai's who was in on the plan. "We don't want the Romans thinking that we're savages who stab their own great teachers." The guard was convinced to lay down his dagger, and he let Yehoshua and Eliezer pass. Once they were outside, ben Zakkai arose from the coffin, presented himself at the Roman headquarters, and demanded to speak to Vespasian, the general in command of the troops and the man who would very soon become emperor himself.

It is here that the controversy over Yohanan ben Zakkai begins.

"If there is a barrel of honey," Vespasian, surprised and more than a little bit irritated by the visit, said to ben Zakkai, "and a snake is wrapped around it, wouldn't [one] break the barrel in order to kill the snake?"[9] It was a simple enough metaphor for ben Zakkai to understand: Jerusalem might have been as precious as a barrel of honey, but the Jewish extremists who now controlled it were like vipers, and the only way to rid Rome of their menace was to smash the beautiful vessel, the holy city they called home.

What should have ben Zakkai said in response? Many of his successors, including the famed Rabbi Akiva, have grumbled that ben Zakkai should have argued, that he should have told Vespasian that no barrels ought to be broken and that snakes could just as easily be removed with tongs—meaning, fight the rebels, but kindly leave Jerusalem and the Temple unscathed.

Ben Zakkai, however, made no effort to save the city. Why? Two possible explanations arose. The first, promoted by the Talmud itself, is perfectly earthly: he was afraid that bold requests—stop the war, spare the Temple—would strike Vespasian as too audacious, in which case he would simply refuse and "there would not be even a small amount of salvation."[10] Better, then, to play it safe and make a smaller, surer request. But later interpreters have offered a second, more metaphysical reasoning. Calamity, ben Zakkai knew, was inevitable; he could no more curb it than he could prevent his own eventual demise. Everything must pass, even things that, like the Temple, have stood strong for centuries and have come to seem eternal. The point wasn't to stand athwart history and yell stop, a privilege reserved only for the Creator. The point was to figure out how to stay alive in whatever it was that came next.

And so, Yohanan ben Zakkai asked Vespasian for three things. First, he said to him, spare the city of Yavneh, a town in central Israel known as a hotbed of Torah study and scholarship. Second, protect the family of Rabban Gamliel, a direct descendant of Hillel and, like his famed ancestor, the spiritual leader of the community at the time. And finally, send doctors to cure my friend Rabbi Tzadok, who, distraught, has been praying and fasting himself to the brink of expiration. Vespasian conceded.

Ben Zakkai's requests may not, at first blush, strike anyone as particularly radical, but their logic is comprehensive, daring, and tremendously insightful. First, ben Zakkai realized, if the community was to survive, it needed to pack up and move. Abandoning Jerusalem was as hard, or harder, for Jews to imagine than it would be for a Frenchman to forget Paris, say, or for a Brit to walk away from a smoldering London. The city had become synonymous with Jewish nationhood, the earthly seat of centuries of religious and political and emotional yearnings. But even a symbol as sacred and as resonant as Jerusalem ought not to be mistaken for more than it was. Jerusalem wasn't Judaism. It was possible, though painful, to start life anew elsewhere, in a town, Yavneh, light on historical baggage and thick with precisely the sort of folk who could take over and do the work of governance and leadership. Ben Zakaai knew he could give the Romans the symbolic victory associated with destroying Jerusalem and still preserve the holy city's meaning—a city of religious learning and community—elsewhere.

But survival wasn't as simple as merely setting up shop elsewhere and announcing that business would be carried on as usual. The loss of the Temple, ben Zakkai understood, would likely produce an effect similar to that felt millennia later by patients who'd lost an organ or a loved one. It would make Jews who were used to Temple life suddenly feel like empty, different, disoriented people, driven to madness by the sensation that everything they'd known about life and about themselves no longer made any sense. This is where ben Zakkai's second request, to protect the descendants of Hillel, came in: By insisting that the same rabbinic dynasty that had been in charge for decades remained in place, he tethered the Jews to tradition, giving them an ember to remind them of the great spiritual fires that once burned bright and making them believe that these same fires may burn bright once again. He gave them, in other words, a piece of their past that wasn't traumatic, that wasn't a reminder of how much they'd lost but rather of the precious things they still had.

The biggest piece of the puzzle, though, was still missing: Even with somewhere to live and someone to trust and something to connect them to their more storied past, what would spiritual, emotional, and public life look like now that the Temple was gone? For centuries, Jews followed the same routines, all of which revolved around pilgrimages and the belief that sins could only be expiated by means of burnt offerings. What did it even mean to be religious, to believe, to follow the faith, without a Temple? And, for that matter, what did it even mean to be human, as no other way of life than one centered around the Temple had been available to Jews for centuries? This is the purpose of ben Zakkai's third and final request. Amid the collective catastrophe, with so many dead and dying, he refused to let the devastation become abstract. He knew that he couldn't help "the Jews," a mass of millions whose faces and names and stories he didn't and couldn't know. But he could help one man, his suffering friend, and by doing so set an example of what he wanted the society he was rebuilding to look like. In ben Zakkai's imagination, the perfect community didn't prattle on about virtue as it stood by idly while its people suffered; it slowed down for long enough to listen to the sobs of just one elderly man, find them intolerable, and step in to help. The Talmud later tells us that when ben Zakkai and Rabbi Yehoshua witnessed Jerusalem burning, the latter was despondent and cried bitterly. Not so ben Zakkai. There was a way to heal, he told his student, and that way was loving kindness and good deeds.[11]

Ben Zakkai's insights hardly materialized out of thin air. The Torah, he knew, delivered detailed instructions on what to do when a loved one passed away, and the destruction of the Temple was another form of bereavement writ large. When a spouse, a child, a parent, or a sibling dies, observant Jews follow the Torah's precise protocol. Its spirit is clear: Mourn, but constructively and never too much. First comes *aninut*, the period beginning with the moment of death and ending with the loved one's burial, which Judaism commands to happen almost immediately, most often before even a single day has passed. A mourner who's just lost someone they loved, the Torah teaches us, is wild with grief and too disoriented and heartbroken to handle anything. That person is therefore relieved of all duties and responsibilities and is allowed to take a moment and be alone with the unimaginable. That moment, however, mustn't last long. The Talmud repeatedly warns that those who grieve too loudly or too excessively will soon find themselves mourning another dead relative, as they've allowed themselves to step aside from the business of living and succumbed to their sorrow instead.

How, though, to keep hearts and minds from collapsing under the weight of so many new and powerful emotions? Judaism's solution is simple: company.

The Torah realized the same exact thing that doctors at Mass General learned in the aftermath of the Cocoanut Grove fire— that grieving people are best served if they are not alone with their grief for very long. To that end, a special period of seven days was designated, known as *Shiva*, during which the entire community is encouraged to visit the bereaved and spend a short while talking about the deceased. Maimonides, the great medieval codifier of Jewish law and himself a physician, already understood what Gerald Caplan would prescribe centuries later, namely that the mere act of allowing bereaved people the opportunity to talk about the person they loved helps them find a path away from rigidly embracing the dead and back into the world of the living. There are several more stages a grieving person must follow, each occurring at specific points in time and each complete with its own set of rules. But the idea behind them all is the same: when disaster strikes, a warm, engaged, caring community is the only engine of survival.

We may now once again take our seat at that disastrous dinner party, the one the Talmud tells us ushered in the mayhem. What were we supposed to learn from the story? Yohanan ben Zakkai gives us the clue we need: learn that by failing to be accountable to each other, the people of Jerusalem brought about the city's demise, and learn also that healing begins—and quite possibly finds closure—when we grieve together and work together to rebuild when possible and mourn when not.

This is why the Bar Kamtza story is presented in such intricate detail and why it strikes us as so strange. The Talmud wants to make sure we stop and consider each player in this drama and ask ourselves what might have been done differently. The servant might have shown some care. The host might have shown some compassion. Bar Kamtza might have shown some humility and swallowed his pride. The bigwigs looking on might have shown some courage and stood up for their humiliated friend. Zekharya ben Avkolas might have shown some backbone and stepped up to resolve this crisis rather than to hide behind technicalities. Even Kamtza himself, the Talmud insists, is to blame, even though he wasn't present. He, the rabbis tell us, might have shown some character by showing up to his dear friend's party without being so prim and waiting for an official invitation. True friends, later generations of rabbis expounded, are obligated to check in on each other constantly, decorum and manners and self-regard be damned.

The late Elie Wiesel captured this idea in a Hasidic tale he shared in several of his works. "One day," goes the story, "the Guerer Rebbe, may his sainted memory protect us, decided to question one of his disciples: How is Moshe Yaakov doing?— The disciples didn't know.—What! shouted the Rebbe, you don't know? You pray under the same roof with him, you study the same texts, you serve the same God, you sing the same songs, and you dare tell me you don't know whether Moshe Yaakov is in good health, whether he needs help, advice or comforting?"[12] This is the true moral of the Kamtza and Bar Kamtza story—"that every man share in every other man's life and not leave him to himself in either sorrow or joy."[13]

It is not insignificant that the closest thing the Kamtza and Bar Kamtza story has to heroes are the Romans. To hear the Talmud tell it, Jerusalem's actual destroyers come off as sensible, charitable, and eminently reasonable. The emperor doesn't fly into a rage at the first mention of a possible conspiracy; he demands that Bar Kamtza provide concrete proof. And Vespasian doesn't merely dismiss ben Zakkai as a lunatic or spy; he listens to the old man and grants him three nontrivial wishes. As it is unusual for anyone, especially in antiquity, to forge a mythology by praising one's enemies while finding fault with each and every one of one's kin, we're left with little choice but to read one more layer of meaning into the story. When the worst happens, the Talmud is telling us, we should resist the urge to blame our stars and find fault instead in ourselves. Others aren't the authors of our misfortune; only we have that power. If we can imagine a story in which we're cruel and caddish, we can also imagine a story in which we're humble and compassionate and wise. We have a choice—be Bar Kamtza or be ben Zakkai.

Astute readers—and the rabbis of the Talmud were nothing if not astute—will notice one more salient feature of the Talmud's twin stories of loss, grief, and recovery: both shy away from the collective and the world-historic in favor of intimate narratives centered around individual choices. If you want to understand how the worst happens and how to bounce back, the Talmud tells us, forget about nations and trends and wars and other ephemeral forces and focus on individuals instead. The power is all ours; so is the responsibility.

This last observation is not incidental. It was the moral and spiritual machinery Rabbi Yohanan ben Zakkai had designed to propel the ideas of the ancient faith into an uncertain future. Where ancient rituals once stood there was now a deep commitment to ethics, to a personal and intimate exploration of right and wrong on an entirely human level with the Almighty hovering somewhere in the background, ever present but unseen in the unfurling of daily life. If you'd like redemption, this new approach quipped, go ahead and roll up your sleeves.

And it was up to ben Zakkai's two celebrated students, who smuggled him out of Jerusalem, to teach this transition to their flock. But how? How to preach to people reeling from a devastating national tragedy so shortly after a war in which nearly everyone lost a friend or a relative? Rabbi Yehoshua and Rabbi Eliezer, in pure Talmudic fashion, took profoundly diverging approaches, still resonant in the ways we teach and think about everything from politics to mental health today.

Rabbi Yehoshua might have felt at home were he to visit a cognitive behavioral therapist, say, because he believed relief would come if we shattered the cycle of obsessive concern and disabused ourselves of habits that only led us deeper into emotional darkness. The Talmud tells an almost comical story in which Yehoshua—a student of philosophy who relished conversations with Roman scholars, an accomplished musician, and a worldly man who shared his teacher's distaste for ecstasy—encounters a group of Jews who are in deep mourning for the Temple. Uninvited and unprompted, he sidles up to them and starts a conversation.

"My children," he kicks things off sweetly, "for what reason do you not eat meat and do you not drink wine?" The mourners are quick to respond: "They said to him: Shall we eat meat, from which offerings are sacrificed upon the altar, and now the altar has ceased to exist? Shall we drink wine, which is poured as a libation upon the altar, and now the altar has ceased to exist?"[14]

It was just the prompt Yehoshua was waiting for. If that's the case, he tells the mourners, you shouldn't eat bread either, because the meal offerings in the Temple contained flour. The mourners admit that this is an excellent point and vow that from that moment on, they'll exclude all bread products from their diets as well. But Rabbi Yehoshua is far from finished. What, he asks, about fruit and vegetables? After all, it was customary for people to bring the first fruits of their trees in gratitude to the priests, so surely fruits and vegetables, too, should now be forbidden. Hearing this, the mourners aren't as quick to agree. The rabbi has a point, they concede, but swearing off all produce is a bit difficult; maybe they should only ban some fruits and vegetables as a token of their intense grief? Maybe just a few symbolic offerings, like grapes and olives and figs and dates? Rabbi Yehoshua, however, does not engage with this arithmetic of self-denial. He was saving the best for last. You know, he tells the mourners, back when the Temple stood, we had a ceremony called the water libation, where water was carried into the Temple while people sang and danced and prayed for bountiful rains. If you're serious about your asceticism and want to cut off anything and everything that reminds you of Temple life, water has got to go as well.

The mourners are stunned into silence. "My children," Rabbi Yehoshua says to them, "come, and I will tell you how we should act. To not mourn at all is impossible, as the decree was already issued and the Temple has been destroyed. But to mourn excessively as you are doing is also impossible."[15]

Like his teacher ben Zakkai before him, Rabbi Yehoshua wasn't telling the mourners anything radical or new, but merely delivering a lesson on the Torah's approach to bereavement. Like Dr. Erich Lindemann, Yehoshua, too, understood that loss—of a friend, of a family member, or even of an institution, like the Temple, that was present in so many facets of daily life—felt like a partial death, a shock so jarring it invited extreme reactions, like depriving the body of sustenance. The key to overcoming this initial shock and making grief sustainable was resisting these inclinations and opting for constructive measures that are instead designed to chart a course back into something resembling normal life. Following up on Yehoshua's conversation with the mourners, the Talmud delivers a few constructive measures of its own. When you paint your house, it advises, leave a tiny strip of wall, just opposite the corner, unplastered. Make it big enough for people to see but not so big as to call immediate attention to it. And when you sit down for a festive meal, leave a small item, no larger than a little fried fish, off the table, just so you remember the days of hunger and want. And when a woman puts on her makeup, she should consider leaving one spot untouched, so that even in her splendor she's not without a blemish to remind her of all that was lost.

This advice, most likely, is the source of the Jewish custom of shattering a glass at weddings: we inject a short and solemn note into an otherwise joyous occasion—not to dampen the celebration but to deepen it, because we understand that joy is all the stronger and longer lasting if it incorporates a remembrance of suffering rather than denying it.

Rabbi Eliezer ben Horcanus, Yehoshua's colleague and intellectual sparring partner, took a very different approach. Born to a family of wealthy landowners, he spent his formative years tending to the family business with his brothers and his father, all of whom considered education a waste of precious time better spent tending to their fields and their livestock. But Eliezer was introverted and intellectually curious, and he looked with awe at the scholars he saw spending their days reading and arguing and grappling with questions of man and God and law. He wanted to be just like them.

One day, the Talmud tells us, Eliezer gathered up the courage and ran away from home. He was twenty-two years old, and he made his way to Jerusalem to see the one man who everyone agreed was the greatest teacher of his generation—Rabbi Yohanan ben Zakkai. He could hardly ask his father for some pocket money or some snacks for the road, and so, reeling with hunger, he ate the only thing he could find by the side of the road, a small heap of cow dung. Naturally, then, when he finally arrived at the house of study, no one wanted to sit next to the smelly stranger. He might have been ignored, dejected, and forced to return home defeated had it not been for ben Zakkai's famed sensitivity. Spotting the silent young man slumped in the corner, the great rabbi walked over to him and asked him if he'd had anything to eat. Eliezer, realizing how horrendous he smelled, said nothing, afraid to open his mouth. Ben Zakkai immediately arranged a meal for him, and intuiting how much the young man must have sacrificed to realize his dream of becoming a learned man, said to him, "My son, just as you now have this bad breath, so will you soon have a good reputation as a great scholar."[16]

Rabbi Eliezer did become a great scholar, and soon. The Talmud treats us to another dramatic account, in which his father, having previously disowned him, sees his son preaching to a gathering of dignitaries and is so moved by the young man's erudition that he immediately bequeaths all of his considerable wealth to Eliezer. This newfound wealth didn't change Eliezer's thinking in the least. He remained a mystic, trying to find the deep, hidden meaning of God's mysterious ways while his colleague, Yehoshua, focused on the present and the observable. But Eliezer, too, had something to say to mourners who asked him how they might contain their grief, and his advice was far from Yehoshua's playful reduction ad absurdum. Instead, Eliezer delivered the following bit of wisdom, as close as an ancient rabbi ever got to a Zen koan: "Repent one day before your death."

Eliezer's listeners were baffled. "But does a person know the day on which he will die?" they asked. "All the more so this is a good piece of advice," he replied quizzically, "and one should repent today lest he die tomorrow; and by following this advice one will spend his entire life in a state of repentance."[17] If you're generous, you may imagine the life Eliezer is prescribing as something like a very long bout of psychoanalysis, with patients forever on the couch, contemplating their actions. Or you may imagine Rabbi Eliezer's credo tacked to the wall of any Hollywood writer's room. "Repent one day before your death" is a pretty decent distillation of the dramatic and moral combustion animating *The Sopranos, Mad Men, Breaking Bad*, or any other pop culture cult classic obsessed with the possibility of healing in an irreparably broken world. Then again, you could also read Eliezer's words as fatalistic, a spin cycle of anxiety and guilt that is more of a blow than a crutch. No sooner had a person recovered from loss than she's informed it was now time to look inward in search of something—anything—to improve. And the improvement, of course, never ends, as the perfection Rabbi Eliezer seeks is reserved only for God. Such moral rectitude may appeal to the few and the impeccably righteous, but it's of little comfort to the many, the tired, the distracted, and the eminently fallible— that is, to the rest of us. Read this way, Rabbi Eliezer's teaching sounds less like an expression of Judaism's practical and communal approach to mourning and more like a solipsistic iteration that echoes the anguished words spoken by that man who'd lost his wife in the Cocoanut Grove fire: "Nobody can help me. When is it going to happen? I am doomed, am I not?"

Eliezer's fellow rabbis thought so, too, and because they regarded their disputations not as esoteric arguments but rather as competing approaches to interpreting the divine will, the scene was set for a major showdown. The rabbis tolerated, even courted, dissent on matters great and small. But on the fundamentals— questions like where we ought to turn to in our time of need or what is the source of moral authority—they couldn't compromise. Which is how we get the single most famous story in the Talmud— arguably its most instructive, certainly its most astonishing—the one about the oven of Akhnai.

One day, the Talmud recounts, the sages were sitting and parsing a fairly complicated question pertaining to purity laws, asking themselves under which circumstances might a certain kind of oven be rendered impure according to Jewish law. As the conversation progressed, the sages all found themselves in agreement, all, that is, save for Rabbi Eliezer, who took the opposing view. The rabbis listened intently; this, after all, was the man about whom their great teacher, Yohanan ben Zakkai, used to say that "even if all the sages of Israel were on one scale of the balance and Rabbi Eliezer ben Horcanus on the other scale, he would outweigh them all."[18] But even after Rabbi Eliezer "answered all the possible answers in the world to support his opinion,"[19] his colleagues were still not convinced.

This made Eliezer furious. "If the halacha is in accordance with my opinion," he thundered, pointing at a nearby carob tree, "this tree will prove it." He was barely done speaking when the tree shook to life, uprooted itself, and, with a dancer's graceful poise, pranced for 150 feet before slumping back to its natural state. Eliezer smiled at this minor miracle, but the other rabbis were indifferent. "One does not cite *halachic* proof from the carob tree," they said. Interpreting Jewish law was none of the tree's business.

This vexed Eliezer. He was now determined to best his friends. He needed a grander miracle. And so, he pointed at a nearby stream and said that if his interpretation of the law was correct, the stream should prove it. And the stream, just like the tree before it, abided, reversing the course of its flow. Watching the river run backward, the other rabbis shrugged. Rivers were rivers, they said, and rivers had no place deciding complicated legal matters.

Eliezer was losing his cool. He needed to give his buddies a shakedown, both figuratively and literally, so he asked the walls of the study hall to come to his aid and prove him right. And the walls, obediently, began to shake. They were just about to cave in and collapse when Rabbi Yehoshua—he, too, growing unamused—scolded them. You stay out of this, Yehoshua said to the walls; this argument is only between us scholars. The walls settled down, and Yehoshua and the others informed Eliezer that they didn't much care for his magic—they still considered his opinion wrong.

This Eliezer simply couldn't bear.

"If the halacha is in accordance with my opinion," he said with the calm of one about to draw the doomsday weapon, "heaven will prove it."

The rabbis grew silent. Calling on God to intervene was unprecedented. And yet no sooner had Eliezer issued his challenge than "a divine voice emerged from heaven and said: Why are you differing with Rabbi Eliezer, as the halacha is in accordance with his opinion in every place that he expresses an opinion?"

Eliezer smiled, relieved, and relished his ultimate vindication. But Yehoshua rose to his feet, and looking up at the sky, said just this: "It is not in heaven."

The phrase is one of the most hotly debated and intricately interpreted in all of Jewish exegesis, but the Talmud affixes a pretty good explanation of what Rabbi Yehoshua had meant: "Since the Torah was already given at Mount Sinai, we do not regard a divine voice, as [God] already wrote at Mount Sinai, in the Torah: 'After a majority to incline' (Exodus 23:2). Since the majority of Rabbis disagreed with Rabbi Eliezer's opinion, the halacha is not ruled in accordance with his opinion."[20] Once God delivered His laws to His human charges, it was up to them—up to us—to interpret these laws, and once we did, not even the Creator of all life had the right to barge in and challenge our decrees.

This is not only an audacious theological argument—the story ends with the prophet Elijah reporting that God was delighted with Rabbi Yehoshua's intransigence, gleefully saying, "My children have triumphed over Me"—but a political and moral one as well. To believe, as the rabbis believed, that ours is the ultimate authority for charting the course of human events—not because we don't believe in God, but because we believe God handed that supreme responsibility down to us—is also to believe that we have an ultimate duty to step in and do the difficult things that

are much too tempting to abandon to higher powers. It is to cultivate what the philosopher Bernard-Henri Lévy, the closest thing
we have today to a Talmudic sage like Rabbi Yehoshua, calls "the
will to see," the courage to engage in the hardest form of the fight
for justice, the one that compels us to look at all of humanity and
see ourselves as beholden to each and every last one of those suffering. This is true for us all, but it is particularly challenging for
people in mourning, who are urged not to get lost in their individual grief but to rush instead to rejoin the community and trade
in their individual emotional burdens for the much heavier, but
much more sustainable, one we all carry together, the burden of
all of humanity's troubles.

This was too much for Rabbi Eliezer to stomach. He couldn't
imagine a world in which human beings had so much leeway,
so much freedom, so much agency, which he took as a license
to unleash disaster and wonder alike. He couldn't live in a
world governed not by strict tradition and revealed instruction
but by human faculties, by reason and logic and rambunctious
discussions that ended in a decision made by a vote. And he
refused to accept the opinion of his peers, which meant they
had no choice but to invoke the harshest punishment at their
disposal—ostracism from their group of scholars. In a solemn ceremony, the other rabbis collected a host of items Rabbi
Eliezer had deemed ritualistically pure and burned them, as if it
were his very opinions they were casting into the fire. Removed
from the community, Eliezer lingered a few more years, sitting
alone in his home in the city of Lod in central Israel, a bitter
and broken man.

The Talmud tells us about his very last moments. Realizing
their ex-friend was at death's door, the sages decided to come and
pay their respects. Still, an excommunication is an excommunication, so even as they entered Eliezer's room, they sat at some
distance from the ailing man. Eliezer looked at them coldly.

"Why have you come?"[21] he asked.

"We have come to study Torah," they answered, not wishing

to tell their former friend that they were only at his side because they feared that his hours were numbered.

"And why," Eliezer asked harshly, "have you not come until now?"

With nothing else to say, really, the rabbis replied that they had been busy. And with that, Rabbi Eliezer broke down. He raised his arms and placed them across his chest. "Woe to you, my two arms," he said, "as they are like two Torah scrolls that are now being rolled up, and will never be opened again." I had learned so much, he cried, and yet my students took from me so little, "only like the tiny amount that a paintbrush removes from a tube of paint."[22]

Eager to make him feel better, the rabbis began asking Eliezer intricate questions about Jewish law, and, for one brief moment, he stirred with answers and ideas and life. And then, he died. Rabbi Yehoshua stood up and announced, for all to hear, that the ban that had been placed on Rabbi Eliezer was now removed.

Which meant that the rabbinic revolution launched by Yohanan ben Zakkai was now complete. In the span of a few cataclysmic years, Judaism had reinvented itself, reborn as an ethical quest for justice that abhors absolutes, demands action, and gives even its humblest practitioners the license to question, challenge, and resist. This gave the rabbis and their followers the spiritual and emotional energy they needed to bounce back from the destruction of the Temple and the loss of their nation, creating a much more democratic—and chaotic, and soulful—society in which everyday people now had to contend with the moral urgencies previously contemplated exclusively by rabbis and priests. It also gave the people grappling with these seminal questions a new motto: It is not in heaven.

Rabbi Yehoshua's line came to him courtesy of Deuteronomy, and its context in the Bible is worth studying. God, talking to the Israelites, reassures them that the laws He was delivering may be tough, at times inscrutable, often demanding, and frequently constricting. But none, He guarantees them, were impossible:

"For this commandment which I command thee this day, it is not too hard for thee, neither is it far off. It is not in heaven, that thou shouldest say: 'Who shall go up for us to heaven, and bring it unto us, and make us to hear it, that we may do it?' Neither is it beyond the sea, that thou shouldest say: 'Who shall go over the sea for us, and bring it unto us, and make us to hear it, that we may do it?' But the word is very nigh unto thee, in thy mouth, and in thy heart, that thou mayest do it."[23]

This affirmation—yes we can—would now become the guiding principle of rabbinic Judaism, shaping everything from how decisions were made to who got to make them. The democratic spirit ushered in by Yavneh and its sages begged for a new kind of thinker, a self-made man or woman driven by passion and brilliance, a dynamo of reinvention who could turn the dirges of destruction into hymns of celebration and joy. It called for people who were, to borrow a few lines from a much later poet who embodied this spirit perfectly, "old and young, of the foolish as much as the wise, Regardless of others, ever regardful of others, / Maternal as well as paternal, a child as well as a man, / Stuff'd with the stuff that is coarse and stuff'd with the stuff that is fine, / One of the Nation of many nations, the smallest the same and the largest the same."[24] And just such a man was waiting in the wings.

CHAPTER THREE

Holding Out for a Hero

or

How to Be Yourself

B Y ALL available accounts, Erich Auerbach didn't much mind it when a letter materialized, in 1934, requiring him to pledge his allegiance to Adolph Hitler.

Sure, he was Jewish, but his family never cared much for the old-timey religion. He was, he felt strongly, a German first and foremost, and the Fatherland had never given him anything but the finest it had to offer. He was born wealthy and grew up in comfort in the poshest district of Berlin. He graduated from the city's best high school and was admitted to Heidelberg University, the nation's oldest and one of its most prestigious academies, the towering institution where Hegel once roared and where Dmitri Mendeleev introduced the world to his periodic table of elements. He pursued a doctorate in law, which was a respectable profession that suited a young man like Auerbach—reserved and obsessive, practical and brilliant, dedicated and hardworking—just fine. But he was soon distracted by a trio of schoolmates, each destined to intellectual superstardom: the Hungarian Georg

Lukács, one of the founding fathers of Western Marxist philosophy; Karl Jaspers, the groundbreaking Swiss psychiatrist; and Walter Benjamin, a fellow Berliner already gaining fame as his generation's finest literary critic.

It's not hard to imagine that such company had its impact on Auerbach, as the reputation of his friends was already making its way across the world and across academic disciplines. Soon, the world of ideas began appealing more brightly than the sedate quarters of the courtroom. After a walk-on part in the First World War—he was shipped to the Western Front, promptly shot in the foot, and returned home with an honorable discharge and the Iron Cross, Second Class—he enrolled in university, in Greifswald, and completed another doctorate, this one in romance languages. He spoke quite a few of them, alongside Greek, Latin, and Hebrew, and enjoyed nothing more than a day spent in solitude, surrounded by books, absorbing the ways different cultures and traditions grappled with war, pride, faith, and the other eternal quandaries of humankind. So when he was offered a job in Berlin's Prussian State Library, he was elated. Here, in the imperious building right in the heart of his hometown—across the street from the Philharmonic and a mile down the road from the Reichstag, the country's parliament—he could thumb through a Gutenberg Bible, spend a few hours with Goethe's personal autograph collection, or hum along to the original manuscript of Beethoven's Ninth Symphony. And if that weren't reason enough to feel chuffed, in that same year of 1923 Auerbach met a young woman named Marie Mankiewitz who shared his interests and was an heiress to the family that owned the largest share of Deutsche Bank. Now enormously wealthy and incomparably educated, Auerbach spent his days writing for little academic journals, translating classical works, and feeling the future was rosy.

Soon, however, his ambitions were peckish for a meatier project. He loved literature because he believed literature could order the world, arrange the seemingly jumbled and broken mess we call reality into discernible and inspiring patterns. Books tell us how to live and what to do and what to think about, and best of all, they give us heroes, men and women who could lead us by example. And if you are seeking someone who ordered all existence into meticulously charted rungs, putting each subspecies of the human animal in its rightful place, showing us the whole cross section of creation from best to worst, you could do no better than Dante.

The Florentine, Auerbach wrote, wasn't merely Italy's brightest light. He was—as the subtitle of Auerbach's book, published in 1929, declares—the poet of the secular world, "striving to involve the whole cosmos in his own experience,"[1] charting the longitudes and latitudes of everything and anything human along the way. The book made Auerbach famous, and an invitation soon followed from the University of Marburg, established in 1527 and nestled in the Lahn mountains, with a lovely river flowing through its town. It was the sort of place where a scholar could concentrate on his studies, far from the distractions of the capital, and the Auerbachs, as their correspondence from the period makes abundantly clear, were deliriously happy with their lot.

They weren't terribly worried when the new National Socialist government passed, on April 7, 1933, the Law for the Restoration of the Professional Civil Service, which barred Jews and other political enemies from all public positions, including as teachers in most universities. A former law student, Auerbach knew that the new ordinance exempted men like him, who'd honorably served in World War I. Nor was he perturbed when his colleague, the socialist economist Wilhelm Röpke, left his position and fled the country, nor when another of his Marburg peers, the Jewish linguist Hermann Jacobsohn, threw himself in front of a train two days after being dismissed. Germany, Auerbach believed, was humanity writ small, and humanity would always return to its senses and prevail. When all professors were called upon to declare their absolute fealty to the Fuhrer, Auerbach signed without too much public reflection or trepidation, and in letters from the time he expressed a remarkably mild-mannered reaction to the violent storm brewing around him. "You know me sufficiently," he wrote to his pal, the philosopher Erich Rothacker, after the latter enthusiastically endorsed the Nazis, "to know that I can understand the motives of your political views. But yet it would pain me much . . . if you wanted to deny me the right to be a German."[2] For more than a year, Auerbach clung on to that right as tightly as he could. On September 15, 1935, however, after the passage of the Nuremberg Laws, which placed onerous restrictions on all Jews in all aspects of daily life, Auerbach finally realized it was time to leave Germany. He was still certain he'd soon return: when he informed the head of the department of his departure, he presented it as a temporary absence and promised that, if conditions allowed, he'd be back by 1941.

Ever fortunate even in the midst of turmoil, Auerbach didn't need to spend much time and effort looking for a new home. A colleague was departing a teaching position at Istanbul University and recommended him for the job, and soon the Auerbachs were Turkey-bound, but not before Erich had his son Clemens, now fourteen, finally circumcised. He was no longer, he realized, a "Prussian of the Mosaic faith," his chosen description before Hitler took power. He was no longer the aloof scholar marveling at the poetry of the secular world. He was now a wandering Jew.

Immediately upon arrival, and after securing a comfortable home in the trendy Bebek neighborhood, overlooking the Bosporus from the European side of the city, Auerbach headed to his new place of employment. He was most eager to see the library, he told his new boss. The dean laughed. "We don't bother with books," he replied. "They burn."[3] As poignant as the statement must have been for someone like Auerbach, who'd witnessed massive book burnings just a few years before, the fact remained that whatever work he would complete next, he'd have to create it not by leaning on volumes of published work but by reaching into the recesses of his mind. And what he found when he looked there was an answer to the question that now struck him as most urgent: how to forge a sense of self that could develop and prevail, emotionally and morally, even if all around it men in droves had lost their minds.

The book he ended up writing took three years to complete. It was called *Mimesis: The Representation of Reality in Western Literature*, and it was so influential that, when it was finally published in 1946, it spawned an academic discipline all its own— comparative literature. Like all seminal works, this one, too, isn't easy to describe. It looks at the ways reality is represented in Western literature, from Homer and Tacitus to Virginia Woolf and Marcel Proust. Its many admirers praised the author's erudition; its few detractors wished he'd delivered a more forcefully articulated theory of everything instead of subtle and penetrating analyses of disparate masterpieces. Yet read *Mimesis* carefully, and its grand theory is right there in the first chapter. We've reason to suspect that Auerbach felt the same way: when the philosopher Martin Buber asked him to write an introduction to the Hebrew edition of the book, Auerbach refused. The first chapter, he wrote cryptically, was already all the introduction Hebrew readers needed.

That chapter, titled "Odysseus' Scar," begins with an analysis of a particularly touching scene in book 19 of Homer's epic. The great hero Odysseus, returning home from his travails, is unrecognizable to his family. His wife, Penelope, asks his old housekeeper, Euryclea, to wash the stranger's feet, and as she does so, she recognizes Odysseus by the scar on his thigh. The old woman is about to let out a cry of joy, but the returning hero, wishing to keep his identity a secret for just a little bit longer, silences her with his right hand while drawing her nearer with his left.

This richness of descriptive detail, Auerbach argues, is what gives the Greek epics their majesty and strength. "Clearly outlined, brightly and uniformly illuminated," he writes, "men and things stand out in a realm where everything is visible; and not less clear—wholly expressed, orderly even in their ardor—are the feelings and thoughts of the persons involved."[4] To read Homer is to bask in the glory of humans in full, heroes whose thoughts and actions alike are kinetic, almost intoxicating.

And then Auerbach turns to the Bible.

Reading the story of the binding of Isaac, he's struck by how sparse it is in comparison. Characters are introduced without names or descriptions. Time is condensed. Major questions go unanswered. Why does God test Abraham so? What is Abraham thinking when he climbs up the mountain where he knows he'd soon slaughter his child? The Bible never tells us. Everything about its way of telling stories, Auerbach writes, is "fraught with background."[5]

Which, Auerbach declares in the book's most astonishing move, is precisely the point. Read the *Odyssey*, and you'll be struck by its "realism," but the text's wealth of description makes it morally circumspect. Homer's world, Auerbach writes, "exists for itself, contains nothing but itself; the Homeric poems conceal nothing, they contain no teaching and no secret second meaning. Homer can be analyzed . . . but he cannot be interpreted."[6] Not so the Bible. The wide gaps it leaves in each story aren't omissions but invitations, urging the reader to answer the very questions the text so deliberately avoids. Why does God test Abraham? What is Abraham thinking when he climbs the mountain where he knows he is to sacrifice his son? That's for us to decide, and our answers determine not only the way we understand the story but, much more importantly, the way we understand our own lives and our responsibilities as moral actors in an imperfect world. Homer gives you heady myths, and it's easy to cast his heroes in bronze and, yearning to be like them, end up just as cold and metallic. The Bible gives you its heroes in fragments, and in putting them together you put together your own self.

And no one in Jewish history, perhaps, embodies this idea better than the Talmud's great sage, Rabbi Akiva.

Who was he? Where did he come from? Akiva is mentioned in the Talmud on 1,341 occasions, more than any other rabbi by far.

Whenever he appears, he's the smartest guy in the room. And he goes on to have an oversized impact on history, not only fomenting a major revolt against the Romans in the year 132 CE but also, arguably, inventing pretty much everything about the Talmud's style of thinking and reasoning. And yet we know almost nothing about him, forcing us, when piecing together this hero's life, to observe our own instead. Rabbi Akiva, *c'est nous*. So it should come as little surprise that this giant is introduced on the scene not with some miraculous creation myth or a legendary feat of strength but with a tender, hopelessly romantic love affair.

Before he met the woman who'd change his life forever, Akiva was an angry young man. Later, when he was a celebrated master, he regaled his students with tales of his youth. Back then, he said, he was animated by a fiery distaste for rabbis. The sages he'd see about town were always aloof, always carrying on with their otherworldly chatter, never truly immersed in the realities that made life here on earth so difficult and yet so gratifying. Akiva, then, crafted a little ditty he'd mutter to himself every time he'd see a rabbi walking by and talking about the Torah: "Who will give me a sage so that I could bite him like a donkey?" Hearing this, the students were confused. "Rabbi," they said to Akiva, "you mean bite him like a dog." But Akiva hadn't misspoken. "No," he said, "a donkey. Because a donkey bites and breaks bones; the dog bites but doesn't break a bone."[7]

What, then, did the daughter of one of the wealthiest men in Jerusalem see in such a hothead? The Talmud simply says that the young woman found Akiva humble and refined. It tells us little else, including the young woman's name, though later accounts identify her as Rachel. Her father was Kalba Savua, the grandee who, for a spell, financed the survival of the besieged Jewish community prior to the destruction of the Second Temple, and his double-barreled name alone urges readers to stop, read carefully, and form an opinion. Both words are Aramaic: *Kalba* means "dog," *Savua* "well fed and satisfied." Was he named that because he was so wealthy and generous that even if one entered his home hungry like a dog one always left with a full stomach and a sense of fulfillment and gratitude? Or was he simply a beastly sort of fellow, himself a well-fed dog who was interested in little else but his bulging belly? From the outset, the story of Akiva is fraught with background.

What happens next, however, is clear. Rachel spots Akiva, by then a middle-aged shepherd tending her father's flock. She falls in love, not, presumably, with the man she sees in front of her but with the man she knows Akiva could someday become, because her pickup line is one for the ages. "If I betroth myself to you," Rachel tells Akiva, "will you go to the study hall to learn Torah?"[8] Akiva agrees, and the two get secretly engaged.

When Kalba Savua hears of his daughter's decision, he is livid. It's one thing for a rich gentleman to feed the poor and give lavishly to those less fortunate. It's another to allow one of those less fortunate to marry your daughter. Kalba Savua kicks Rachel out of his home and curtly informs her that she may no longer expect to benefit from his property. But she doesn't much care. She marries Akiva, and, impoverished, the two move into a hayloft. It's winter, and they're cold, but also very much in love. In the mornings, the Talmud tells us, Akiva would sweetly pick the straw from his bride's hair and make her promises of a rosier future. "If only I could," he would say to her, "I would give you a 'Jerusalem of Gold,'"[9] a bejeweled tiara shaped to resemble the ancient city's walls and the ultimate luxurious accessory of the time.

Pretty soon, however, Akiva makes good on his promise and takes off to a far-off house of study to start learning the Torah, and Rachel is left alone in the frosty hayloft. She remains there, the Talmud tells us, for twelve long years, until one day, the town is abuzz with a rumor: a great rabbi named Akiva will soon arrive. Rachel rushes to greet her husband and is elated but likely not surprised when she spots him, from a distance, accompanied by twelve thousand students who were now his adoring disciples. Before the joyous reunion can take place, however, fate intervenes. An unnamed old man sees Rachel and mocks her bitterly.

"For how long," he asks her, "will you lead the life of a widow of a living man, living alone while your husband is in another place?"

We'd do well, if only as a tribute to Auerbach, to stop here for a second and think about this old man and his motives. Is he being a jerk? Maybe. But it's also quite possible, as the scholar of Jewish classical texts Barry Holtz notes in his biography of Akiva, that the old man is a stand-in for us all. Sure, Rachel's self-sacrifice and perseverance is the stuff of legend; but we're not legends. We're human, and all too fallible, and if a husband or a wife were to come to us and take his or her leave for over a decade, it's likely that we, too, would stop and ask, as the old man had, what good is a life lived apart and alone. Just as we wondered why Rachel would toss away comfort and fortune for Akiva's sake, we ask again what it was about him that made her endure twelve years of solitude. Both questions force us to think about what it is that we value—in ourselves, in our significant others, in our relationships, in life.

Rachel, however, gives us no clues. "If he would listen to me," she icily tells the old man, "he would sit and study for another twelve years." Akiva overhears this exchange and knows just what to do. "I have permission," he tells his students, and he retraces his steps, heading out of town and straight back to the study hall.

Twelve more years go by. Again, a rumor swirls, but this time the buzz is even greater. Akiva has become even more renowned, and he's now accompanied by twenty-four thousand students, double his earlier entourage. So giddy are Rachel's neighbors that they urge her to borrow some nice clothes; it would be unseemly, they scold her, to greet the famous rabbi wearing a poor woman's rags. Again, Rachel refuses to budge. Quoting Proverbs, she quips, "A righteous man understands the life of his beast,"[10] meaning that even if she may appear as bedraggled and lowly as an animal, her husband will still recognize the beauty of her soul.

But as Rachel tries to make her way to the front of the greeting line, she's squeezed by the throngs of well-wishers and hangers-on who've come to catch a glimpse of Akiva. She finally breaks through and throws herself at Akiva's feet. When a few of his students, having no idea who she is, grab the wild and weeping woman and begin dragging her away, Akiva thunders, "Leave her alone! What's mine and what's yours truly belongs to her."

The story, however, has one more order of business to address. Kalba Savua, the Talmud goes on to tell us, is thrilled to hear that a great sage is passing through town. He's not sure who the sage is—a rich man has no time to concern himself with learning the names of rabbis—but he knows the man is wise and celebrated, precisely the sort of studious chap who might help him out of a pickle. Now an elderly man, Kalba Savua is growing increasingly remorseful about the vow he'd made all those years earlier, the one denying Rachel her inheritance and kicking her out of his home. Shortly after Akiva's return, he goes to see the great rabbi and, having no idea who he is, tells him the whole story.

Akiva listens without saying a word. When Kalba Savua is done, Akiva poses one simple question. When you took your vow, he asks his unsuspecting father-in-law, did you ever think this Akiva would become a great man?

If I thought that, Kalba Savua replies, if I believed he'd learn even one chapter of Torah or even one Jewish law, I wouldn't have been so harsh. It was all Akiva needed to hear. He rises and says, "I am he." Falling on his face, Kalba Savua kisses Akiva's feet and immediately gives him half of his worldly possessions.

The repentant wealthy man, the public showdown, the reversal of fortune and the honoring of the sage with large sums of money—we've seen it all before with Rabbi Eliezer's origin story. But whereas the Talmud took care to tell us everything we needed to know about Eliezer and his journey to greatness, with Akiva, it plunges us into mystery, giving us far less than we'd like to know. Akiva is the anti-Odysseus, a hero whose journey remains entirely invisible and whose good qualities remain to be seen. Who was this man, and was he worth all the fuss?

Before we answer the question, it's worth considering the particular historical context into which Akiva emerged. He was born in the year 50 CE, which means he was twenty when the Temple fell. Most legends insist that he was forty years old when he married Rachel, which means that he would have returned to her twenty-four years later, around the year 114 CE, giving him a twenty-one-year tenure, until his death in 135 CE, as the most important sage of his or any other day.

What were these years like? The rabbis living in the first generation after the Temple's destruction understood their mission well—transform Judaism from a sacrifice-based religion to a faith system predicated on personal, intimate prayer and communal practice. That much is clear. But *how* to do so remained a much thornier question. The sages, as we've seen, were a quarrelsome bunch, and each had his own ideas, his own approach, his own ego. And their bickering was getting in the way of building something sustainable, cohesive, and lasting. If you can't even agree on which of the Bible's books ought to be canonical, and if half of the geniuses in the study hall believe that the only admissible teachings are the ones passed down from previous generations while the other half holds that the correct approach must rely on individual and original interpretation, you're not likely to come up with any solid foundation.

The rabbis, in short, were having the sort of problem Auerbach recognized all too well. They excelled at being like Odysseus, wholly expressed, orderly even in their ardor. They were very good at arguing, epically, for their particular, and unchanging, points of view. What they couldn't do was be more like Abraham, the sort of person who was always evolving, forever growing, busily contemplating his own positions and everything around him.

And if Judaism was to survive—if it was to become anything but a thicket of warring tribes, each with its own settled mythology—the rabbis needed someone who could show them how to develop a sense of self, how to remain every bit a thinking, feeling individual who could take in all these traditions and teachings and distill them, brilliantly and respectfully, into something that felt at once in line with centuries of observance but also fresh, entirely immediate, and completely personal. They needed an adjudicator, a convener, a leader who could seize the different strands of thinking and teaching and weave them together into one coherent story that moved and inspired—a story we today call religion, though the idea was foreign to the rabbis of antiquity, for whom life independent of worship made little sense. That transformational person, almost by definition, would have to be someone who was strong yet flexible, smart yet humble, determined yet sensitive, common yet exalted. And the Talmud doesn't spare us stories to convince us that Akiva was just that guy.

Or rather, he eventually *became* that guy. Early on in his rabbinic career, we see Akiva nearly intoxicated by both his own extraordinary abilities and the sheer profundities of studying the Torah. One famous tale recounts Akiva sitting at the feet of his teachers, Rabbi Yehoshua and Rabbi Eliezer, and begging them to teach him just one law. The two rabbis comply, and Akiva retires to a corner to think. He returns shortly thereafter with questions. It's not enough for him to grasp the general ideas and principles at play. If you believe that the Torah is divine, he argues, then that means that each sentence, each word, even each letter, has a very specific purpose that must be clearly understood. Why was this letter *alef* written, he asks Yehoshua and Eliezer? And this *bet*? Why was this said? Why was that? The two rabbis, these most revered scholars, "were reduced to silence."[1] You hardly have to believe in the Torah—or, for that matter, in God—to admire Akiva's radical move. Like a brilliant philologist, he argues that if your world now consists not of symbolic actions—slaughtering sheep so that God may forgive you for your sins—but of symbolic words—spinning stories into laws that govern behavior—you'd do well to read these words very, very carefully. His approach is simultaneously utterly liberating and completely terrifying. It holds that a bright mind may, on its own, unlock all the secrets of creation. It follows then that if you can, just by reading and hard thinking, get everything about life right, you can also get it all wrong. The power to interpret the world into existence is awesome; use it well, and you'll become better and make life better for all around you. Use it poorly, and your own brilliance may cause your downfall.

It was a lesson Akiva would eventually learn too well. But starting out as a scholar, it hadn't occurred to him yet. He was busy establishing his dominance. Before too long, he triumphed over the other bright young man of the day, Rabbi Ishmael, who believed that the "Torah speaks in the language of human beings," meaning that there was nothing about scripture that was innately mysterious, coded, or difficult to understand. Akiva vehemently disagreed; to him, scripture was a puzzle, and logic and exegesis the tools to solve it. He agreed with Auerbach: The Torah was fraught with background. And unlocking its mysteries called not only for an agile mind but also for a healthy ego.

The ascending rabbinic eminence seemed blessed on both counts. Later rabbis told an apt parable about Akiva. Once upon a time, there was a stonecutter who was quarrying in the mountains. People passing by saw him sitting on the ground, shovel in hand, hitting the rock and breaking it into tiny pebbles. They asked him what he was doing. "I am uprooting the mountain," he replied, "and moving it to the Jordan River." This amused the passersby, and they informed the stonecutter that no matter how good he was at his job, he couldn't possibly uproot an entire mountain. But the stonecutter ignored them. He continued to smash the side of the mountain with his shovel until he reached an enormous boulder. He crawled under it and pushed it until it tumbled into the river below. "This is not where you belong," the stonecutter declared triumphantly as the large boulder began to roll downhill; "that is where you belong." This, the rabbis concluded, "is what Rabbi Akiva did to Rabbi Eliezer and Rabbi Yehoshua."[12]

The latter of these two teachers was delighted with his pupil's ascent. The former was more troubled. Eliezer, the rabbi who took such pride in never saying anything he didn't directly learn from his own teachers, looked askance at the upstart who was now drawing bold new interpretations from the scriptures, squeezing new meaning out of the ancient, well-known words. The older man had spent his entire life avoiding having anything like a sense of self, seeing himself as nothing more than a recorder for the wisdom of others. The younger man was convinced that without a sense of self through which to judge everything and anything, all the wisdom in the world didn't matter.

The Haggadah, a text read on Passover, contains a small vignette showing us these two divergent attitudes at war. In it, Eliezer is trying, and failing, to one-up his young disciple. The two rabbis, together with Rabbi Yossi HaGelili, are trying to understand precisely what was meant by the account of the Ten Plagues. Influenced, perhaps, by Akiva's style, Yossi takes the first stab. The Bible, he argues, mentions that when the Egyptian sorcerers witness the plagues, they tell the baffled pharaoh that what he's seeing is "the finger of God."[13] Later, as the pharaoh gives chase, the Bible notes that "the Lord's great hand"[14] came down and struck the Egyptian king and his chariots in the Red Sea. It's simple math, Yossi concludes: If one finger equals ten plagues, and a hand has five fingers, then the Egyptians giving chase were struck by no less than fifty additional plagues.

Nice try, says Rabbi Eliezer, but not quite right. Read more carefully and you'll learn in Psalm 78, verse 49, that "He sent upon them the fierceness of His anger, wrath, and fury, and trouble, a sending of messengers of evil." Count them, Eliezer concludes: "wrath" is one, "fury" two, "trouble" three, and "a sending of messengers of evil" four. So the ten plagues were really forty plagues, and the Egyptians giving chase were struck not with fifty plagues but with fifty times four, or two hundred plagues.

But it's Rabbi Akiva who has the final word. Read even more carefully, he tells his elderly teacher. "The fierceness of his anger" is one; only then come wrath and fury, trouble, and the messengers of evil, which means that you ought to multiply each plague not by four but by five: fifty in Egypt, 250 later.

Analyzing this exchange, Barry Holtz sees it as a comical, perhaps even parodic, example of the Talmud's style of discourse, a style that owes much of its existence to what Holtz calls "Akiva's interpretive creativity."[15] And most of the readers racing through the first section of the Haggadah, eager to conclude the story and get to the part where the festive meal is served, likely dismiss it as yet another example of rabbinic obfuscation, too clever by half. But the Talmud itself would have none of it. Akiva's method, his way of interrogating every detail, no matter how minute, is, the Talmud tells us, the correct path forward.

It's an emotional argument as much as it is a methodological one. There are, as Auerbach so insightfully told us, two main ways for us to understand life and our role in it. We can read our reality like a Greek epic poem, all action and thick with detail, and end up right back where we started—at home, slowly forgetting how great our journey was. Or we can understand it to be a biblical account, maddening and inscrutable and demanding that we investigate and complicate every intricacy until it all makes sense to us, allowing us to grow the more we understand.

In Tractate Menachot, we're treated to an unusual tale of miracles affirming this very point. Moses, the Talmud tells us, dies and goes to heaven. There he sees God painstakingly decorating the Hebrew letters of the Torah with beautiful calligraphy, "tying crowns" on each letter.[16] Moses is confused; why was God taking such care with adorning each and every letter?

"Master of the Universe," he asks the Almighty, "who is preventing you from giving the Torah without these additions?"

God is quick to reply. "There is a man," he tells Moses, "who is destined to be born [several generations after you], and Akiva ben Yosef is his name; he is destined to derive from each and every thorn of these crowns mounds upon mounds of *halachot* [Jewish religious laws]. It is for his sake that the crowns must be added to the letters of the Torah."

Naturally, Moses is curious. There he is, the Bible's greatest teacher and prophet, the man chosen to receive the Torah in person, hearing that another man would soon arrive who would possess such awesome powers. He asks God if he could possibly meet Rabbi Akiva, and God acquiesces, sending Moses zooming through time, into the future, straight to the eighth row of Akiva's study hall. Moses listens eagerly, but the more he hears, the more crestfallen he grows. Try as he might, he can't understand a word of what Akiva is saying. The rabbi's teachings are just too intricate, too brilliant, too complex. Moses, the Talmud continues, grows weary, thinking that maybe his knowledge of the Torah is deficient. But just as he's about to sink into despair, a student quizzes Akiva about some matter. "My teacher," the student says, "from where do you derive" your opinion? And Akiva, not missing a beat, says, "It is a halacha transmitted to Moses from Sinai." Moses's mind is set at ease; he understands that although Akiva may have advanced Moses's reasoning, he still sees himself as a link in the same chain of tradition that began with the receiving of the Torah on Mount Sinai. When he returns to heaven and meets God once again, however, he's curious. "Master of the Universe," he asks God, "You have a man as great as this and yet You still choose to give the Torah through me. Why?" God doesn't answer. "Be silent" is the best He can muster.

God in this story may be speaking to us just as much as to Moses. When faced with anything cataclysmic—good and bad alike, major opportunities or terrible tragedies—we tend to retreat to the same befuddled cry: Why me? Very few of us believe, in these moments, that we have what it takes to weather the storm, to lead, to thrive, to overcome. Self-doubt and humility are not only normal but desirable; without them, we run the risk of being devoured by vanity and pride. But self-doubt and humility are only useful if applied conservatively, so that they don't overpower our innate potential and hamper us from becoming what we were meant to be. That's why God urges Moses—and us—to stop fretting and instead learn from the example of the great teacher, Rabbi Akiva.

At the height of his success in the study hall, a later midrash (rabbinic exegesis) tells us, Akiva was revered in previously unimaginable ways. One time, the story goes, he arrived late to

class, and not wanting to interrupt his teacher, Rabbi Eliezer—
perhaps knowing that their relationship was already fraught—he
sat outside and waited for Eliezer to conclude his teaching. Inside,
the old rabbi asked his students a question; he presented them
with some quibble, and then inquired, "Is this the law?" The students didn't skip a beat. "The law is outside," they said. Eliezer
was confused by their answer, but continued teaching and again
asked his students if something he'd just mentioned was in accordance with the Torah. "The Torah is outside," the students said.
Eliezer, still not understanding what they meant, asked a third
and final question, and finally, the students couldn't hold back
anymore. "Akiva is outside—make room for him." Dumbfounded,
Eliezer had to stop teaching and wait for his student to come in
and sit down.

Try and put yourself in Akiva's sandals, and you'll likely soon
feel your head spinning. To go from chasing sheep to being so
admired by your peers that they describe you as being the equal
of the Torah itself could make anyone lose their grounding. It's
not hard to imagine a lesser person succumbing to self-regard and
treating others with imperious disdain—it's why so many of our
dramas and novels and plays are about the high and the mighty
and the conceited falling from grace. Akiva, however, resisted,
growing to become just the man Rachel had always known he
could be. The Talmud—working, as it always does, not in straightforward narratives but in vignettes, peppered throughout disparate tractates that require some assembly—tells us how he did it.

It's a story of putting together a self. It may sound absurd—
aren't we all endowed, by virtue of being thinking, feeling people,
with a strong sense of self?—but the Talmud, like Auerbach and
others of our finest critics, understands that the self is a tricky
thing. Many of us, it knows, go through life simply reflecting
whatever is projected onto us. Our family histories, our national
pride, our religious affiliations, the prejudices of our peers—that
is what we become. Tell us we're great and we'll believe you. Tell
us we're worthless and we'll believe that, too. Tell us, in short,

what to believe and we'll believe it. That is why the Greeks, masters of mythology, fashioned their gods and their heroes the way they did: Odysseus needs no introspection because Odysseus doesn't reflect; he simply does, and the outcome of his efforts is preordained. The tragic hero always lays defeated by the end of the final act.

Judaism requires the opposite. It demands that we question—everything, everyone, always—and that we cobble together whatever answers we've collected into the mental mosaic we call the self. And then it demands that we apply this self of ours to navigate our way through life, refusing to succumb to anything, from mass movements to collective delusions to religious fanaticism, that might distract us from the hard and essential task of reading our own life's story, in real time, with a critical eye.

Few did it as well as Akiva. Just as he was in his prime, we learn, the small community of rabbis to which he belonged was rocked by a nearly unprecedented power struggle. As we've already seen, the Romans, acquiescing to Yohanan ben Zakkai's plea, allowed the family of Rabban Gamliel to continue to lead the community, and Gamliel's grandson, known as Gamliel II, was now the Nasi, or leader. But whereas the grandfather was beloved and admired, the grandson was feared. Maybe it was because he felt he had much to prove with such a sparkling pedigree, or maybe it was the uncertainty of having to flee the Romans long enough for ben Zakkai to advocate on his behalf, but whatever it was, Gamliel II took to his office with an iron fist, tolerating no dissent or disrespect.

One time, two people came to Gamliel II and testified that they'd seen the waning moon in the morning in the east, and later that same day observed the new moon in the evening in the west. Lacking clocks, calendars, or any other modern modes of astronomical calculations, the rabbis relied on testimonies to determine when one month ended and the next began. Gamliel II had a chart hanging in his office with the various shapes of the moon, from crescent to glowing orb, that he used to grill anyone who came and said they looked to the heavens and believed the new month had arrived. These two particular witnesses were especially important because the month in question was Tishrei, the seventh month of the Hebrew calendar and the one in which Jews celebrate the High Holidays, including Yom Kippur, the Day of Atonement, the holiest day of the year. Gamliel II listened to the two fellows, looked at his notes, did some math, and decided that their report made sense. It was now Tishrei, he announced, and Yom Kippur would be ten days hence.

Wrong, said Rabbi Yehoshua. It's impossible to see the new moon so soon after the previous month's waning moon. The witnesses were incorrect, and Gamliel II's calculations were off by a day. Because setting the calendar was one of the Nasi's most important roles, Gamliel II was livid to hear Yehoshua question his authority. He sent a message to the dissenter: "You must appear before me with your staff and with your money on the day on which Yom Kippur occurs according to your calculation."[17] The decree stunned Rabbi Yehoshua: Jewish law strictly prohibits carrying things and using money on Yom Kippur; Gamliel II wasn't just rejecting Yehoshua's argument, but forcing him to violate his beliefs by desecrating, in public, the day he believed to be the year's holiest.

Enter Akiva.

Sensing his teacher's distress, Akiva visited Rabbi Yehoshua. How to comfort the older teacher? Naturally, with a close reading of a text. In Leviticus 23:4, Akiva noted, it says the following: "These are the appointed seasons of the Lord, sacred convocations, which you shall proclaim in their season." The emphasis here, Akiva continued, is on the word *you*; the moon's orbit is objective, absolute, and independent of all human judgment, but the Torah specifically says that it's humans who get to make proclamations about dates, which means that the calendar isn't a divine mystery for us to guess at but a human construct, fallible and arguable like all others. Therefore, Akiva concluded, there was really no problem. Yehoshua should submit to Gamliel

II's will. Barry Holtz sums it up nicely: "Akiva is saying that by bowing to the will of authority as represented by the Patriarch [Yehoshua], would not be compromising his principles and violating Yom Kippur; he would be acknowledging the fact that human courts decide the calendar and [Yehoshua] has simply been outvoted."[18] It's not only a feat of Torah interpretation; it's also a masterclass in forging and fashioning a self. Yehoshua was convinced; he grabbed his staff and his purse and went to see Gamliel II, and the two enjoyed a heartfelt reconciliation.

Herein lies the greatness of Akiva's insights. Proving Auerbach's point that reading helps us order our lives and rediscover meanings and possibilities we never knew existed and that we ought to make sense of our own lives just as we try to make sense of a great work of literature, Akiva plumbed the depths of the Torah not only as an esoteric intellectual pursuit but as an urgently ethical and interpersonal one.

But why bother reading at all? After all, wouldn't it be enough if we all did our best to be good, decent people who treat others kindly? Isn't that commonsensical, and do we really need religious instruction to direct us to this rather obvious goal? Couldn't we craft that elusive sense of self by simply trying to be nice?

Very early on in his career, Akiva asked himself this same question. Eager to show his teachers that he was serious and committed to his new rabbinic vocation, he told them that he'd found a dead body by the side of the road, most likely the victim of a murder. Akiva picked up the corpse, carried it to the nearest cemetery, and buried it. He was expecting his teachers to praise him, but instead they issued the strongest rebuke: With every step you took, they told a stunned Akiva, it's as if you had committed murder yourself.[19] Then the rabbis proceeded to teach Akiva about the Jewish approach to burial. They told him it is forbidden to tarry before laying the deceased to rest, as the soul does not begin its journey to the World to Come before the body is properly buried. Akiva thought he was following that belief by carrying the corpse the distance to the cemetery. He found out that he would've done much better if he had simply buried the man by the side of the road where he was discovered without further ado.

There is subtle beauty in this tale. It teaches us to slow down and pay attention to minute details. It reminds us that the right thing to do isn't always obvious. And it instructs us to be very close readers—of our traditions, of the situation, of our selves. Akiva grasped that early on in his studies, and now he was teaching this idea to his teacher, Rabbi Yehoshua, with considerable success.

So when Gamliel II, a little while later, again picked on poor Yehoshua, driving the other rabbis to take the drastic step of voting Gamliel II out of office, Akiva thought his time had finally come. Who else was more worthy of leadership? Who else wiser, more astute, more learned, more worthy of the rabbinic throne? He braced himself for his coronation, the pinnacle of so many years spent studying and arguing and navigating his way in the rarefied world of the study hall. And he watched as his peers instead elected Elazar ben Azarya, an affable sixteen-year-old from a well-off family, to the highest office in the land.

Why was Akiva rebuffed? The Talmud delivers a straightforward yet harsh explanation. The sages, it tells us, convened to discuss who to appoint now that Gamliel II was out of the picture. They couldn't, they agreed, appoint Rabbi Yehoshua, because he was "party to the incident for which [Gamliel II] was deposed," and "appointing him would be extremely upsetting for [Gamliel II]."[20] Nor, they sighed, could they elevate Akiva, "as he lacks the merit of his ancestors to protect him." Akiva, in other words, wasn't the son of a well-established rabbinic lineage. He was a nobody who came out of nowhere, which was precisely why he could be so innovative and so bold. But if the rabbinic enterprise wanted to survive, it couldn't simply celebrate every arriviste, no matter how absolutely brilliant he was. It had to balance its desire to promote exciting and capable outsiders with the more prudent instinct to also promote scions of solid dynasties who could capably preserve and protect the old traditions. Champion the former, and you run the risk of the radicals throwing out all the laws and customs that have been passed down from generation to generation and replacing them with something strange and unfamiliar that would soon lose the respect of the Jewish people. Champion the latter, and you run the risk of these laws and customs growing stale, ossified, and irrelevant. A system of belief and behavior could only keep on keeping on if it found equilibrium, which meant that Akiva, the rebel in chief, was needed as a gadfly but that he couldn't be elevated.

Still, it's hard for readers, particularly modern ones, to read this story without feeling irate. The idea of solid dynasties, of the right family, of the accidents of our birth determining the course of our lives is profoundly dispiriting. So much so that you'd be hard pressed to turn more than ten or twenty pages in any classic novel without some meditation on this very theme. We may understand the logic behind the rabbis' rejection of Akiva, but our hearts may still swell with anger. How did Akiva feel?

The Talmud very rarely comments on the emotional state of its heroes, but in this case, the Yerushalmi, the Talmud compiled by the sages who remained in the land of Israel, makes an exception. "Rabbi Akiva sat," it tells us, "and was sad; he said, not that he is a greater Torah scholar than I am, but he comes from a greater family than I do; hail to the man whose forefathers created merit for him, hail to the man who has a peg to hang on."[21]

Right then and there, in the lowest point of what was otherwise a career consisting of nothing but peaks, Akiva must make a choice. Does he storm out and remove himself from the community, as other great rabbis before and after him had done under similar circumstances? Or does he take this occasion to prove to himself and to his peers that when it truly matters, he can put his considerable ego aside and choose humility? It's a question most of us have had occasion to ask ourselves when slighted by bosses or colleagues or friends or family. And it is, in a way, a question of whether or not you're ready to meet your self.

The Greeks, to return for a moment to Auerbach's helpful

distinction, generally weren't. Selves were of little use for the muscular he-men camped outside of Troy and waiting for war, which is why the *Iliad* is an epic poem of unchecked pride leading to immense suffering. No one grows, no one changes, no one stops to think. Agamemnon refuses to give Achilles his just rewards. Achilles is outraged. Achilles refuses to fight. Everyone dies. At no point does anyone snuggle up in their tent and wonder whether or not it's worthwhile to lose friends and brothers over Helen's fling. The Greek hero, in other words, is proud for the same reason he's a hero—because he's a perpetual motion machine who constantly acts and rarely reflects. The biblical hero, on the other hand, only becomes a hero when he grapples, wrestles, struggles, and overcomes the urge to act without contemplation.

Akiva is very much in the latter mold. When he is tested, he answers with poise and grace, acknowledging his hurt, nursing his wounded pride, and making sure he can find, even in his hour of misfortune, reason to feel genuinely happy for his young friend ben Azarya.

Akiva wasn't merely being the bigger person. He'd learned his lesson, and he understood that simple, instinctual thinking about right and wrong was a very flimsy foundation for living. To him, the only true wisdom could come from the Torah, and the Torah had told him just what to do: "Thou shalt not avenge," it says in Leviticus 19:18, "nor bear any grudge against the children of thy people, but thou shalt love they neighbor as thyself." The more he studied Torah, the more it seemed to Akiva that this one verse ought to be amplified, internalized, and practiced until it became second nature. His humility, then, wasn't just an emotional reaction, which, by definition, is mercurial and subject to change; it was a deliberate work in progress, the mindfulness of a master who realizes that if he truly wants to embody the values he studies, he has no choice but to learn the art of accepting rebukes.

And learn it he did. The Sifre, a Talmudic-era commentary on Deuteronomy, gives us a heartwarming little story about four rabbis sitting together and discussing this very issue. I swear, says Rabbi Tarfon, that there's no one in our generation who is able to rebuke another person—all are just too timid nowadays. That's not the real problem, responds Eleazar ben Azarya; the real problem is that there's no one in our generation who is able to properly receive a rebuke. Not so, says Akiva, it's not knowing how to rebuke the right way that's the issue. The story gives Rabbi Yohanan ben Nuri the last word: "I call heaven and earth to witness for me that Rabbi Akiva was rebuked because of me more than five times before Rabban Gamliel in Yavneh," he says. "I used to complain about Akiva, and Rabban Gamliel would rebuke him. But I truly know that each time Akiva was rebuked, he loved me more and more."[22] Akiva, then, had mastered the art of self-control by reading the same verse that inspired Søren Kierkegaard to later wax poetic: "If it were not a duty to love, then the concept of neighbor would not exist; but only when one loves one's neighbor, only then is the selfish partiality eradicated, and the equality of the eternal preserved."[23]

To benefit those of us who have some difficulty eradicating all manner of partiality, the Talmud delivers a slew of stories about Akiva's humility, each touching in its portrayal of such a larger-than-life figure in such approachable, intimate settings. One of the finest tells of the rabbis sitting in the study hall, discussing a legal question and learning that a valued sage, an old man by the name of Dosa ben Harkinas, had issued a ruling that struck all present as incompatible with their understanding of the issue. As Rabbi Dosa was already feeble and nearly blind and could no longer leave his home, Rabbi Yehoshua decides to pay him a visit and ask him to explain his ruling. Immediately, Elazar ben Azarya and Rabbi Akiva join him.

When Dosa's servant ushers them into the old rabbi's sitting room, Dosa recognizes Yehoshua. He doesn't know ben Azarya, but when he's introduced to Akiva, he's elated. "You are Akiva ben Yosef, whose name has spread from one end of the world to the other?"[24] With such an introduction, Akiva would've been forgiven had he simply thanked his host for his kind words and then asked his question without further delay. But loving thy neighbor is an exhortation to always put yourself in your neighbor's place, and no man, particularly one who is aged and weary, would enjoy a perfunctory visit, particularly one revolving around a potentially thorny disagreement. And so, Akiva begins asking Dosa a host of unrelated questions, letting the older man teach him and share his wisdom and erudition. Skillfully, however, Akiva navigates the conversation to the matter at hand, and, to his surprise, Rabbi Dosa delivers a different answer than the one he was rumored to have delivered, an answer that is totally compatible with Akiva's own understanding of the question. Akiva is curious; why, he asks Dosa, did I hear people attribute to you a very different ruling?

Dosa is amused. "Did you hear that Dosa ben Harkinas issued this ruling," he asks Akiva, "or did you hear that it was stated by ben Harkinas?" We can imagine that Akiva, the stickler for every letter and every word, was taken aback by the question. "On your life, Rabbi, we heard simply ben Harkinas," he replies. "If so," Dosa quips, "it is no wonder, as I have a young brother who is the firstborn of the Satan. And his name is Yonatan. . . . It is he who issued this ruling."

The three sages thank Dosa and set out to find the younger brother, but Dosa warns them: "That Yonatan, he said, is as vicious as he is sharp, and for every question you ask him he'll confound you with 300 of his own." A short while later, Akiva comes across Yonatan, and the two have a fierce debate. Yonatan raises a hundred objections; Akiva answers each one. Still, Yonatan isn't impressed.

"Are you Akiva ben Yosef, whose name has spread from one end of the world to the other?" he asks in mock repetition of his brother's earlier and genuine praise. "Be happy that you have merited a great name, and yet you have not yet reached the level of cattle herders." Akiva doesn't lose his temper; he doesn't sulk or skulk away. "And I have not even reached the level of shepherds," he replies to Yonatan, not only alluding to his previous lowly profession but also identifying himself with an even lower class of people than cattle herders, as shepherds were considered so ill educated that they were not even permitted to testify in a court of law.

In his ability not only to exercise restraint but to practice true and joyful humility, Akiva managed to achieve something very close to transcendence. In what is perhaps the most famous and furiously debated story about Akiva, the Talmud tells us that he and three of his fellow rabbis entered the Pardes. The word is Hebrew for "orchard" and where we get the term "paradise." The story, concealing more than it reveals, implies that through mystically meditating, the rabbis were able to enter God's own celestial abode, a magical heavenly domain few if any had ever seen. The first, Ben Azzai, looked at the divine presence and immediately perished. The second, Ben Zoma, lost his mind. The third, Elisha ben Abuyah, became a heretic and was, from that moment on, known simply as Acher, or "the Other." Only Akiva, we're told, entered in peace and left in peace.

Why? Jewish scholars have spent centuries offering various intricate explanations, but Akiva's is best. "It is not because I am greater than my colleagues," he is quoted as saying in a midrash, "but because of the teaching in the Mishnah, 'Your deeds will bring you near and your deeds will keep you far.'"[25] Just as his status as a self-made man of low lineage kept him from receiving the highest honor on earth, so did his deeds enable him to receive the highest honor in higher, celestial spheres. In Yavneh, the kid from nowhere could never be appointed Nasi; in paradise, he and only he is welcomed and protected. Even the angels themselves, the Talmud tells us, resented Akiva this privilege and sought to push him out, but "the Holy One, Blessed be He, said to them: Leave this Elder, for he is fit to serve My glory."[26]

It's an amazing story, but to embrace it too closely would be to run afoul of Auerbach's hard-won insights about learning to become the sort of person we truly wish to be. To see Akiva as a mortal besting the angels is to Greekify him, to turn him into another airtight Odysseus, an unchanging and impenetrable figure that is larger than life and therefore irrelevant to it. The Talmud seems to understand this risk well, because after many fantastic tales—including one about marrying the wife of a Roman bigwig who abandons her husband and her paganism alike for Akiva's sake—comes the great rabbi's tragic end.

Or maybe "tragic" isn't the right term, at least not in its Greek connotation. Watching or reading Sophocles's play *Oedipus Rex*, the poet W. H. Auden noted, we are moved by seeing the great hero follow the preordained path we know can only lead him to his doom. As the young man goes about the business of killing his father and wedding his mother, Auden imagines us in the audience muttering "What a pity it had to happen this way." But a very different feeling emerges when we watch Shakespeare's Scottish play: As Macbeth contemplates his lot in life and then, out of his own free will, proceeds with the carnage, we sigh, "What a pity it had to happen this way when it might have been otherwise."[27] One hero is tragic because he never had a choice; the other precisely because he always did.

Did Akiva? His end is fraught with background. Volumes might be—and have been—written about the circumstances of his demise, but a brief account will do just as well. Ever since the destruction of the Temple, the Jews in the Land of Israel lived in the hope that one day soon, a Roman emperor would reign who would allow them to rebuild the Temple; and if not a temple in all its glory, then at least a small altar where priests could once again go about the business of making burnt offerings. A succession of emperors rose and fell, each giving a bit of hope but ultimately doing nothing. Not so Hadrian: From the moment of his ascension in 117 CE, Rome's new monarch had little love for the Jews, and he didn't take long to announce that Jerusalem would soon be razed and replaced with a garrison town called Ilia Capitolina that would only welcome imperial soldiers. And if that wasn't enough of an insult, the new metropolis's beating heart would be an eye-catching temple to Jupiter, built on the exact spot where the Temple once stood.

The Jews, already grumbling about Rome's onerous taxes, decided to revolt, inspired by a charismatic and mysterious warrior named Shimon Bar Kochva. *Kochav* is Hebrew for "star," which makes "Bar Kochva"—literally, the son of the star—sound like he was heaven-sent, the chosen one who would lead the Jews out of despondency and degradation and into a new era of national glory and independence. In the Talmud Yerushalmi, one rabbi suggests that it was Akiva who gave the military commander his moniker, based on the biblical verse "there appeared a star out of Jacob."[28]

Akiva believed that the young man was, quite literally, the Messiah. Or maybe not *the* Messiah but *a* Messiah. In Jewish tradition, there are not one but two redeemers; the first, Moshiach ben Yosef—the Messiah, son of Joseph—will usher the Jewish people through the practical considerations of redemption, including erecting an army and restoring self-rule, and will most likely die while in service. At this point the second, Moshiach ben David, will arrive and elevate the Jews to the spiritual perfection of the end-times. Bar Kochva, Akiva believed, was a Moshiach ben Yosef par excellence.

Others disagreed. The general, they argued, was a great tactician, able to lead his small army to impressive early military victories. But he was a fanatic and a zealot: to test the courage and fearlessness of his men, for example, he had each soldier who pledged his allegiance cut off a finger, a practice many rabbis at the time argued was in direct violation of the Torah's prohibition against self-mutilation. Akiva didn't much mind the finger-cutting bit; a fervent nationalist, he was swept up in the promise of Bar Kochva. In contrast, increasingly horrified, Akiva's peers took to calling the leader Bar Kuziba, or the son of deception.

Bar Kochva's rebellion lasted three years. It swept across vast swaths of the Land of Israel. And it ended in utter disaster. The Roman historian Cassius Dio put the number of Jewish dead at 580,000, many of whom were Rabbi Akiva's students. In one particularly cryptic passage, the Talmud informs us that twenty-four thousand of Akiva's disciples perished one year during the rebellion, "because they did not treat each other with respect."[29] It's safe to assume that Hadrian's troops had something to do with their death as well. Many of the period's leading rabbinic lights, too, met a bitter end, which meant that the de facto patriarch of the Jewish community was now . . . Akiva. The earthly honor he had craved for so long was finally his, but he was no longer free to relish it. Identifying him, most likely, as the rebellion's spiritual leader, the Romans sent a warrant out for Akiva's arrest. His fellow Jews, who may have been disheartened by Bar Kochva's faltering, showed the great rabbi little love. The Talmud tells a story of Akiva, on the lam, entering a town and seeking refuge, only to meet with closed doors. He sleeps outside in the field and miraculously evades the Romans, who sack the town at night as they look for Akiva and arrest every Jew they see. The rabbi celebrated for his humanity and his humility doesn't seem moved by the townspeople's fate, but does praise God in the Talmudic telling—but merely for showing him kindness and saving his life.[30]

Eventually, though, the long arm of Rome reaches Akiva. He is put in prison and for several years continues to lead his rabbinic circle from his cell. Eventually, he's released, but the reality he now encounters is different and dismal. Livid at the cost of suppressing the rebellion, Hadrian not only razes, as recent archaeological findings confirm, literally every Jewish village and town in the Land of Israel, but also forbids the Jews who remain there from studying and teaching the Torah. How would Akiva respond to such a decree? The Talmud tells us.

One day, Akiva convenes a large assembly of students and teaches them Torah in public in defiance of Hadrian's decree. A man named Pappos ben Yehuda comes to him and asks if he isn't afraid of the Romans. Akiva answers with a parable.

"To what," he asked, "can this be compared? It is like a fox walking along a riverbank when he sees fish gathering and fleeing from place to place. The fox said to them: From what are you fleeing? They said to him: We are fleeing from the nets that people cast upon us. He said to them: Do you wish to come up onto dry land, and we will reside together just as my ancestors resided with your ancestors? The fish said to him: You are the one of whom they say, he is the cleverest of animals? You are not clever; you are a fool. If we are afraid in the water, our natural habitat which gives us life, then in a habitat that causes our death, all the more so."[31]

The moral, Akiva continues, is simple: If Jews left their natural habitat, which is the study of the Torah, they would no more survive than would fish out of water, and besides, the Romans—the fox in this parable—would eat them anyway.

Was Akiva brave? Foolish? Some combination of the two? Should he have acted more discreetly and by doing so guaranteed not only his survival but also his ability to teach more students for a longer time? Or was his stance heroic and all the legacy we need, with its urging us to focus on what truly matters in life even if external forces offer great punishments or great rewards to distract and dissuade us? These questions have occupied rabbis and scholars for centuries. They still do. But the Talmud couldn't abandon Akiva without a properly dramatic farewell.

A few days after his bold public lesson, we're told, Akiva is arrested again. Pappos ben Yehuda is arrested, too. When he sees Akiva, he weeps, feeling bitterly sorry that Akiva was seized for engaging in Torah study and he, Pappos, for "engaging in idle matters,"[32] which are, sadly, not defined. Not surprisingly, Akiva is swiftly sentenced to death, and the hour of his execution happens to coincide with the time to recite the Shema, Judaism's seminal prayer, affirming God's majesty and oneness.

"And they were raking his flesh with iron combs," the Talmud continues, "and he was reciting Shema, thereby accepting upon himself the yoke of Heaven." Akiva's students, watching their master calmly recite the ancient words even as he was being severely tortured, stand beside him and ask him how he could possibly be praying even as he suffers so. "All my days," Akiva replies calmly, "I have been troubled by the verse: With all your soul, meaning: Even if God takes your soul. I said to myself: When will the opportunity be afforded me to fulfill this verse? Now that it has been afforded me, shall I not fulfill it?"

Ever the incomparable reader, Akiva took the biblical exhortation to love God with all of your soul literally and yearned for an opportunity to put the verse to the test. "He prolonged his uttering of the word: One, until his soul left his body as he uttered his final word: One." And with that, a voice descends from heaven and says, "Happy are you, Rabbi Akiva, that your soul left your body as you uttered: One."

If Akiva's end infuriates you, you're in good company. In a vaguely postmodern interpretation that would have surely delighted Auerbach, the Talmud acknowledges that saying to a righteous man that he should count himself lucky because— despite unbelievable suffering—he died with a prayer on his lips isn't exactly the sort of explanation most people find soothing. Nor do most celestial creatures: The story continues with the angels in heaven, shocked and furious, accosting God. "This is Torah and this is its reward?" they inquire. If this is how you repay a pious scholar of your laws, why should anyone bother studying the Torah?

God seems to take this to heart. Immediately, the divine voice is heard again on earth with one more addendum: "Happy are you, Rabbi Akiva, as you are destined for life in the World-to-Come."

Why does God test Akiva so? What are Akiva's students thinking when they watch their teacher flayed alive? Do they buy into the bit about the reward in the World to Come justifying such sorrow and suffering in this world? Do we?

These questions were never meant to be answered. Answers, like heroes, are finite things that eventually expire. These questions were meant to trouble us, to spur us into action, to urge us to wrestle even (or especially) with the thorniest of questions, like the one about why very bad things happen to very good people.

Akiva, the sage who remade his life by reading so brilliantly and so boldly, dies interpreting text. He is his old self again, introspective and reflective even under the direst circumstances. We can almost imagine him smiling, looking at his gathered students and knowing that they're paying attention, and that they, too, will follow his lead.

CHAPTER FOUR

Romance in the Dark

or

How to Win in Love and Marriage

B Y THE TIME Eleanora Fagan was nine years old, she was dragged before juvenile court, found guilty of truancy, and sent to a reform school named the Good Shepherd, where she was forced to spend nearly a year. She hated it there, but her home wasn't much better: she never knew who her father was, and her mother, Sadie, worked on commuter trains and was absent most of the time. By the time Fagan was eleven, she dropped out of school for good, and not long after that a neighbor crept into her apartment and tried to rape her. Fagan fought back, but when she agreed to testify against her attacker, she was once again removed from her house—for her own protection, she was told—and returned to the Good Shepherd. When she was released, she found a job running errands for a neighborhood brothel. The only thing that brought her some solace was spending time with her elderly great-grandmother, who was born enslaved on a Virginia plantation and had sixteen children by the white man who owned it.

One night, Fagan and her elderly relative lay down to bed. "I woke up four or five hours later," she later recalled. "Grandma's arm was tight around my neck and I couldn't move it. I tried and tried and then I got scared. She was dead, and I began to scream. The neighbors came running. They had to break Grandma's arm to get me loose. Then they took me to a hospital. I was there for a month. Suffering from what they said was shock."[1]

When she was released, she found comfort in music. She loved Bessie Smith, and she could listen to Louis Armstrong play "West End Blues" over and over again. "It was the first time I ever heard anybody sing without using any words," she remembered. "It had plenty of meaning for me—just as much meaning as some of the other words that I didn't always understand. But the meaning used to change, depending on how I felt. Sometimes the record would make me so sad I'd cry up a storm. Other times the same damn record would make me so happy."[2]

She started singing herself and realized she had a nice voice, but no one, she thought, would pay just to hear her croon. So she kept on listening to records, especially ones where a singer would have a duet with a saxophone or a clarinet. This, she thought, was what true love sounded like, a feeling much purer and more harmonious than the crude and often violent advances she received from the men around her.

One day, the fifteen-year-old Fagan returned home to her apartment on 139th Street in Harlem to find her mother in a bitter state. The rent was past due, Sadie told her daughter, and if $45 didn't materialize by morning, the two would be out on the street. It was a freezing night, but Fagan didn't care. She ran out onto Seventh Avenue, storming into every restaurant, café, bar, or club she could find and demanding rather than asking for a job. One joint after the next turned her down, and she was reaching the point of contemplating crime when she walked into a club called Jerry's. She told the owner she'd like to wait tables, or dance, or do whatever needed doing for a few bucks. Jerry asked her to show him some of her moves. He observed no more than two steps before telling Fagan that he was very sorry but that she was neither graceful nor beautiful enough for anyone to look at. She was already making her way out when he stopped her with one more question: "Girl, can you sing?"

Sure, Fagan said, adding that she didn't see why that mattered. In those days, girls who worked in clubs were referred to as "ups," and they'd just shimmy from table to table for hours, collecting cash tips off tables while wearing skimpy outfits. But Fagan was desperate, so she asked Jerry's pianist if he knew one of her favorite sad tunes, telling Jerry she didn't feel like belting out anything too cheerful. The pianist knew the song and played it. Fagan started singing.

Within seconds, the place was dead silent. Within minutes, several of the guests were sobbing. Within hours, Fagan walked out the door with $57 and a job singing at Jerry's. On her way home, she stopped to buy a whole chicken and baked beans, Sadie's favorite, and when she walked in the door she told her mom she didn't have to worry anymore. But "Eleanora Fagan" didn't exactly roll off the tongue; if she was going to be an entertainer, she needed a name people would remember. She thought about women she admired; Billie Dove came to mind, the actress who'd played opposite Douglas Fairbanks in *The Black Pirate*. And the man she believed was most likely her biological father was named Clarence Halliday, a name that, with some tweaks, could sound memorable and cool. And so, when she returned to work the next day, Eleanora Fagan was reborn as Billie Holiday.

For a few years, she sang in a handful of New York clubs. Her fans, and more and more of them were coming to hear her every night, commented on two things: her ability to use her voice like a musical instrument, improvising and playing with its registers to a hypnotic effect, and her capacity to deliver the full emotional weight of whatever song she was singing in an understated, natural, and utterly devastating way. John Hammond, the record producer who would later launch the careers of Bob Dylan, Leonard Cohen, and Bruce Springsteen, to name but a handful of many stars, was one of those early fans, and he signed Holiday up in November of 1933. Her first single, a collaboration with Bennie Goodman, sold three hundred copies. Her second, released shortly thereafter, sold more than ten times as many. Holiday was on her way to stardom.

And so, at the exact same time and playing in many of the same clubs, was Lester Young. He was a few years older than Holiday and was raised first in New Orleans and then in Minneapolis in a family that made its living traveling around the country and performing in carnivals. His father was the bandleader, his brother Leonidas played the drums, and his sister Irma sang. Young Lester got his start on the violin and was pretty handy with both the trumpet and the clarinet, but from the moment he first picked up the tenor sax, he hardly bothered with any other instrument. Learning to master the mouthpiece, however, was one thing; being told he had to use separate restrooms and water fountains from the white folks who'd come to hear him play was another. Increasingly, Young felt sickened by having to tour the segregated South, and when his father insisted that the family didn't have the luxury of turning down paying gigs, Lester, then a teenager, quit the band and moved to Kansas City.

Anytime Young played with a band, however, someone would tell him he should play more like Coleman Hawkins, the dominant sax player of the day whose forceful style was described by his biographer John Chilton as sounding like "rubbery belches."[3] Young refused. Sensitive and introverted, his approach to playing was more relaxed, almost meditative; years later, the jazz pianist Leonard Feather called it a "liquid, nervous style."[4] You just had to look at Young to know he was an original. Unlike other musicians, who held the sax straight and vertical, he swung his instrument high and to the right at a sharp angle, as if his grasp was somehow tenuous and slipping. And when Young spoke, he improvised as well; he was the first, according to jazz historian Phil Schaap, to use the term "cool" to mean hip and desirable,[5] and would often come up with terms to more lyrically describe things that struck him as too painfully mundane. When he wanted to ask how much a gig would pay, for example, a subject that always made him feel awkwardly self-conscious, he'd say, "How does the bread smell?" Sometimes, words would strike him as altogether inadequate, at which point he'd simply say something like "ring ring!" and trust that whomever he was talking to understood what he meant.

In 1934, Young and Holiday, the jazz scene's two ascending stars, stumbled across each other. They became fast friends and, quickly, roommates. Lester was living in a seedy Harlem hotel, and one day he opened his dresser drawer to discover an enormous rat glaring at him while nestled among his shirts. Shaken, Young ran out and sought refuge with Billie and Sadie, living in the hallway of their two-bedroom railroad apartment. He was always, Holiday reported in her memoir years later, the perfect gentleman, calling Sadie "Duchess" and giving Billie a nickname that was true to her: Lady Day. She, in turn, named him Prez, the president of jazz; together with trumpeter Buck Clayton, they called themselves "the Unholy Three" and spent the long bus rides while touring with Count Basie's band smoking pot and drinking a concoction of port and gin they'd invented and dubbed the "top and bottom." They were everyone's favorite bandmates, always ready with a rowdy joke or a good yarn, but those paying close attention could tell that they were both tormented, delicate souls rattled by the hardships of their circumstances, from having to make a living as touring musicians to facing the racism and sexism of the day. "You never got an idea that she wasn't enjoying life," the trombonist Benny Morton, who toured with Holiday and Young, recalled years later, "but to me this was a cover-up. The laughter, this was a top, this also goes for Lester. He was one of the nicest men I've ever known, so very kind, but I think he felt the world had short-changed him."[6]

All their pain, however, disappeared once they stepped onstage. Listen to "Romance in the Dark," "He's Funny That Way," "Travlin' All Alone," or any other of the numbers Holiday and Young recorded in the late 1930s, and you could sometimes feel that sax melt into voice and vice versa, that the two people onstage aren't so much performing a duet as disappearing into each other, thinking and playing as one.

But then the show would be over, and Young and Holiday would return to a life that was increasingly nasty and brutish and, sadly, short. Young served in the army during the Second World War, spending much of his stint in prison after a racist commanding officer discovered he had a white common-law wife, raided his locker, found marijuana, and alerted the military police. Holiday didn't fare much better. After she insisted in 1939 on recording "Strange Fruit," Abel Meeropol's gut-wrenching song about a lynching, she became a national celebrity as well as the target of Harry Anslinger, the head of the Federal Bureau of Narcotics, a tiny government agency in peril of big budget cuts and in need of a high-profile case. An African American woman performing night after night before white audiences and singing boldly and bravely about white supremacy was a convenient target.

In May of 1947, agents burst into Holiday's New York apartment and arrested her for possession of narcotics. She was in such poor shape that she pled guilty just to expedite her transfer to the hospital. From there, she was sent to the Alderson Federal Prison Camp in West Virginia, where she spent the lion's share of the next year. "It was called 'The United States versus Billie Holiday,'" she later wrote about her ordeal, "and that's just the way it felt."[7] There was no peace awaiting Holiday once she was released: she tumbled from one abusive romantic relationship to another, beaten, used, and abused by a string of husbands and lovers.

Neither Holiday nor Young ever recovered from their respective ordeals. They tried to capture the transcendence of their earlier collaborations, but their legal troubles and tumultuous personal lives distracted them and eventually led to a fight that resulted in years of losing touch. Young was repeatedly admitted to a string of hospitals, first, in 1955, for a nervous breakdown and later for alcohol-related ailments. In 1959, while flying from Paris to New York, he suffered from internal bleeding due to cirrhosis of the liver. He died a few hours after landing. He was forty-nine years old. In a cab on her way to Young's funeral, Holiday told a friend she'd be the next to go. Four months later, she was admitted to New York's Metropolitan Hospital after losing nearly 20 pounds and suffering from heart and liver problems due to years of abusing alcohol and drugs. Anslinger sent federal officers to her hospital room, arresting her for possession of narcotics as she lay dying. Her friends went to court to insist that her guards be removed and that she be allowed to recover in peace. They won, but recovery never came. She died on July 17, 1959, at 3:10 in the morning. She was forty-four years old and had 70 cents in her bank account when she passed.

Despite living in a different era and facing different circumstances, Bruriah, born sometime in the second century CE, could probably relate both to living in a sexist environment that discounted the talents of women and to finding solace in a nurturing relationship with a man who valued the same things as her. The daughter of one prominent rabbi and the wife of another, she is the sole female sage of the Talmud, an exception that has made her the subject of intense scrutiny for millennia. But before we can meet her in all her incandescent, impatient, and, ultimately, tragic glory, we would do well to know a little more about the rules of the world she inhabited, a world that found love often at odds with duty and ambition at war with tradition.

What, then, was the Talmudic world like when it came to relations between the sexes? The question is so vast and intricate that it has kept a few centuries' worth of scholars merrily busy, but a good primer would necessarily focus on two critical questions. The first one has to do with society at large: What did this culture, forged by the rabbis, value most? Who did it elevate, and who did it denigrate? And was it even remotely accommodating of anyone except the usual suspects—the wise old rabbis with their long, white beards?

Take a quick, cursory look, and you may be forgiven for thinking that the answer to that last question is, alas, no. After all, the rabbis believed that the most important thing a person could do was study the Torah and perform its commandments. And because many of these commandments, like praying, applied only to men, they occupied a more elevated sphere of public life, confining women, along with the unlearned, the mentally and physically disabled, and all gentiles to the lower castes. Such a worldview wouldn't have been out of sync with most of the region's contemporary cultures; but no sooner had the rabbis begun to explore its consequences than they stumbled upon one major logical fallacy. If the above statement was true, and the virtue they truly cherished was a person's ability to excel in the study of the Torah, didn't that mean that anyone smart and passionate enough about studying the Torah could prove themselves a brilliant student and ascend to the highest level?

In one heated discussion, the rabbis contemplated this thorny question. Rabbi Meir—Bruriah's husband, and a rabbi so revered in his days that his colleagues readily admitted that they often failed to understand the brilliance and depth of his arguments— offered a definitive answer. Read Leviticus, Meir taught, and you'll see that the Bible simply says that "a person" ought to live by God's commandments. The Bible, Meir explained, didn't say that "only priests" or "only the most learned" or even that "only Jews" ought to observe the commandments. The Torah was clear: all people are called upon to obey and delight in God's laws. "You have therefore learned," Meir concluded, "that even a gentile who engages in Torah study is considered like a High Priest."[8] You didn't have to be Jewish; study the Torah, whoever you are, and you can obtain the same level of holiness as the most elevated servant of God.

Herein lies the uneasy and imperfect answer to the first and most crucial question about Talmudic times. What kind of society did the rabbis have in mind? Certainly, one fairly strict about distinctions—between Jews and gentiles, between the learned and the unlearned, between men and women—but also one that left sufficient room for movement and growth, an aspiring meritocracy that was willing, however begrudgingly or irregularly, to confer its greatest privileges on any individual that broke through its biases. Which leads us to a second, even more complicated question: Where did that leave women?

Let's eavesdrop on one seminal discussion about this very question. A few rabbis we've already met are sitting and talking about the importance of procreation. Having kids, says Rabbi Eliezer, is such a crucial commandment that anyone who chooses not to is basically shedding innocent blood, because no sooner does God, in the Bible, command us to be fruitful and multiply than he introduces us to Cain, humanity's first murderer, who chose not to procreate but to snuff out his brother's life instead. Pleased with this teaching, the young Elazar ben Azarya riffs on the same theme and says that if man was created in the divine image, then anyone not procreating is disgracing the divine image, a sin even graver than murder. Listening to this, a rabbi named Ben Azzai chimes in, saying that not having children is as bad as all that and more. At this point, the other two rabbis look at him coldly.

"There is a type of scholar who expounds well and fulfills his own teachings well," they say to him haughtily, "and another who fulfills well and does not expound well. But you, who have never married, expound well on the importance of procreation, and yet you do not fulfill well your own teachings." Ben Azzai listens patiently. "What shall I do," he finally replies, "as my soul yearns for Torah, and I do not wish to deal with anything else? It is possible for the world to be maintained by others, who are engaged in the *mitzvah* to be fruitful and multiply."[9]

What to make of Ben Azzai's answer? "The absolute and contradictory demands of marriage and commitment to the study of Torah remained one of the greatest unresolved tensions of rabbinic culture,"[10] explains historian of religion Daniel Boyarin, adding playfully that, under the circumstances, one could almost refer to the Torah as "the other woman," tempting men away from the demands of house and home and into an ecstatic, almost erotic, relationship. Rearrange a few of the particulars, and you'll see the same tension still simmering today, albeit with a different type of career often taking the place of studying Torah, as unresolved as it was during the time of the Talmud. Should I be there to have dinner with my young kids, or should I stay late at the office to make sure my team nails the big account? Should I marry young and have kids, or should I live a little first, go to grad school, make some money, and stand on my own two feet? Everywhere we go, we're expected to settle down and start a family. Everywhere we go, we're pressured to get that promotion, that raise, that status. These goals are incompatible. We can't have it all. Something's got to give.

Enter Bruriah.

Her father was Rabbi Hanina ben Teradyon, a contemporary of Rabbi Akiva's who also found himself on the wrong end of Roman justice. Like Akiva, Hanina, too, refused to refrain from teaching the Torah. Like Akiva, Hanina, too, was soon arrested and sentenced to death. But whereas the Romans were content to merely tear at Akiva's flesh with iron combs until he died—a relatively merciful death, considering the Empire's smorgasbord of ways to torture the condemned—they had something altogether different in mind for Hanina. A man like him, known for his great piety, deserved something special. If Hanina loved the Torah so much, mused the Romans, let's wrap him up in a Torah scroll and set him ablaze. And to make sure he experienced every excruciating moment in full, let's wrap him first in wet wool, just to make sure he wouldn't pass out or burn too quickly.

Watching their teacher roasting slowly, Hanina's students stood by and wept. But the elderly rabbi comforted them with a mystical vision. Look, he said, and you'll see the scroll burning and its letters floating freely in midair. It hardly took a great Torah scholar to decipher Hanina's message: even as his body was being consumed by the fire, his soul remained tethered to its eternal source of life, the timeless teachings of God. Listening

to this conversation, the Talmud tells us, Hanina's Roman exe-
cutioner grew misty-eyed, moved by the dying rabbi's grace and
fortitude. If I remove the wet wool, he asked Hanina, will you
guarantee that I, too, will have a place in the World to Come?
Hanina gave his word, and the Roman soldier yanked out the wet
wool as promised. Watching Hanina burn to death, the Talmud
tells us, drove the Roman to despair, and he, too, quickly jumped
into the pyre and perished.[11]

The rest of Hanina's family hardly fared better. His wife, the
Talmud informs us, was summarily executed, as was his son, who
had abandoned the old-timey religion and become a bit of a brig-
and. His unnamed daughter was seized by soldiers and sold off
as a prostitute, which left his other daughter, Bruriah, alone in
the world.

Or not exactly alone. By the time her family was eradicated,
Bruriah was married to Rabbi Meir, Rabbi Akiva's most brilliant—
and most difficult—student.

How difficult? So difficult that his other teacher, once Akiva
was out of the picture, was the scandalous Elisha Ben Abuya, a
fiery rabbi who chose to abandon Judaism and, from that moment
on, became known simply as Acher, or the Other. So difficult that his colleagues speculated that Meir was a descendant
of the supposedly mad Roman emperor Nero, who, according
to the Talmud—but in defiance of all other available sources of
antiquity—had secretly converted to Judaism.[12] So difficult that
the sages of the Talmud weren't even sure if their friend's name
was really Meir; the name, some speculated, was only given to
him because it means "the luminous one," a fitting moniker for
such a brilliant guy.[13] Which, when it came to Meir, didn't strike
anyone as far-fetched. His contemporaries, a cantankerous bunch
forever quick with a jab, a barb, or a put-down, spoke of Meir in
terms they applied to few, if anyone, else. When one of his pals
was asked to describe what the great Meir was like, Rabbi Yossi
ben Halafta waxed poetic. Rabbi Meir, he said, was "a great man,
a holy man, a humble man."[14]

You'd expect such a phenom to be his generation's uncontested leader, but the rabbis knew better. One moment, they'd watch as Meir argued that a ritually impure item was actually pure, applying brilliant arguments and talking so fast they could hardly follow them. Then, without catching a breath, Meir would argue the opposite, explaining why a ritually pure item was impure. "He was so brilliant," the Talmud tells us, "that he could present a cogent argument for any position," even if his argument wasn't consistent with halacha. Simply put, laws applied here on earth, and Meir seemed to live in higher planes of existence, where every question was nothing more than an invitation to get a little bit closer to God. So disdainful was Meir of anything and everything mundane that each week he took all the money he had left over after buying food and paying rent and donated it to impoverished Torah scholars. When his friends urged him to put some aside so he'd have something to leave to his children, Meir shrugged his shoulders. If his children grew up to be righteous, he said, God would support them, and if they didn't, well, let them take care of themselves. This harshness of Meir's, coupled with his impenetrable erudition—he once wrote down the entire book of Esther from memory, making not one single mistake—led his peers to decree that Meir should never be the final arbiter when it came to deciding the law. He was simply too smart for his own—or anyone else's—good.

This bothered Rabbi Meir not a bit. He had a routine he loved and which made sense to none but himself. As stringent as he was about interpreting the Torah as commanding a total separation between Jews and gentiles, he spent much time debating with Roman philosophers and intellectuals, engaging in fascinating discussions, many of them preserved in the Talmud, about life, nature, God, art, and pleasure. And as much as he believed that Torah scholars ought to be held in the highest regard, which meant they could and should avoid spending any time with anyone but their learned peers, he treated poor and unlearned people with tremendous kindness and respect. One Friday night, the

Talmud tells us, Rabbi Meir was giving his usual sermon, which
he did at blockbuster gatherings during which the eloquent orator
would teach some Torah, say a few words about Jewish law, and
then regale the audience with delightful fables all could understand. One person in attendance was a hardworking, unnamed
woman, who was so riveted by Meir's flow of words that she
stayed until the very end of his talk, returning home so late at
night that the Shabbat candles she'd lit earlier that afternoon had
already burnt out.

The woman's husband was the brutish sort; immediately, he
suspected her of having an affair. The woman denied this and
told her husband the truth: she was listening to a rabbi give a
talk. That assurance did little to appease the churlish man. "I
swear," he roared, "that you will not enter this house until you
go out and spit in the eye of this rabbi who kept you out so late!"

Scared, confused, and hurt, the woman had no idea what to
do next. Spitting in Rabbi Meir's eye was out of the question. In
her despair, she walked out to her garden and stood there, sobbing quietly. Her neighbors came over to inquire what had happened, and the woman, fighting back tears, told them the whole
story. You've no other choice, the neighbors said after thinking
things through for a few moments; you have to go see Rabbi Meir
and ask for his advice.

As they were making their way to see the holy man, the Talmud tells us, Rabbi Meir had a vision. He saw the woman about
to approach, saw her heart, and understood exactly what had
happened and what she was feeling. So when the woman and
her neighbors walked into his house of study, Meir shut his eyes
tightly, threw himself on the floor, and started moaning. My eyes,
he wailed, my eyes! They hurt so! I must have caught some rare
disease! Quick, someone spit in my eyes and help me rinse them!

The woman and her neighbors stood frozen, not sure what
to do next, but Meir was adamant. He opened one eye, looked
straight at the woman, and in a loud and calm voice asked her to
kindly come near and help him out by spitting in his eyes seven

times. Quickly, the woman did as Rabbi Meir had ordered, and when she was done, Meir got up, wiped his face, and smiled. "Now go home," he told the woman, "and tell your husband that you spat in my eye not once but seven times."

Watching this scene unfold, Meir's students were livid, and when the woman finally left, they tore into their teacher. How, they demanded, could the great rabbi, who so often preached about the respect we owe wise Torah scholars, allow himself to be denigrated like that? Had you said a word, they groused, we would've gone over and beaten the husband into submission rather than allow you to be humiliated in this way.

Meir smiled. The Torah, he told his fuming disciples, teaches us that in order to uphold peace between man and wife, we are even allowed to erase the explicit name of God. And if God is willing to forgo His honor for the sake of a happy marriage, then I, too, am glad to suffer a bit of humiliation for this sacred cause.[15]

What sort of woman would such a man—punctilious yet warm, aloof yet kind, brilliant yet almost comically ill-suited for life—take to be his wife? The Talmud takes the question seriously, giving us a surprising number of scenes from the marriage of Meir and Bruriah. Rabbi Akiva and Rachel may have had their meet cute, but that is an exception. Other rabbis were married, yet their wives are never mentioned by name and, at best, are referred to in passing—bit players in the rabbinic drama performed exclusively by men. But if it were to say something meaningful about love and marriage and the ways they so often clashed with the construction and constrictions of society, the Talmud needed its own Lady Day and Prez, two people connected on the deepest level imaginable, to show us what a more equitable and emotionally gratifying relationship might look like.

We know nothing about Bruriah and Meir's courtship. From their very first appearance—just a few pages into Berakhot, the Talmud's first tractate—they are already intertwined, a two-headed unit there to teach us something about couplehood. Let us observe them.

"There were," the Talmud recounts, "these hooligans in Rabbi Meir's neighborhood who caused him a great deal of anguish." Who were these bullies? And how, exactly, did they upset Rabbi Meir? The Talmud doesn't tell us, and so invites us to write ourselves into this nasty dispute between neighbors. How does the great Meir deal with this conflict? Poorly, as was his wont when it came to all things earthly. He prays to God to have mercy on the brutes and end their miserable lives. He means it sincerely, almost sweetly: in his world, if a person isn't a brilliant and accomplished scholar, a person may as well be dead.

Bruriah, hallelujah, knows better. "What is your thinking?" she asks. It's much more than a bit of throat clearing. If she simply chastises her husband for his ridiculously harsh position, she knows, he'll likely just walk away, telling himself that his wife doesn't understand him or, worse, doesn't understand the intricacies of the divine teachings that propel him to such conclusions. To engage with Meir, Bruriah knows, she has to be a Billie to his Lester, speak Meir's language to create this duet that makes real communion possible. Luckily, it's a language she knows as well, if not better, than her incomparably brilliant husband. "On what basis do you pray for the death of these hooligans?" she continues. "Do you base yourself on the verse, as it is written, 'Let sins cease from the land' (Psalms 104:35), which you interpret to mean that the world would be better if the wicked were destroyed? But is it written, let sinners cease? Let sins cease, is written."

By now, we can imagine, Bruriah has Meir's attention. She uses his own method of understanding the world to prove him wrong, and she might be forgiven for stopping at that. But her husband, Bruriah knows, isn't a man who does anything by half measures; if she wants his respect—and, more importantly, if she wants to truly help him out of this neighborly pickle—she has to argue the way he argues, with abandon. And so, she goes on: I know what you're thinking, she tells Meir. The same verse in Psalms ends by saying, "And the wicked will be no more," which is probably the reason you think it's OK to ask God to smite these particular wicked gents next door. But if that's what you think, you're wrong. It's simple logic: Here's a verse that first says the sins should cease, and then tells us that the wicked will be no more. Clearly, what the verse means to say is that once sins cease, the wicked will no longer be wicked. In other words, they'll still be very much alive, but no longer evil. The Bible isn't telling us to pray for the death of bad guys; it tells us to pray for bad guys to repent. Problem solved. "Rabbi Meir," the Talmud concludes, "saw that Bruriah was correct and he prayed for God to have mercy on them, and they repented."[16]

The story is remarkable for several reasons, not the least of which is its introduction, barely ten pages into the Talmud, of a renegade female sage. For one thing, we see Meir, the smartest guy in any study hall, humbled in his own living room and treated not only to a healthy dose of common sense but also to a lesson in the Torah, his field of expertise. For another, we see a stunning reversal of the gender roles that were then—and, sadly, are still now—perceived as essential and that portray men as inherently cool and reasonable and women as emotional and impulsive. Plato, as per usual, captured this worldview neatly; interestingly, he did so while riffing on the very same subject Meir and Bruriah were discussing, namely, how to deal with the wicked person down the block. "Now while in general the wrong-doer and he that has these evils are to be pitied, it is permissible to show pity to the man that has evils that are remediable," Plato wrote, "and to abate one's passion and treat him gently, and not to keep on raging like a scolding wife. . . . It behooves the good man to be always at once passionate and gentle."[17] The Talmud gives us a smooth inversion of Plato's dictum. Rabbi Meir is the nagging wife, quick to anger and unable to see the world through any lens other than his own. Bruriah is the passionate and gentle husband, learned and even-keeled and, above all, merciful.

Or is she? A far funnier book than we give it credit for being, the Talmud follows this story with another, raunchier one. No sooner have we met Bruriah and known her to be a sweet and sensitive soul than the Talmud gives us a very different version of her. In what is billed as "another example of Bruriah's incisive insight," the Talmud tells us that she was accosted by a spiteful heretic. The Bible, the man gleefully cited, said the following: "Sing, barren woman who has not given birth."[18] Really? A woman should sing and rejoice because she *didn't* have kids? Isn't that the opposite of the prime biblical command to be fruitful and multiply?

Bruriah, however, was far from perturbed by this gotcha moment. With none of the tenderness she'd previously shown to her badly behaved neighbors, she looked the man straight in the eye. "Fool!" she scolded him, "go to the end of the verse, where it is written: 'For the children of the desolate shall be more numerous than the children of the married wife.'" What the Bible is really saying here, she concluded with gusto, is that pious women sing and rejoice because they didn't have children who are bound to go to hell, like you.[19]

What to make of this barbed exchange? Why give us one version of Bruriah only to deliver a distinctly alternative one a moment later? Still another Bruriah story helps answer this question.

One day, we're told, Bruriah was sitting outside her house when Rabbi Yossi HaGelili, one of his generation's finest minds, ran into her. Yossi was headed to the town of Lod and didn't know the way. "Tell me," he asked Bruriah, "in which way should I go to the town of Lod?"

It was all Bruriah needed to hear. "Foolish Galilean," she snapped at him, "didn't the sages say: Don't talk much with women? You should have asked your question more succinctly: Which to Lod?"[20]

She was hardly being needlessly churlish. As soon as Judaism transformed itself from a sacrifice-based religion into one dedicated to personal and communal ethical conduct, no question was more pressing than how, precisely, should people go about interacting with the opposite sex. Or, even more awkwardly, with sex in general. The rabbis, uncommonly for men of their time, all agreed that because sex led to procreation, it was sacred, and because it was sacred, it had to be exercised in very particular and mindful ways. This meant, of course, that it could only be enjoyed between husband and wife, but also that it could never be practiced without explicit consent, or even joy. Whatever dominance men had elsewhere, when it came to the bedroom, the Talmud makes it explicitly clear, again and again, that any application of force or coercion was strictly forbidden.

Which gave the rabbis some guidelines, but not too many. Being men—often, young men—and spending their days in the exclusively masculine confines of the study hall, the rabbis talked about sex, openly and bluntly. And, being rabbis, they tried to figure out where it fit into the larger and intricate set of behaviors commanded of each observant Jew. One famous story tells of a prominent rabbi who was making love to his wife. The couple, the Talmud tells us, were having a great time, laughing and talking and enjoying each other's bodies, when, all of a sudden, they heard a creaking sound come from under the bed. Looking down, the rabbi saw one of his disciples, himself a prominent rabbi, just lying there and observing. Livid, he asked the younger man why on earth he was peeping in on such an intimate moment, but the student was unapologetic. "It is Torah," he told his teacher, "and I must learn it."[21] If sex is so holy, in other words, let me get it just right by observing the master at work.

This anxiety, this desire to keep the carnal appetites in check lest they take over and occupy hearts and minds and loins, is the source of some of the Talmud's most outlandish—and instructive—interactions. One rabbi, for example—Yohanan the son of Dabai—once regaled his colleagues by stating that the Ministering Angels themselves had revealed to him the secrets of proper sex. Lame children were born, he said, because their fathers had allowed their mothers to be on top during intercourse, which was unnatural and therefore unadvisable. Mute children were born because men engaged in oral sex; the sin of pleasuring a woman with one's mouth resulted in the punishment of a child who cannot speak. Deaf children we owed to fathers who talked to their wives during sex, which robbed the holy conduit of procreation of its mysterious might, and blind children to fathers who spent too much time staring at their wives' private parts.[22] It's not hard to follow the rabbi's logic here—any action that isn't directly tied to the possibility of conception is nixed. Thankfully, the Talmud goes on to reject both this mad list and the claim that it was somehow divinely inspired, offering instead a much more cheerful assessment: anything that brings husband and wife pleasure—including, fascinatingly, activities, like anal sex, that cannot result in pregnancy—is permitted, encouraged, and celebrated. Just have fun.

Which, alas, hardly relieved anyone's jitters. The rabbis were in a bind. They could not, as Christian monks later did, declare themselves too holy to marry or reproduce, as marriage and children were deemed absolutely essential. Nor could they deny their wives sexual satisfaction, a promise written directly into the ketubah—the Jewish marriage contract—which mentions neither God nor love but does require the husband to provide his wife with all of her earthly needs, gratifying sex included. Which meant that as mighty as these men might have been in the public sphere they'd so diligently constructed, they had no special authority and no claim to anything but a slight advantage in their domestic lives. Even the most eminent rabbis had to ask his wife's permission to spend prolonged periods of time in the study hall, and if he was absent for too long, he could expect not only her rebuke but also that of his male colleagues.

Naturally, then, some rabbis sought to double down on the distinctions between men and women, arguing that women's inherent qualities made them too frivolous to take seriously. Thus, they could be excluded entirely from the only realm that mattered, that of studying the Torah. The Talmud tells us that a certain unnamed wise woman once came to Rabbi Eliezer with a very good question. Read the Bible, she asked the old eminence, and you see that all the Israelites bore equal responsibility for the sin of the golden calf. Yet the Bible then says that different culprits died in different ways: some who prayed to the calf perished by plague, others died by the sword, and yet others succumbed to an intestinal illness. Why, the woman asked, this discrepancy? Why not punish all sinners in the same way for the same transgression?

"There is no wisdom in a woman except weaving with a spindle,"[23] Rabbi Eliezer replied, rudely and curtly. Women weren't capable of understanding the intricacies of the divine words and therefore need not concern themselves with asking questions about anything but domestic chores.

The story, maddening as it is, tells us two things. First, it strongly suggests that it was customary—or at least not unheard of—for Jews to teach their daughters Torah as diligently as they had taught their sons; the unnamed woman's question suggests both a sharp and well-trained analytical mind as well as deep and intimate familiarity with scripture. Second, it shows us just how uncomfortable—and sometimes downright dismissive—some of the rabbis were in their relations with women. As if to bookend this anecdote about Rabbi Eliezer, the Talmud later gives us a brief cameo by his wife, Imma Shalom—the name literally means Mother Peace—delivering a touching, if nearly comical, account of Eliezer's lovemaking. "My husband," she says, "does not converse with me while engaging in sexual intercourse, neither at the beginning of the night nor at the end of the night, but rather at midnight. And when he converses with me while engaging in sexual intercourse, he reveals a handbreadth of my body and covers a handbreadth, and he covers himself up as though he were being coerced by a demon and is covering himself out of fear." Naturally, Imma Shalom is curious, and she asks her husband to explain his strange behavior in the bedroom. Rabbi Eliezer replies by saying that he's terrified of accidentally thinking about other women during intercourse. If a man makes love to his wife and thinks of another woman, he explains, his soul becomes entangled with that of the other woman, and the children his wife bears him are therefore mamzers, or illegitimate.[24]

For Eliezer, the physical aspects of lovemaking are torturous stumbling blocks, keeping him from attaining the spiritual purity in which he feels most comfortable.

This male discomfort with—or, really, fear of—women is a thread the Talmud records faithfully. In Pirkei Avot, the part of the Mishnah that records the ethical teachings of the great rabbis, we hear one of them, Yose ben Yochanan, share the following advice: "Engage not in too much conversation with women. They said this with regard to one's own wife, how much more [does the rule apply] with regard to another man's wife. From here the Sages said: as long as a man engages in too much conversation with women, he causes evil to himself, he neglects the study of the Torah, and in the end he will inherit gehinnom," or hell.[25]

It was this popular dictum Bruriah was referring to when she berated Rabbi Yossi HaGelili for asking her for directions to Lod. If you truly believe this idea, Bruriah tells her interlocutor, that it is incumbent upon you, as a pious man, to refrain from speaking very much to women lest your thoughts turn impure—then choose your words carefully and ask your mundane question in the pithiest way possible, muttering not even one single unneeded word. But if you don't believe in this idea, then give me the respect I deserve, and rather than merely asking me for directions, sit and dignify me by speaking a bit about the Torah, as you would have done had you come across any of your male colleagues. Again wielding her sharp mind and sharper tongue as weapons, Bruriah claims her place in a male-dominated world.

And the Talmud goes out of its way to celebrate her for it. It would have been easy, almost natural, for the redactors of the Talmud to decide that having a woman sage was simply too confusing, leaving unanswered the many questions about how to balance the clear distinctions Jewish law makes between men and women on the one hand and the obvious and innate ability and desire of women like Bruriah to engage in traditionally male pursuits, like Torah study, on the other. Instead, the Talmud returns to Bruriah again and again. Here she is, in the midst of one hyperspecific legalistic discussion, waiting for her brother to give the wrong answer before jumping in with the correct one, and receiving the praise of the elders.[26] And there she goes, set up as an example when a wise old rabbi scolds one of his lazy students by telling him that he should be more like Bruriah, who learned three hundred Jewish laws each day from three hundred different sages.[27] We even see her playfully kicking a young man who was praying too softly for her taste; a person who is secure in his love and devotion to his studies, she scolds the student post-kick, should raise his voice, not whisper.[28]

Why give Bruriah, the exception to every rule, so much space and so much attention? One obvious answer is simply that she was a brilliant woman, and the rabbis, no matter what else they believed, had the deepest admiration for anyone who could match or surpass them in learnedness. Their world, ultimately, *was* a meritocracy, and Bruriah had earned her stripes. A less obvious answer goes a bit deeper. The tension between men and women, the rabbis realized, was as eternal as it was innate. A guide to life could only be worthwhile if it went beyond acknowledging this tension to also amplify it enough to study all of its intricacies. By placing a female sage in the middle of the male drama, and by making her not only the triumphant hero of every interaction in which she is mentioned but also a muscular firebrand who is quick with a kick and an insult, the Talmud is demanding of us, whoever we may be, to challenge any and all preconceived notions we may have on how a man or woman ought to behave.

But there's a third, even more profound reason, for the ascendency of Bruriah, and it has everything to do with marriage.

Let's return, for a moment, to Billie Holiday. Hers is a story that continues to resonate because it hums with aspirations and frustrations we all, men and women alike, can fully understand. How maddening must it have been to be so talented, so passionate, so wise, and yet find, at every turn, that your fate lies in the hands of men, frequently your artistic inferiors, often callous, and sometimes cruel. How terrible to feel like following your heart came at the steep price of everyone, from your husbands and boyfriends to the federal government, unleashing their fury in return. Holiday fought back, sometimes literally, getting into fisticuffs with drunk bigots who called her horrible names. And she sang "Strange Fruit" night after night, defiant and courageous. But such acts of bravery, inspiring as they may be, ended with Holiday in an early grave, heartbroken and broke.

We still care about Holiday today not only because of her singular talent, but because we admire her tenacity in the face of such great prejudice. Society still places different values on male and female behavior and achievement, and it still makes contradictory demands—Raise a family! Have a career! Spend more time with your kids! Hustle harder at work!—that offer no clear and simple path out. It is tempting, perhaps almost inevitable, to come and see this conundrum as nothing more than a battlefield on which men and women are destined to forever grapple for power, wounding each other in an unending series of skirmishes designed to carve out just a little more pay, just a little more autonomy, just a little more recognition.

Bruriah, like Holiday, is here to tell us that such an approach is doomed to fail. Love isn't a battlefield; it's a convalescent ward, a place to lay broken and heal from the blows you suffer simply by virtue of being alive. Holiday and Young, Bruriah and Meir— both couples found a channel through which to connect almost telepathically, transcending the earthly frustrations and resentments and exhaustions that mar so many relationships and experiencing something more powerful and pure.

One of the most heartbreaking midrashim tells us that one Saturday afternoon, both of Bruriah's children suddenly died. They were grown men by then, and the story has little to add about why both suddenly succumbed, but it does give us a very detailed account of what Bruriah did next. Carefully, she covered her dead children with a sheet. Later that evening, Rabbi Meir returned home from the house of study, and as soon as he walked in the door, he asked to see his sons. Where, he asked Bruriah, are they? Calmly, Bruriah replied that they had left and gone to the house of study. Strange, said Meir, I was just there and didn't see them. Quickly, Bruriah handed her husband a cup of wine so that he would recite the havdalah prayer, which marks the end of Shabbat. Eager to spend time with his sons, Meir again asked after them, and Bruriah again assured him that they were on their way. She served Rabbi Meir his dinner, and as he was eating, she began to speak.

"Rabbi," she said, taking the unusual step of referring to him by his honorific, "I have one question to ask you."

"Go ahead and ask," Meir replied.

"Rabbi," Bruriah continued, "earlier today, a man came and gave me something as a deposit, and now he has returned and he wants his property back. Shall we give it back to him or not?"

"My daughter!" said Rabbi Meir, shocked by the question into using this term of endearment, "do you really believe that someone given something as a deposit isn't obliged to return it to its rightful owner?"

"Rabbi," Bruriah said, "if you hadn't told me so, I wouldn't have."

And with that, she took him upstairs, motioned for him to approach the bed, and then removed the sheet, revealing the two dead men. Seeing his sons lying there, lifeless, Meir began to weep bitterly. "My sons! My sons!" he wailed, but Bruriah refused to let him sink into despair.

"Rabbi," she said softly, "is this not what I told you—do I not need to return the deposit to its owner?" The book of Job, she continued, is very clear on who is the real proprietor of all human life: "The Lord has given," it states, "and the Lord has taken; may the name of the Lord be blessed."[29] The children were merely a deposit God gave to their parents to have and to hold, she said, and now He has claimed them back. This argument, a well-known one among rabbis at the time, comforted Meir, and his mind, the story ends by telling us, became composed.[30]

It's easy for us moderns to read this story and feel little but a shiver. Bruriah's composure is eerie, almost inhuman. We expect a bereaved mother to grieve, to show emotion, to weep and rage and shout. But Bruriah knows two very big things about life, and these twin insights guide her behavior. First, she knows that no matter how hard you try, some things in the physical world can't be changed. Life is unfathomable. Bad things happen. Often, we are powerless to change them. People make rules, many of them unfair. We are powerless to change most of them, too. Prejudices persist. Perfection is out of the question. The realm in which we live and work and love is this wretched earth, so holy—and whole—precisely because it is so very broken. And second, she knows that—to quote a much later rabbinic eminence, Leonard Cohen—"love's the only engine of survival."[31]

Instead of trying for power and glory and vindication, Bruriah realizes that the society she lives in—or, for that matter, *any* society that *anyone* lives in, then and now and forever—is thick with indignities and injustices. She fights—hard, well—for a place of her own, choosing to excel in the existing hierarchy rather than trying to bring it down and risk losing a host of traditions she cherishes and knows are vital. Yet she realizes that the greatest role she can play—the greatest role any living person can play— isn't as a sage or a celebrated eminence or a very respected person but as a loving spouse, child, or sibling. As her sons lie there, dead, she puts aside the surging emotions she must have felt and instead thinks about how to break the news to her husband, who she knows is both a great man and a man not easily given to understanding the vicissitudes of human life. She could sacrifice for the sake of her love just as easily as she could scold for the sake of her dignity; be just one or just the other, she knows, and you fall short of this harrowing and beautiful human journey, one that, by design, requires the company of others.

The Talmud, then, gives us so much of Bruriah and Meir because Bruriah and Meir are a paradigm for how to do marriage right: assemble two strong people, each only too happy to fight for their place in the world; bind them around a set of values they deeply share; and then abandon all pretense and expectation and do whatever works, even if it is hard or requires self-abnegation. If the wife is the one who is more logical, more rational, more practical, let her lead. If the husband is the one who is more emotional, more mystical, more unmoored, let him follow when necessary. Instead of turning marriage into a jousting match, a tally of grievances and slights, approach each other in a way you know is sure to appeal, like Bruriah addressing her husband by reciting Torah verses because she understands little else will resonate. Outside the home, fight for your rights. Inside the home, give your all to the ones you love and who love you back, and watch your love change minds and open hearts.

It's a lesson so tender and so beautiful and so inspiring, you'd expect it to become a popular paragon of Talmudic lore, the sort of maxim you see crocheted on pillows. But Bruriah was the victim of a harsh afterlife. At some point, the Talmud tells us, Rabbi Meir had to flee to Babylonia. Why? Either because he displeased the Romans, the Talmud opines, or because of the Bruriah Episode.

What was the Bruriah Episode?

It's a question that has sent rabbis into fits of obsession for millennia. The first and, sadly, most prominent answer came hundreds of years after the Talmud was redacted, in a commentary by the medieval French scholar Rabbi Shlomo Yitzchaki (1040–1105), better known as Rashi, far and away the most famous—and definitive—author of commentary on the Bible and Talmud. Rashi's commentaries are printed side by side with the text in the Talmud and are studied as closely and as diligently as the source material on which they expound. And here's what Rashi had to say when trying to understand what the Talmud meant by the Bruriah Episode: One time, Rashi explained, Bruriah mocked the rabbis for arguing that women's minds are easily swayed. Rabbi Meir was unamused by what he perceived to be his wife's disrespect, and he promised her she'd come to regret her words. Then he went to one of his students and ordered the young man to "seduce her into sin." The student worked hard at it, until, finally,

Bruriah succumbed to his charms. "And when she discovered the truth," Rashi concludes, "she strangled herself, and R. Meir fled due to shame."[32]

The story is astonishing. First, it requires us to believe that Bruriah and Meir, who we'd seen interacting warmly and lovingly on numerous occasions, had suddenly transformed into two completely different people, engaged in a battle of wills, vindictive and disdainful and uncaring. Next, it suggests that Meir, the person who was only too happy to have a stranger spit in his eye just so that she could have peace with her husband, would wage war against his own wife—or that he, a deeply pious man, would subject his wife to a grievous sin, and sin himself, just to prove a point. And finally, it urges us to ignore the fact that such a seminal occurrence, for some reason, was never mentioned by the Talmud itself and only appeared, mysteriously and unaccountably, nearly a thousand years after Bruriah and Meir's deaths. Why, then, had Rashi delivered this harsh and shocking verdict?

For a very long time, rabbinic Judaism's finest minds troubled themselves with this question. None believed that Rashi simply made it up, as he was known for being extremely meticulous and made regular notes about his sourcing, freely admitting if something could not be confirmed from additional, external sources. Some rabbis attempted to smooth the story's jagged edges, opining that the student Rabbi Meir had dispatched to tempt Bruriah was a eunuch, so there was never any risk that the two might consummate their relationship. Others read it as metaphor, yet another reminder of how powerful the evil urge is and how careful we ought to be lest we allow our desires to get the best of us. Still others noted its similarity to folktales prevalent at the time and suggested that Rashi might have confused one of these yarns for Talmudic reality, an unlikely occurrence.

In 2015, a young American-born Israeli rabbi named Eitam Henkin set out to solve the mystery. With a detective's keen eye, he looked at the first ancient manuscripts to include Rashi's note and came up with a simple but startling theory: Rashi, he proposed, never wrote the controversial opinion in question. Back in medieval times, he explained, parchment was precious, and so scribes who copied text often made their notes in the margins of existing works and, if space was limited, even in between the lines. Some later scribe, Henkin theorized, must have heard the folktale about the woman who mocked the rabbis and the husband who decided to test her, and wrote it in a footnote next to Bruriah's name, as the Talmud featured no other husband-wife team so prominently. And later scribes, Henkin concluded, must have seen that note, mistook it for Rashi's own work, and copied it into future iterations, making the story canonical.

Before being brutally murdered by Palestinian terrorists—he and his wife were driving home with their four small children when gunmen opened fire and killed both parents—Henkin offered a solution of his own, one that has since grown in stature. What was "the Bruriah Episode"? Simple, Henkin said; it's all right there in the Talmud.

After seeing her sister sold off into prostitution, the Talmud tells us, Bruriah was despondent. Recognizing her own limitations, she knew she couldn't simply walk into the brothel and rescue her sibling. And so, she asked her husband to intervene. Which, of course, was a lot to ask of a man like Rabbi Meir, as it required the esteemed sage to go into an unholy place and risk significant damage to his reputation should he be seen. In his usual fashion, however, Meir decided that the matter was truly not up to him but up to God. If the sister hadn't transgressed— that is, if she had refused to have sex with any man who offered her money—God would save her, and if she had transgressed, no miracle would occur. Armed with this sense of certainty, Meir dressed up like a Roman soldier, took a big purse full of coins, and made his way to the brothel.

Immediately upon entry, he found Bruriah's sister, offered her the cash, and demanded sex. The sister refused, saying that she was menstruating and therefore could not have intercourse. "I will wait," Rabbi Meir said, eager to test the sister, and she, in turn, pleaded with him. "There are many women in the brothel," she said, "and there are many women here who are more beautiful than I." This pleased Meir mightily, as he realized that Bruriah's sister must have said the same thing to any man who sought her company and had therefore remained chaste.

It was time, then, to save the sister. But how? Meir took his purse of coins, walked over to the guard, and said, "Give her to me." No can do, said the guard; if I let her go, the government might punish me. Meir shoved the purse in the guard's hand and told him to keep half and pay half to the government as a bribe. The guard wasn't easily convinced. "But when the money is finished," he whimpered, "what shall I do?" No worries, said Rabbi Meir. I will teach you a secret, mystical code, a spell you can say and be sure that everything will be alright. The magic words, he thundered, are these: "God of Meir answer me!"

Nice story, said the guard, but how do I know it works? Observe, said Meir. He picked up a clod of dirt and walked right toward a pack of vicious, wild dogs roaming outside the brothel. He threw the dirt at the animals and immediately the dogs pounced. "God of Meir answer me!" Meir shouted, and immediately the dogs backed off and skulked away. Convinced, the guard gave Bruriah's sister to Meir. She was saved.

A while later, the Talmud concludes, the Romans found out about the guard's perfidy, arrested him, and walked him to the gallows, but when he, too, shouted "God of Meir answer me!" a miracle occurred, and the hanging failed, again and again and again. The man was set free. The Talmud then goes on to recount numerous other miracles related to Meir, including another close call with the authorities that drove him, once more, to enter a brothel. At this point, we get the cryptic line about Meir fleeing because of the Bruriah Episode.[33]

No need to overthink it, wrote Rabbi Henkin. Miraculous as the saving of Bruriah's sister might have been, it still involved the sensitive and celebrated Meir cavorting with prostitutes, entering a house of ill repute, and paying money to purchase a woman.

It's easy to imagine, Henkin continued, that a man like Meir, deeply uncomfortable with earthly life under the best of circumstances, would have felt deep shame at having had to do all of this. He did it, of course, because he loved his wife dearly and was only too happy to sacrifice on her behalf just as she had on his. But once the deed was done, he needed a change of scenery, a fresh start, a new community where the story of his sweep through the brothel wasn't known. "We are no longer forced to accept the story in Rashi as part of Bruriah's life history," Henkin concluded.[34] Instead of yet another fallen icon, another destitute Billie Holiday plucked in her prime, another too-proud femme fatale punished for rattling the foundations of society, we now have Bruriah and Meir back, two difficult people who softened their hearts when it mattered most to remind each other, and us, that we've no better cure than love.

CHAPTER FIVE

Everything in Order

or

How to Make Sense of the World

THE ARRIVAL of the nineteenth century found the north-western corner of New York State in a particularly feisty mood. For fifty years, starting in 1800, the block of land that lay between the Finger Lakes and Lake Erie shimmered with radical ideas about how best to organize the world. In no short order, the good people of Allegany, Niagra, and Oneida Counties and their environs gave us the Millerites, who were convinced that believing passionately enough in Jesus could lead to immortality; the Latter Day Saints, whose founder, Joseph Smith Jr., claimed to have been led by the angel Moroni to the golden plates that he found near Palmyra, which allowed him to translate the holy Book of Mormon; the Fox Sisters in Hydesville, who introduced the country to séances and birthed the Spiritualist movement that sought to break down the barriers between the living and the dead; the Oneida Society, which tried to eradicate all unhappiness by orchestrating mass-scale arranged marriages through a commit-tee and insisting that all children be raised communally; and the

Ebenezer Colonies, which aimed to restart life on this continent afresh and in glorious seclusion in the woods. Add to that a thick layer of the Shaker religion, and you understand why historians have come to call this corner "the burned-over district." Too many conflicting ideas about how human life ought to be ordered, too much passion, too many unfulfilled promises and fallow prophecies left this region and its residents exhausted.

But not, thankfully, all of them. On December 10, 1851, Joel and Eliza Dewey, sellers of boots and shoes and members of several breakaway churches that once hummed with passion, welcomed their second son. They named him Melville Louis Kossuth, after the Hungarian democratizer and freedom fighter, and they brought him up in an austere way they believed was essential to raising worthy children. "Praise to the face is an open disgrace" was Eliza's favorite saying, and Joel, who believed fewer words could always say much more, would occasionally drill his boy with his own pithy mantra, "Don't waste."[1] Above all, the boy was expected to grow up and become an accomplished person, which, in the Dewey household, paragon of burned-over idealism, meant discovering some new way to make sense of anything and everything. As soon as he had a little bit of money, young Melville bought himself a pair of cuff links with the letter R engraved on each; it was to remind him that he was born to be a great reformer, redacter, reorganizer of all things human and fallible.

But what to reform, and how? The answer came to Dewey slowly, almost mystically. He was born on the tenth day of the month. When he was thirteen, he walked exactly 10 miles to the bookseller in the nearby township of Watertown to buy an unabridged dictionary, his most prized possession. The number ten began to loom larger and larger in his mind. Soon Dewey trained himself to sleep exactly ten hours each day, and when he wrote letters, which was often, they seldom came in at more or fewer than ten pages. His obsession grew fiercer in high school, when he realized that his birthday marked the fifty-second anniversary of the French Assembly adopting the platinum meter bar as the nation's standard unit of measurement. They did so after a committee measured the shortest distance from the North Pole to the equator, passing through Paris, and determined 1 meter to be precisely one ten-millionth of this globe-spanning distance. A system that divided everything by ten struck young Dewey as almost poetically beautiful, and for a while he toyed with the idea of introducing it to a continent lumbering with miles and inches. But he was still a rebel without a cause, pulsating with energy and entirely unsure about what to do next.

The answer revealed itself in a fiery fashion. On January 29, 1868, Dewey, then sixteen, was in class at his high school, the Hungerford Collegiate Institute, when a fire broke out. Most students ran out of the building as quickly as they could; Dewey kept running back in, grabbing as many books as he could and saving them from the flames. He inhaled so much smoke and developed such a bad cough that for a brief stretch, his doctor doubted that he'd make it. But Dewey was nothing if not resilient, and before too long, he recovered and decided that if his near-death experience taught him anything, it was simply that books were his life's calling. He enrolled in Amherst College and got a job at the library. Almost immediately, he alighted on the seminal question haunting librarians since at least the third century BCE, when Callimachus, a Greek poet working in Alexandria, was entrusted with cataloging its fabled library's tens of thousands of scrolls. How to arrange so much knowledge, making it easily accessible and useful?

Callimachus's answer was the Pinakes, the plural Greek word for "tablets." First, he divided all the library's collection into two categories—poetry and prose. Works of poetry were then divided into subcategories like drama or epic poetry and works of prose into subjects like philosophy or medicine. All entries were sorted alphabetically, and each author was identified by a brief biography and complete bibliography, which is why the Pinakes took up 120 volumes, a comprehensive if not always inviting index.

The problem of how to organize vast collections grew far

more dire when print made owning books much easier. Samuel Pepys, for example, valued size above all else, arranging his massive library strictly according to the height and width of each volume. Sir Robert Cotton, the seventeenth-century nobleman who owned the greatest private collection ever held by a single individual—it included the original codex-bound manuscript of *Beowulf*, the seventh- or eighth-century Lindisfarne Gospels, and a fifth-century Greek Bible—kept all the volumes in a bookshelf-lined room that was 26 feet long and 6 feet wide, with a bust of a different Roman emperor decorating each bookshelf. If you wanted to see how Grendel was doing, for example, you had to mosey over to the bust of Vitelius and look on shelf number 15, a system that must have made sense to its proprietor but which continues to baffle scholars today.

Cotton left his vast collection to the British Museum, which, in turn, had its own way of organizing books: according to color. "In the British Museum," observed the English book publisher Joseph Cundall in 1848, "books of Divinity are bound in blue, history in red, poetry in yellow, and Biography in olive colored leather. This is an excellent plan in a large library."[2] By the time Dewey was born, the system developed by the Frenchman Jacques Charles Brunet, a bookseller's son, was growing more popular. He divided all books into five major categories: theology, jurisprudence, sciences and arts, belles lettres, and history.

In most libraries, however, books were placed on shelves by their order of acquisition. This made each library a mystery knowable only to its custodians, leaving readers in the dark. That chemistry book you enjoyed while visiting a library in Boston would be on a very different shelf in Chicago, and this was the kind of chaos Melville Dewey couldn't bear. Gradually—first at Amherst, then in Boston, and finally as the head librarian of New York's Columbia University, where he founded the school of library economy—he developed a better way of arranging books on shelves, one that could help librarians and readers alike quickly and effortlessly find whatever they needed anywhere they went. To do so, he summoned the ultimate method of counting to ten: the decimal system.

By now, Dewey's invention is so deeply ingrained in the culture—it is used in nearly a quarter of a million libraries in virtually every country on the face of the planet—that it hardly seems to be anything to think about. But his ideas—that each subject will receive a three-number classification, that subcategories could be added by adding more corresponding numbers, and that each title would be shelved in precisely the same place in any library that applied the method—were radical and immensely attractive when first introduced. So attractive, in fact, that it took observers a while to realize that Dewey's way of organizing all printed knowledge was more than a little bit colored by his own raging biases.

A sexual predator—he was forced to resign from the American Library Association, an organization that he had founded, after groping several female colleagues on a 1906 ALA trip to Alaska, and in 1929 settled out of court for $2,147 after being sued by a woman he'd forcibly kissed and caressed—Dewey had originally assigned the books pertaining to women right next to the books pertaining to etiquette, which reveals more than a little about his state of mind. As an avid anti-Semite who had explicitly banned Jews from the club he'd founded in Lake Placid, he assigned the first ninety spots in the religion classification to Christianity—its history and ideas—leaving the last ten spots to "other religions" and assigning the very last two spots to Judaism and Islam. And being an open and committed racist, he tended to place books by Black authors, including works of poetry and literature, in category 325—International Migration and Colonization.

These decisions reveal a hard truth that Dewey, a man dedicated to erecting all-encompassing systems of arranging human interactions, would never admit: namely, any attempt to organize our lives is bound to be steeped in our ideological biases—sometimes hideous ones—emotional predilections, likes and dislikes. No system designed by mortals to make sense of human life could ever be free of the species' inclination to confuse personal attitudes with the absolute good. Nor should it: it's precisely our fondness for our own idiosyncrasies that may lead us, if we're mindful enough, to marvel at the radically different choices made by our peers. Particularism is not the antithesis of universalism, but its prerequisite.

Toward the end of his life, Dewey drifted further and further from even the mere pretense of impartiality. Now residing part-time down South, he couldn't stand the asymmetry of owning two homes in two different towns with two different names, and so convinced his neighbors in the Sunshine State to rename their hamlet Lake Placid, Florida. By the time he died of a stroke, in 1931, his reputation was just like that of his home district, a burned-over testament to what too much enthusiasm and too little restraint could do to anyone who believed they had what it took to sort out the world. The Dewey decimal system has been subject to numerous revisions, each one aspiring to tamper with or eradicate the founding father's bigotry. By 2019, the ALA removed Dewey's name from its most prestigious prize.

But the problem to which Dewey devoted his life, the problem of organizing knowledge, was never really resolved. In fact, it became much more prevalent as the available information grew from a trickle to a torrent. The advent of the Internet meant that each of us could now, just by glancing at a smart phone or laptop, summon an enormous volume of facts, figures, manuscripts, photographs, videos, audio recordings, documents, and maps that would have made Callimachus weep twice, first with delight and then with despair. By itself, all this information is less a fountain of knowledge and more a riptide, likely to suck you under, which is why so much of our economy is powered by corporations that offer new and increasingly intricate ways of helping us access the data we want. It's no coincidence that the chief of these information-peddling behemoths, Google, eventually changed its name to Alphabet, a final admission that it was no longer in the search engine business but rather in the business of restructuring all forms of human literacy, teaching us how to read the world anew, from scratch. And, like Dewey, Alphabet, too, insists that its products are systematic and scientific rather than bundles of biases and commercial interests.

Where, then, does that leave the rest of us? In a bind, because, whether we like it or not, we are all now in the sorting business as well. Most of us can no longer do our jobs without mastering at least a handful of systems, platforms, and applications designed to help us take, keep, find, and share information. No sooner do we return home than we're lured in by books that promise to teach us how to cull our belongings or television programs that show us how to more neatly arrange our homes. These days, we are all amateur taxonomists, irrepressible rearrangers forever worrying if everything, or anything, is truly in its right place. Which would have made Rabbi Yehuda HaNasi, had he dropped by for a visit approximately eighteen hundred years after his death, feel right at home.

"From the days of Moses and until the days of Rabbi Yehuda HaNasi," the Talmud tells us with brio, "we do not find unparalleled greatness in Torah knowledge and unparalleled greatness in secular matters, including wealth and high political office, combined in one place, i.e., in a single individual."[3] Hillel was wise and compassionate, teaching his followers how to adjudicate justly and kindly. Akiva was fiercely brilliant, inventing a whole new way of understanding the ancient tradition and applying it to everyday life. But it fell to Rabbi Yehuda HaNasi to make sure that the teachings that the Jews believed had been passed down from God to Moses remained both approachable and unchanged. How to organize so much information in a way that not only made sense but also, egad, inspired? For taking on this task and giving us the Mishnah, the cornerstone of the Talmud, Rabbi Yehuda HaNasi was honored by being referred to simply as Rebbi, or teacher, without further description or distinction, suggesting he stood elevated and alone.

Did he really have a choice? His father, Shimon ben Gamliel

II, was the Nasi, communal leader, as was his grandfather, the fearsome Gamliel II, who was a descendant of Hillel and, before that, of King David himself. According to the Talmud, Rebbi was born at the exact moment that Rabbi Akiva was martyred, which "teaches you that a righteous person does not leave the world before an equally righteous person is created."[4] From the very moment he emerged into the world, then, Rebbi was expected to grow up and become another in a long line of major Jewish leaders. Early in his life, this struck him as totally unfair.

One day, the Talmud tells us, when Rebbi was still a boy, he and a friend fancied some delicious figs. Both of them being the sons of prominent rabbis, they had studied their halacha inside and out, and the halacha, they knew, was very clear on the subject of figs: as long as you were laboring in the field and picking the fruit, you could eat your fill, but once the figs were put into storage, you had to set aside a portion of the fruit for the priests and the poor. This raised the question of what constituted a proper storage place; the yard, the rabbis agreed, qualified, but because people rarely stored fruit on the roof, any produce that found its way there was exempt from tithing. Rebbi and his friend, then, grabbed a few basketfuls from the yard and were making their way up the stairs so that they could eat on the roof without paying their dues. An older rabbi spotted them and showered them with invective for this bit of trickery. Akiva, he told them, was always careful to eat fruit and vegetables only after he was certain the poor had gotten their share. "Look," he cried out, "what the difference is between you and the earlier generations."[5]

But Rebbi didn't remain a boisterous boy for long. Soon, he was sent to the house of study, and there he met his great frenemy, his polar opposite, his catalyst, the man who drove him to become the eminence everyone had always told him he was destined to be: Rabbi Elazar ben Shimon.

Whereas Rebbi's childhood was sheltered and privileged, Elazar's was the stuff of legend. His father was Rabbi Shimon bar Yochai, or Rashbi, one of Akiva's best students and the person who many believe wrote *The Zohar*, the seminal work of Jewish mysticism, the Kabbalah. Like Akiva, Rashbi, too, was wanted by the Romans, and so left his home and hid in the house of study. Elazar, still a boy, decided to join him, unable to bear the thought of being apart from his beloved father. For a brief while, the two passed their days studying Torah and talking, but soon Rashbi grew worried. His wife, Elazar's mother, came by every day to bring them bread and water; if the Romans captured her and tortured her, Rashbi argued, she might break and give them up. It was time to move to a more secure location.

The hideout Rashbi chose was a small cave near Peki'in, in the Galilee. If his son worried at all about finding food or drink, he didn't have to worry for very long: as soon as Rashbi and Elazar entered their new abode, the Talmud tells us, "a miracle occurred and a carob tree was created for them as well as a spring of water." Because they hadn't a change of clothes, father and son would undress, cover themselves in sand up to their necks, and study Torah, dressing again only to pray. Their practice, the Talmud continues, went on for twelve years, until the Roman emperor died and his decrees were annulled. The Prophet Elijah himself stopped by to break the news to the monastic pair of fugitives.

Emerging from their cave, father and son saw people plowing and sowing in the field. The sight enraged them. Here we are, they said to each other, abandoning all worldly concerns for more than a decade and dedicating ourselves to the Torah, while these people selfishly care only about their own sustenance! So great was their fury, the Talmud reports, that "every place that Rabbi Shimon and his son Rabbi Elazar directed their eyes was immediately burned." Immediately, a divine voice spoke up. "Did you emerge from the cave in order to destroy My world?" it said angrily. "Return to your cave." And return they did, spending twelve more months in study and contemplation. When they emerged again, they were changed men. Or, at least, one of them was: "Everywhere that Rabbi Elazar would strike," the Talmud tells us, "Rabbi Shimon would heal." The father had grown reconciled to the idea that people couldn't just expect trees and fountains to appear; they needed to work in order to live. The son, however, was still enamored of his glorious, sacred seclusion; he might have left the cave, but the cave had not left him. "My son," Rashbi tried to comfort the young Elazar, "you and I suffice for the entire world," because we study Torah so intensely it more than makes up for everyone else's spiritual faults.

The story has a touching ending. "As the sun was setting on Shabbat eve," the Talmud recounts, Rashbi and Elazar came across an elderly man holding two bundles of myrtle branches. Why two? they asked. Simple, said the old man: the Bible tells us that we should both "remember the Shabbat day, to keep it holy"[6] and "observe the Shabbat day, to keep it holy,"[7] and each of these commandments deserves to be celebrated with its own lovely and fragrant decorative branch. This touched both men deeply. "Their minds," the Talmud concludes, "were put at ease" as they realized that while not all Jews were as learned and as intense and as devoted as they were, all loved God and His commandments in their own way.[8]

Imagine, then, being the brightest in your class, the son of the Nasi, and being told that the new kid in school is the fabled young zealot who'd spent his entire childhood eating miracle carobs and literally doing nothing but studying Torah. At first, the Talmud tells us, Rebbi and Elazar were friends, drawn to each other's erudition. When one floated an opinion, the other rushed to dig up a verse that supported it, and when one found himself questioned by the older rabbis, the other hurried to his defense. But the study hall wasn't big enough to contain two such enormous talents, especially as one, Elazar, was still very much the incandescent absolutist who strove to elevate earth and bring it nearer to the heavens while the other, Rebbi, was still very much the pragmatist interested in practical solutions to small but meaningful problems. It was bound to end poorly. And one day it did.

As was customary in the study hall, the more senior teachers sat on benches in the front of the room while their students sat on the floor. One day, the Talmud tells us, the study hall was abuzz. It made no sense, groused the students, that Rebbi and Elazar still had to sit on the floor, as they are incredibly brilliant and teach their peers as much as the older rabbis do. Fetch them two benches of their own, went the demand, and the elders, being very fond of their dynamic duo, readily assented.

But the sight of his son stretching his legs up front bothered Shimon ben Gamliel II, Rebbi's father. Why? Perhaps it was because he was, like many rabbis of his time, keenly aware of the "evil eye" and was worried that elevating the boy too quickly was asking for some surge of bad luck to befall him. Or perhaps, closer to home, he didn't want anyone tsk-tsking that Rebbi was enjoying his elevated and comfortable new digs because he was the boss's son. Quickly, Shimon ben Gamliel II said to the study hall's teachers, take away Rebbi's bench; he is perfectly fine sitting on the floor.

The teachers now had a conundrum. One of them, Rabbi Yehoshua ben Korha, raised an objection: Rebbi and Elazar, he said, are both brilliant, but one of them has a father who cares deeply about his well-being. So shall we punish the other, Elazar, just because he's less fortunate? If we're going to demote Rebbi back to the floor—which, all agreed, was a good and pious and humble thing—let's do the same to Elazar as well.

And so, both boys were sent back to the floor, but whereas Rebbi's father told him precisely why he'd made this request, no one bothered explaining the situation to poor Elazar. Naturally, he grew angry. "You are equating Rabbi Yehuda HaNasi to me," he said, "by demoting us together. In fact, I am much greater than he is." Gone was the cheerful young man who had found his first friend after a lifetime of solitude in a cave; instead, Elazar was once again the emblem of fierceness, burning down—this time figuratively rather than literally—anyone he deemed less competent with his fiery gaze. Now, any time that Rebbi began to speak, Elazar interrupted. I know exactly what you're going to say, he quipped haughtily, so before you waste your breath, let me tell you why you're wrong. Dejected, Rebbi went to his father to complain, but the old man had little soothing to say. "My son," he replied bluntly, "do not let his actions offend you, as he is a lion, son of a lion, and you are a lion, son of a fox." In other words, admit defeat—Elazar and his father both are the superior scholars of Torah.[9] Giving us a savage coda to the story, the Talmud skips to the future, to the moment right after Elazar's death. Rebbi, we're told, goes to his former friend's widow to ask her hand in marriage. She dismisses him with a sneer. "A vessel which was used in holiness," she asks him tauntingly, "should be used in a profane way?"[10] Why would I lower my standards and go from the holy and wise Elazar to an ordinary man like you, however wealthy and elevated?

The Talmud isn't the place to go for intricate accounts of feelings and states of mind, but it doesn't take too much insight or even empathy to guess what Rebbi must have felt. Mad, hurt, and heartbroken, any person in his position would have likely opted for one of two courses of action: either double down on being celebrated as a great scholar, which would mean going head to head with any and all challengers in the house of study, or take the opposite path and focus on raw political power, tormenting those scholars who rebuked him by virtue of his now being the Nasi. Either of these choices would have been perfectly understandable and entirely normal. Rebbi chose neither, or, more accurately, he chose to struggle with both.

Instinctively, he picked up and moved, settling down in the town of Beit She'arim, close enough to the great study halls of his day but sufficiently far away as to send a clear and distinct message that the Nasi wasn't really a part of the scholarly crew. Being a close friend of the Roman emperor, Antoninus Pius, Rebbi enjoyed unprecedented privileges, including the right to grow *afarsimon*, a plant known for its precious oil and which some scholars have theorized may simply be the fruit we now know as persimmon. This made him an extraordinarily wealthy man, and he was savvy enough to realize that money, like knowledge, only meant something if it allowed its possessor to benefit from advantages otherwise unavailable. One time, the Talmud tells us, Rebbi hosted an opulent dinner, and in walked the son of a very wealthy man named Bonyas. Immediately, Rebbi declared that the Bonyas boy should be given a prime seat at the table, as he hailed from a wealthy family. A few minutes went by, and another well-off lad joined the feast; looking at him, Rebbi assigned him an even better spot. Discreetly, Rebbi's aides whispered to him that Bonyas was much wealthier than the newcomer's dad and that, if anything, Bonyas's boy deserved primacy of seating. "When you reach his father," Rebbi replied coldly, "tell him: Do not send him to me in these garments. Dress him in accordance with his wealth and status, so that he will be honored accordingly." The Talmud goes on to tell us, as if further explanation was necessary, that Rebbi really honored the wealthy.[11]

If the story rubs you the wrong way, if it makes you see Rebbi as nothing more than the well-heeled son of a patrician family who lorded his privilege over his peers, you're not alone. Some of Rebbi's peers were incensed by his attitude as well. When he threw a lavish wedding for his son, one of his pals by the name of Bar Kapara was shocked to find himself uninvited—the guests were all carefully selected from among the community's richest families. Shortly before the wedding, the Talmud tells us, Rebbi's house was vandalized with what may very well be the first graffiti in recorded Jewish history: 24,000 dinars were spent on this wedding, said the scribble, and yet Bar Kapara wasn't invited.[12]

A man of Rebbi's stature could have easily arranged for Bar Kapara, the likely culprit of the prank, to be arrested, possibly even punished severely, especially as his pal Antoninus gave Rebbi, and him alone among all of Rome's subjects, the power to condemn the people under his jurisdiction to death. Or, less dramatically, he could have simply surrounded himself with sycophants, a popular option then as now. Rebbi did neither. Immediately, he apologized to Bar Kapara, invited him, and said nothing even as his guest tormented him throughout the feast by making him do embarrassing things, like interpreting all of the Torah passages pertaining to the lewdest sex acts.

Why would a man so keenly attuned to matters of wealth, class, and status suffer such disrespect? Because the Nasi, Rebbi knew, wasn't just another powerful man. He was the leader of the community, which meant that he was beholden to all of its members, even those who were churlish or outright rebellious. He had to suffer Bar Kapara for the same reason he had to insist on giving the wealthiest their due: because he was the embodiment of the social order and because he knew that upending that order exerted a great price. If you were a community's leader—and the Nasi was a potent combination of spiritual paragon, legal adjudicator, and executive authority—you had no choice but to uphold social norms and beliefs, even those that struck you as somewhat odious. And you had no choice, either, but to allow anyone who needed to blow off some steam the chance to do so. Like Moses, Rebbi had to suffer his stiff-necked people, spending his days sitting in judgment while everyone around him judged him right back.

To make sure he was at least given the benefit of the doubt by his grumbling subjects, he balanced his deference to the rich by practicing radical humility. Despite his own great wealth, he made a point of not indulging in any luxuries and lived an austere, almost ascetic, life. Again and again and again in the Talmud, we also see this celebrated eminence readily admitting that he doesn't know the answer to a certain question or humbling himself before those he realized were wise and worthy of respect. When Pinchas ben Yair stopped by one day, for example, Rebbi went out of his way to invite the sage for dinner. Pinchas, he knew, rarely dined with fellow rabbis, and his piety and learnedness were legendary. So when this holy man told Rebbi he'd love to stay and dine, Rebbi was delighted. And yet, when the hour came for the feast, Pinchas announced he would not be coming after all, for as he was walking by Rebbi's house, he noticed that the Nasi had a few white mules, and white mules meant trouble.

Did Pinchas mean, as the Talmud then suggests, that he believed the mules were wild and was afraid of a kick or a bite? Or did he simply grow queasy by Rebbi's ostentatious wealth, a herd of handsome beasts in the yard being the Talmudic equivalent of a few Bentleys parked out front? Hard to tell, but Rebbi didn't care. I'll sell them, he said to Pinchas; just come for dinner. If you sell them, Pinchas replied, you'll only be passing on the same problem to some other schlub, which is a very unkind thing to do. Alright then, said Rebbi; I'll declare them ownerless. Even worse, said Pinchas, because without anyone to care for them, the animals will suffer needlessly. Fine, said Rebbi, growing desperate, I'll kill them all. Worst one yet, replied Pinchas; you can't just destroy a thing of value, and an animal is just that. Finally, the Talmud reports, Rebbi felt as if "a mountain rose between" him and Pinchas, and he started crying. "If during their lifetimes it is so that the righteous are great," he wept, "after their death it is all the more so true."[13] Even as he was being rebuked, Rebbi could still recognize—and admire—Pinchas's pure heart, and he envied him his freedom to focus on his spiritual practice without worrying about any worldly drudgeries.

These drudgeries were Rebbi's full-time job, and he took them so seriously that, often, he found himself at odds with the sages he admired. Grappling with widespread poverty, he balked at the rabbinic ordinance that prohibited Jews from buying bread baked by gentiles, an opinion that scandalized the more stringently observant of his peers. To improve morale, he argued that Tisha B'av, the day commemorating the destruction of the Temple, should no longer be observed: Jews living in the Land of Israel and enjoying a reasonable measure of independence, he argued, had no business dwelling on past catastrophes. Whenever he could, he cut down taxes. Wherever possible, he found some creative way to make life a little bit easier.

That left him with as many bitter detractors as reverent fans. Many believed he was, quite literally, the Messiah, soon to usher in the beginning of the end of time. Others saw his kindness as an invitation to play dirty politics, and increasingly his days were spent minding the thicket of competing aides in his orbit, each jockeying for position. In his despair, Rebbi wrote a prayer, which so resonated with its listeners that observant Jews still recite it every morning. "May it be your will," it reads, "my God and the God of my fathers, to save me today and every day from arrogant men and from arrogance; from an evil man, from an evil companion, from an evil neighbor; from an evil mishap and from the destructive Satan; from a difficult judgment and a difficult opponent, whether he is a fellow Jew or not a fellow Jew."[14] It's the prayer of a man who has no one to trust.

All this rancor could make a man sick, which was soon the case with Rebbi. He developed a terrible and incurable toothache and shortly thereafter a debilitating intestinal illness. The Talmud tells us that Rebbi had so many livestock that the man running his stables was wealthier than the king of Persia and each day, that stableman would take care to feed the animals at precisely the moment that Rebbi went to the bathroom, so that the sounds of the herd eating drowned out Rebbi's anguished screams. It didn't work. Rebbi, the Talmud states, was in so much pain and screamed so loudly that his anguished cries "overcame the sound of the livestock, and even sailors heard it out at sea."[15] Even more tragically, the more Rebbi suffered, the more his fans cherished him, believing that his pain was payment for the sins of the community and that the righteous Rebbi was atoning for all Jews. Years after Rebbi's death, the Talmud recorded sages saying that as long as he persisted in his suffering, "no pregnant woman had a miscarriage in the Land of Israel."[16]

But one man taking it all on himself, Rebbi knew, wasn't a long-term solution. Even if he'd been the wisest, the sharpest, the most learned—and he was soulful enough to know he wasn't—he couldn't carry the tradition on his back and expect to pass it down to future generations in working condition. People who have been in positions of power—bosses, teachers, parents—believe themselves to be at least a little bit irreplaceable, which is a natural reflex that makes carrying the immense burden of responsibility easier. But we are all replaceable, which is life's greatest joy, not its grimmest tragedy. It's what makes life go on. But for life to go on according to some sort of plan, for it to make sense to future generations in more or less the same ways it made sense to their grandparents and great-grandparents before them, you needed to grapple with the same problem that so vexed Melville Dewey. You needed to come up with a system of ordering the world.

From the very start, Rebbi was clear on what to do—take the Oral Torah and write it down. Scholars still argue whether "write it down" meant committing it to parchment or merely structuring it as the books we know now and continuing to transmit them orally for a few more generations. The bigger question was how: how to arrange such a massive amount of information, how to make it accessible, how to make it into something other than another Pinakes, reams upon reams of data too impossible to plumb and thus foreboding for anyone to apply.

Much has been written about the redaction of the Mishnah, the seminal project for which Rebbi is best known, yet for all of its fame, this foundational work of Jewish thought is still too often read as a dense codex of commandments rather than as a nearly unparalleled exercise in empathy. Consider, then, the many and excellent questions Rebbi asked himself while compiling the Mishnah.

The first, and most radical, is this: What do we know and how do we know it? For centuries before Rebbi was born, if not longer, the Jews had an easy answer: they knew the laws they believed to be divine, and they knew them because they were passed down from one generation to the next. But not all Jews, Rebbi knew better than most, were learned, and even the learned ones were struggling to consolidate the various teachings they'd heard from disparate teachers. If you wanted to streamline this knowledge, then, you could appoint one ultimate arbiter, the path eventually chosen by the Catholic Church by instituting a system of popes. But that didn't guarantee you much, as a Supreme Decider could well decide to overrule his predecessor's rulings or, worse, to uphold them blindly, which would eventually create a rigid system with little room for reform or innovation. Writing all of these ideas down in a book seemed like a better idea, and a more Jewish one, considering the absolute centrality of the five books constituting the Torah to Jewish life and thought.

But confining knowledge to a book was a dangerous proposition. Because Rebbi spoke Greek at home—almost alone among the sages of his day—and was both well educated and in constant dialogue with non-Jews, it's likely that he was familiar with Plato. In the *Phaedrus*, the Greek giant has his teacher, Socrates, launch an assault against the very notion of writing anything down. "I cannot help feeling," Socrates tells his unfortunate conversation partner,

> that writing is unfortunately like painting; for the creations of the painter have the attitude of life, and yet if you ask them a question they preserve a solemn silence. And the same may be said of speeches. You would imagine that they had intelligence, but if you want to know anything and put a question to one of them, the speaker always gives one unvarying answer. And when they have been once written down they are tumbled about anywhere among those who may or may not understand them, and know not to whom they should reply, to whom not: and, if they are maltreated or abused, they have no parent to protect them; and they cannot protect or defend themselves.[17]

It's not hard to imagine Rebbi advancing a similar argument. At the study hall, anyone who made an assumption or assertion had to defend it against wave after wave of inquiry. If you were misunderstood, you had ample chances to explain yourself. If you were wrong, you eventually had to admit it. But take this same vibrant conversation and replace it with a series of written statements, and you lose the very lifeblood of the rabbinic way of making sense of the world. This, naturally, was unacceptable to Rebbi. He had to find a better way to translate the sweaty, shouty, passionate, often jagged, always lively energy of the study hall into prose.

The first instinct of anyone seeking to preserve a religious tradition would have probably been to keep it simple: Write down the laws and commandments, the thou shalts and the thou shalt nots, as clearly as you can, so that anyone wondering when, exactly, is the correct time to say the prayers, or what to do in the case of divorce, or precisely how much of one's harvest ought to be tithed could simply look it up. But do that, and you risk running into two major hurdles, both of them fundamental to the way humans live in the world. The first is that people, generally, have too much confidence. The second is that they haven't nearly enough.

If what he produced was merely a book of laws, Rebbi knew, it was likely that someone, somewhere soon would thumb through it and then declare that it was all nice and well but that little of it still applied. Being a reformer who often pushed to change or amend tradition—even arguing that entire days of observance should be scrapped now that historical circumstances have changed—he realized that the first thing that would happen if you gave people, and especially people who'd spent the last few centuries in study halls arguing about every letter, a written document is that many of them would giddily find creative ways to dismiss, amend, or altogether ignore vast chunks of it at will. Plato was right; books had no parent there to protect them, and no sooner did they argue that prayer time was such and such many minutes past sunrise, say, than anyone with a bit of knowledge could come along and espouse other ideas.

This is particularly true given the second observation: As the Nasi, Rebbi spent his days sitting in judgment and knew intimately the ways people presented their problems and circumstances. Coming before a court, they unfurled their cases in great detail, and these details mattered. So while people may be boisterous in approaching a book of rules and arguing that they shouldn't be compelled to observe all of its laws in the precise way prescribed, they are likely to also be hesitant to seek concrete answers that applied to their specific problem. And, as Melville Dewey could have told you, it's exceedingly difficult to create a taxonomy of everything, a system both clear and flexible enough to contain every category and subcategory for every circumstance that ever appeared or might suggest itself in the future. Fine, your rule book says prayer is a few minutes past sunrise, but what if I slept in? What if I'm on the road and unable to stop and pray? What if I'm on the road and able to make a quick stop but happen to be driving through an area known for not being safe, and I'm afraid of getting mugged? And by "pray," do you mean out loud, or can I just recite it silently in my heart, because God can read our minds anyway? And does it matter which language I choose? Or if I've had breakfast before praying?

This litany of questions is how we humans—maddeningly solipsistic, annoyingly specific, wonderfully inquisitive—see the world. We alight on a grand category, a big question, and then immediately drill it down for more detail. Books and larger systems of producing meaning frustrate us because they can't answer our questions fast enough. This is as true, if not more so, for the minute things in our lives as it is for the momentous ones; left without recourse, without answers to the very particular problems that haunt us, we'd sooner dismiss any system of knowledge, no matter how wise, as not being the right fit.

And so, Rebbi realized a solution: Instead of writing down the answers, focus on the questions.

The rabbis, he knew from experience, quibbled over everything. Their method of understanding the divine laws was taking each one and examining it from every given angle. That often meant engaging in elaborate games of what-if, which imagined every conceivable circumstance a person might encounter, reasonable as well as remote. They then imagined how the laws might apply to each one. Rebbi came up with the idea of writing down all these quibbles. Open a page of Mishnah today, nearly two thousand years after it was redacted, and it's likely that you won't receive much clarity on anything. What you would get is a faithful record of discussions—often, if not always, very, very animated discussions—between the great rabbis of various eras. Because Rebbi took care that the Mishnah be written in exceedingly clear and sparkly language, anyone can follow along. And because little attention is paid to pestering things like chronology, anyone can feel like they're entering right into the study hall, mid-argument, and are expected to have an opinion on whatever it is that's being discussed. In turn, everyone is expected to roll up their sleeves and follow the logic of the conversation, sweat the small stuff, learn the corresponding verses, and come up with exceptions or objections. No one studying the Mishnah may remain passive, and no one studying the Mishnah is ever alone.

This literary creation would have been enough to win Rebbi his place in the pantheon, but he was just getting started. Bigger problems lay ahead, none more challenging than the one that had bedeviled organizers from Callimachus onward, the problem of order. How to arrange all of God's commandments, which, naturally, extended to almost every realm of human existence, into a book or set of books? How to organize centuries of rabbinic disputations in an approachable and inspiring way? What goes first, what follows, and why? Rebbi's answer was almost shockingly modern. Human life, he theorized, began with a seed, like all natural things. And, at least if lived according to the teaching of the Torah, it aspired to something much loftier, to godliness, to honoring the divine in whose image it was created. As the thirteenth-century commentator Nachmanides argued in his commentary on the Bible, God speaks in the very first chapter of the book of Genesis, saying "Let us make man in our image, after our likeness,"[18] using the plural form to indicate that man was always designed as a dualistic creation, one part earth and one part heavenly soul. In this idea, Rebbi, long before Hegel, saw a dialectic; if, as the Bible informs us, God "formed man of the dust of the ground, and breathed into his nostrils the breath of life,"[19] then there was necessarily tension between these two poles, the dusty and the divine. And to resolve this tension, we needed a synthesis, which was human society. People, Rebbi believed, looked for affinities in and affiliations with each other so that they might collectively elevate themselves above the primordial dirt from which they came and erect communal constructs that took them a few steps closer to sanctity.

With this idea in mind, Rebbi was ready to start organizing. The Mishnah, he decreed, would have six parts, called—could it be any different?—*sedarim*, or orders. The first two, *Zera'im* (Seeds) and *Mo'ed* (Festivals), will pertain to all matters agricultural, natural, time- and earth-bound. The middle two, *Nashim* (Women) and *Nezikin* (Torts), will address all social constructs, from marriage contracts to lawsuits. And the last two, *Kodashim* (Sacred Things) and *Tohorot* (Purity), will deal with the intricate matters of how to properly worship God.

You don't have to be the greatest Torah scholar of all time to see the clear and lucid patterns at play here, but the man who most deserves the title—Rabbi Moses ben Maimon, better known as the Rambam, or Maimonides—celebrated Rebbi's choices in his own introduction to the Mishnah. "Without food, a person cannot worship God," Maimonides stated plainly, which is why we begin with seeds, the source of all sustenance. And as Jewish festivals are, to a large extent, tethered to the natural agricultural cycle—Shavuot, for example, the holiday celebrating the giving of the Torah on Mount Sinai, coincided perfectly with the beginning of the wheat harvest in ancient Israel—it makes sense to simply follow their pattern.

Why, then, do the middle two orders of the Mishnah deal with women and torts? Just look at Exodus 21:7, Maimonides explained: "And if a man sell his daughter to be a maidservant, she shall not go out as the menservants do. If she please not her master, who hath betrothed her to himself, then shall he let her be redeemed: to sell her unto a strange nation he shall have no power, seeing he hath dealt deceitfully with her."[20] The concepts of servants and masters and of women sold into forced marriages are rightfully offensive to us. But Rebbi's decision to arrange these two orders as he did, Maimonides wrote, gives us an inspiring prescription for pursuing justice. Unlike rabbinic quibbles over the meaning of one verse or another, lawsuits and court cases don't deal in theoreticals and hypotheticals. They address the concrete distress of real people, and because the cornerstone of all social construct is the family, we ought to begin by looking at family dynamics first and only then at the justice system writ large. The Rambam chooses a telling verse: The maidservant in question, wronged by her deceitful master, isn't merely a sui generis person when she comes to plead her case in court; she's a poor soul who ended up in service because her father had sold her, and any system bent on delivering true justice should take a pause and remember her father's action initiating her plight before passing judgment. The reason for juxtaposing women and torts, then, is to bring the human individual into an often faceless bureaucratic system.

But if the soulful move, when dealing with the relationship between one person and another, is from the individual to the communal—beginning with the intimacy of the family home and ending up in the austere light of the courthouse—the move, when dealing with the relationship between the individual and God, is exactly the opposite. Consider sacred things, which largely meant the communal sacrifices undertaken by the priests in the ancient Temple. Only then are we at liberty to think about questions of purity, which involve highly personal and emotional situations like how to behave when we're near the body of a recently deceased family member.

Reading the Rambam's explication of Rebbi's arranging principles, you might feel intrigued but not moved. There's nothing innately sweeping about the work of taxonomy in general; no one enters a library and feels immediately becalmed by a sudden sense of order and well-being that comes merely from seeing that Charles Dickens's novels are not far from Joan Didion's. The rush we get from cleaning out our desk or reshuffling the linen cabinet is always short-lived, a quick bout of satisfaction followed by a sinking feeling that by bringing a little bit of order into one tiny corner of our lives, we've done very little to mitigate the uncertainty that lurks everywhere else. And Rebbi's logic when determining the Mishnaha's six orders, while it could have impressed Melville Dewey and his coterie of librarians, gives us a lot to think about but very little to feel.

And that, Rebbi realized, was a problem, because a system of organizing the world must never become a mere abstraction. For it to be relevant, it must be stirring on a deeper level, so that it's not dropped, like so many New Year's resolutions, a week or a month in. The problem of trying to organize life wasn't just that life, by definition, resisted order—or at least, what with so many sharp turns and sudden tragedies, happy accidents and uncanny coincidences, any order that a mortal could truly understand. The real problem was that even if we committed ourselves to some intellectually impressive way of making sense of the world around us, our pesky feelings will always get in the way. I know this diet plan says I'm not allowed to have carbs on Tuesdays, but I had a really bad day at work and this leftover slice of cake is so tiny that nothing really bad will happen if I eat it, and besides, I could always make up for it by exercising twice as hard tomorrow morning. This is us in our silliest, in our most profound and fallible glory. We're ever so ready with these sorts of excuses not because we're weak-willed or lazy or otherwise deficient but because we're overwhelmed by too much. Any one of the Mishnah's orders is a lot to handle, and yet here we are, asked to think not only about seeds, or where our sustenance will come from, but also about family, and society, and our relationship to God and law. It's a lot.

A good way of ordering the world, then, needs to be a lot like what the Dewey decimal system ended up being. It needs to pulsate with our biases—although not with toxic, violent, and harmful ones—and our personal preferences, our fears and our discontents, and then somehow sublimate this writhing mess into something coherent, something we can use in our day-to-day life.

How did Rebbi achieve this? It's enough to peek into one of the Mishnaha's orders to answer this question.

Take, for example, Nashim. Here's a fun exercise in Talmudic thinking: Imagine you were by Rebbi's side, and the aged sage tells you that he's got a bit of a tummy ache and wishes to lie down for the day. You go ahead, he continues, and help out with this whole business of organizing the Mishnah. I'm up to the part that deals with family life, so tell me how to organize it. If this were the case, and if you were trying to think about family— your own, but also in the broadest possible sense—you'd probably want to begin right at the beginning. When does a family begin? A Talmudic discussion would likely ensue. Some may say with marriage, as the union of two people is what makes family possible. Others would point out that there are plenty of single parents out there, which means that any discussion of what constitutes a family ought to begin by paying attention to childbirth. Rebbi made a startlingly different choice, one that has puzzled scholars for millennia. Rebbi chose to begin with *yibbum*.

One of the Torah's most fascinating concepts, the idea behind *yibbum*—or levirate marriage, as it is often, and unhelpfully, translated—is simple. Suppose a man and a woman get married, and before they have had the chance to have children, the husband dies. This, the Bible tells us, is a problem for two reasons: First, it means that the man will then be "obliterated from Israel,"[21] meaning deceased without leaving someone behind to continue his line and his family. And second, and more pressingly, it means that the woman, in a patriarchal society, will be left alone, without protection or sustenance. *Yibbum* was designed to solve both problems: If such a tragedy occurs, the Bible instructs us, the man's brother is then obligated to offer the widow two choices. He may perform the *yibbum*, in which case he must marry her, support and sustain her, and do his best to have the children his sibling never could. Or, if neither he nor she are keen on the arrangement, he may perform *halitza*, an arcane ceremony by which the woman is released of any affinity with her dead husband's family and is now free to marry anyone she chooses.

The idea may sound deluvian, but when King Henry VIII's older brother, Arthur, died childless in 1501 just six months after his marriage, the famous royal wed his widow, Catherine of Aragon, in what is arguably history's most famous levirate marriage. Seeking to annul it when Anne Boleyn came along, and because his only male child with Catherine had died, Henry relied heavily on Talmudic scholars—some actual, others wily pretenders—to find biblical grounds for extricating himself from his sticky situation. When he failed, he took an innovative way out by simply establishing the Church of England, which then allowed him to do as he pleased.[22]

Why, then, begin the family section of the Mishnah, the written account of God's laws for life, by talking about this bizarre— and, frankly, depressing—institution of levirate marriage? Shortly before his death in 1935, Rabbi Abraham Isaac Kook, considered one of the most influential thinkers in religious Zionism, devoted a lecture to this very question. If something is real and ideal and timeless and true, he argued, then it's real and ideal and timeless and true under any circumstance, even—or especially— when "the natural structure has broken down and the family is destroyed."[23] Decades later, in his introduction to Kook's published talk, Yeshiva University's Rabbi Shalom Carmy explained this idea further.

"There is something in R. Kook's insight that is at odds with popular modern attitudes," he wrote. "Our culture tends to assume, sometimes almost unthinkingly, that life is tolerable, and spiritually meaningful, only if it is getting better. The rapid pace of technological innovation and the attainment, by the middle classes, of luxuries unimagined by the wealthiest of our predecessors, fuel our expectation of unlimited progress in all areas."[24] It's why Ronald Reagan reassured us it was morning in America, and why Bill Clinton urged us not to stop thinking about tomorrow.

Tomorrow, everything will be better, and if not for us then for our children.

But what if that's not true? There's a popular story in Orthodox Jewish circles about Rabbi Chaim Soloveitchik, a celebrated Talmudic scholar who lived in Poland in the late nineteenth and early twentieth centuries. When World War I broke out and killed so many, one of Rav Chaim's students cried bitterly and told his rabbi that he could only find this amount of senseless death and destruction meaningful if he could be sure that messianic redemption would soon follow. Rav Chaim was horrified. Absolutely not, he said, because once you start thinking like that, you end up seeing life as a grotesque transaction in which immense suffering now is worth some imagined comfort later. And that's not just delusional—none of us can be sure that comfort will eventually come—but also downright dangerous, because it can make us numb to just how immense the current suffering is and just how urgently we should act to curtail it. Closer to home, the historian Christopher Lasch eloquently expressed the same idea in his last book, *The True and Only Heaven: Progress and Its Critics.* "Hope," he wrote, "does not demand a belief in progress. It demands a belief in justice: a conviction that the wicked will suffer, that wrongs will be made right, that the underlying order of things is not flouted with impunity. Hope implies a deep-seated trust in life that appears absurd to those who lack it."[25]

Real hope, then, comes not from expecting that tomorrow will somehow be better; it comes from doing whatever we can to make today less bad. This, Rabbi Carmy explained, was how faith, at its best, worked. Rav Kook, he wrote, called *yibbum* "redemption," using that most loaded of words in the entire religious lexicon to teach us a lesson: "Redemption is not always about progress and a new, better beginning. Sometimes, and paradigmatically so, redemption is about the restoration of what was destroyed: sometimes redemption is the attempt to recreate the sober authenticity of the past (of course no recreation is ever the same as the original!) without the glittering assurance of the better future."[26]

This may not sound like the kind of stuff you'd find on a Hallmark card, but considered properly, it's an idea with immense generative powers. Levirate marriage is not romantic. It harbors no illusions of passion. But it is redemptive because it insists that we do whatever we can to make sure we don't leave our loved ones behind in their greatest time of need, and while we cannot overcome death, we can brighten its aftermath by stepping in and providing the bereaved with an affirmation that we care and with another shot at a good life. Redemption, the idea of levirate marriage suggests, is a DIY project. Stop waiting for the cavalry to arrive. It's not coming. It doesn't matter. Save yourself. And even if you don't, at least do whatever you can to make the time you have here on earth a bit more tolerable.

What, though, does any of this have to do with the family? Simple, explained one of our most inspiring contemporary scholars, Rabbi Dovid Bashevkin: "You never really become a part of a family until you weather your first tragedy together."[27] Sure, marriage proposals are great. Everyone loves a great, fun wedding, and the honeymoon is sweet bliss. But it's when disaster strikes, when the unexpected happens, when you meet the circumstances beyond your control that your commitment to each other is truly tested and proven. It's being there for each other in our darkest moments, when the future we'd imagined is extinguished, when hope is hardest to see, that counts the most. "And as difficult as that moment can be," Rabbi Bashevkin wrote, "when the winds subside and the storm passes, and you're still huddled together protecting one another, connected to one another—you know this family is now a part of who you are."[28]

How, then, should we think about the family? Rebbi's answer was by imagining the worst first and building from there, which defies logical order but which allows us to exercise an even more important faculty, our empathy. Rather than try to order our world by thinking about what fits into which category, Rebbi is challenging us to do it by projecting ourselves into situations, especially painful and disastrous and surprising ones—the sort that, when encountered in real life, often send us into a tailspin—and then gives us the comfort of teachings and laws and centuries of rabbinic disputation, all there to help us try to imagine the unimaginable.

The Mishnah is formed by this logic. It's why Rebbi chose to start the order of seeds not by talking about the concrete laws of working the land—a subject on which Judaism has much to say—but by considering blessings. Because "seeds," as such, is an amorphous concept, but the outcome they produce, food, is much clearer and present. And because observant Jews are commanded to recite a blessing before they eat, Talmudic discussion of agricultural law begins by contemplating blessings. First, we imagine ourselves at the dinner table, reciting words of gratitude for the meal we're about to enjoy. Only after we've said the blessing, with its emotional expression of gratitude, are we ready to invest ourselves in a more intellectual conversation. First comes dedication, only then discussion. The mind must follow the heart.

It's the opposite, sadly, of the popular perception of the Talmud, a book too often denigrated as being too difficult, too cerebral, too obtuse. Rebbi's work was anything but. The Mishnah is immensely demanding, but only because it is designed not to impose its own order on us but to demand that we commit ourselves, body and soul, to making sense of the world ourselves. The laws are there to guide us, but the laws are meaningless if they remain not much more than lines in a book. Making sense of the world is a full contact sport, not a head game.

Having completed this immense project—six orders divided into sixty-one individual tractates, for a total of 523 chapters of discussion about pretty much everything even remotely pertaining to human life—Rebbi was ready to be rid of his miseries. On his deathbed, the Talmud tells us, "he raised his ten fingers toward Heaven and said in prayer: Master of the Universe, it is revealed and known before You that I toiled with my ten fingers in the Torah, and I have not derived any benefit from the world even with my small finger. May it be Your will that there be peace in my repose." Immediately, a divine voice made itself heard, soothing Rebbi with a quote from the prophecy of Isaiah: "He enters in peace, they rest in their beds."[29] His work was done. It was time to rest.

But his disciples could accept no such fate. They revered their rabbi so much that in their grief they ignored the core part of his teaching, the bit about redemption coming from below, not from above, and about supporting each other in grief rather than raging about what's inevitable. The source of their wisdom and their comfort and their strength, they believed, was Rebbi himself. And so they decreed that he mustn't die. They congregated by his door, declared a fast, and begged God for mercy, but that, they decided, wasn't enough. More extreme means of guaranteeing Rebbi's survival were necessary. "Anyone who says that Rabbi Yehuda HaNasi has died," his disciples decreed in their sorrow, "will be stabbed with a sword." If we don't speak of it, it will not happen.

Realizing the touching absurdity of the situation, the old woman who was Rebbi's longtime maidservant climbed up on the roof and, matter of factly, presented her case to the heavens, sounding considerably calmer and more reasonable than the wailing men gathered below. "The upper realms are requesting the presence of Rabbi Yehuda HaNasi," she said, "and the lower realms are requesting the presence of Rabbi Yehuda HaNasi. May it be the will of God that the lower worlds should impose their will upon the upper worlds." She completed her plaintive prayer and took the stairs back down. There she saw Rebbi, frail and suffering, running in and out of the bathroom in anguish, ravaged by his disease. She climbed back up on the roof. "May it be the will of God," she said, "that the upper worlds impose their will upon the lower worlds." But she herself could barely hear her prayer, drowned as it was by the din of the rabbis huddled downstairs by the front door, crying and begging for God to save Rebbi. And if she couldn't hear her own words, she reasoned, how would God? She took a big jug lying nearby and threw it down

on the ground, watching as it shattered with a loud and fright-
ening crash. The noise distracted the rabbis below; they stopped
praying for a moment, and just then, the Talmud tells us, Rabbi
Yehuda HaNasi died.[30]

His students, then, were left with a comprehensive, recorded
set of teachings, but no teacher. It was now incumbent on them
to continue Rebbi's work, to do as he wished, to exercise empathy, to elucidate the Mishnah, to expand on it and continue the
painstaking task of ordering the world. And to do that, they soon
realized, they had to rely on the most precious source of renewable energy at their disposal: each other's friendship.

CHAPTER SIX

Thank You for Being a Friend

or

How Fighting Can Bring You Closer

"FRIENDSHIP," C. S. Lewis once wrote, "is not a reward for our discrimination and good taste in finding one another out. It is the instrument by which God reveals to each the beauties of all the others."[1]

Yet on the day he met the man who would soon become his best friend—who would spark his conversion to Christianity, who would inspire his greatest literary accomplishments, and who would, eventually, break his heart—Lewis didn't see much that struck him as beautiful.

It was Tuesday, May 11, 1926, and Lewis, a junior tutor in English at Oxford University's Magdalen College, was invited to English tea, the charming name for the old institution's faculty meeting. That afternoon's topic of discussion was Oxford's English curriculum and what should or shouldn't make the cut. Lewis, twenty-eight years old, felt passionately that English literature flourished in the aftermath of Chaucer and that works from the 1400s onward should be favored. A colleague seated nearby, the Rawlinson and Bosworth Professor of Anglo-Saxon, argued that only Old and Middle English texts should make the cut, meaning that students should be on a literary diet of works dating from the seventh to the fifteenth centuries only. They duked it out for a while, but ended up agreeing that no one writing in the nineteenth century should be taken seriously. Returning home that evening, Lewis captured his impressions in his diary.

J. R. R. Tolkien, he observed, "is a smooth, pale, fluent little chap. . . . Thinks the language is the real thing in the school—thinks all literature is written for the amusement of *men* between thirty and forty." And then, a few lines later, a final judgment: "No harm in him: only needs a smack or so. His pet abomination is the idea of 'liberal' studies. Technical hobbies are more in his line."[2]

Despite this lukewarm first impression, Lewis and Tolkien soon became friends. They had too much in common to keep them apart. Neither could drive. Both were shipped to the Somme early in the First World War—Tolkien taking part in several major assaults before being gnawed at by lice, contracting trench fever, and being returned to England, and Lewis wounded by a British shell missing its mark. And both believed, fiercely and truly, in literature and the power of stories to change the world.

So when Tolkien invited Lewis to come join the Kolbiters, the young tutor was thrilled. The society—the name was a playful allusion to those who sat so close to the fireplace on cold winter nights that they may as well be biting the coal—was devoted to reading ancient Icelandic texts. Lewis came for the *Poetic Edda*, a medieval manuscript considered one of the most important sources of Norse mythology, but soon realized that it was Tolkien he was really there to see. When the meetings were over, the two men stayed behind and talked, often at great length and often about myths.

"Up till 2:30 on Monday," Lewis wrote to his friend Arthur Greeves on December 3, 1929, "talking to Anglo-Saxon professor Tolkien, who came back to College from the society and sat discoursing the gods and giants of Asgard for three hours, then departing in the wind and rain—who could turn him out, for the fire was bright and the talk was good."[3]

But it wasn't Asgard Tolkien really wanted to talk about. It was Middle Earth, the fantastical realm he'd begun creating, the culmination of his belief that myths and languages were the double helix that formed and informed every aspect of existence. Late in 1929, Tolkien sent Lewis one of his epic poems, all about the brave Beren, a mortal who steals a jewel from the dark lord Morgoth, and of his love for the elf princess Lúthien. Lewis stayed up all night reading it and responded with a rapturous report. "I can quite honestly say that it is ages since I have had an evening of such delight: and the personal interest of reading a friend's work had very little to do with it."[4]

Larger in size and cheerier in disposition than his friend, Lewis quickly became not only Tolkien's closest reader but also his most impatient booster. He wanted to see the tales of Middle Earth published; not yet, said Tolkien, not until he'd perfected Oromëan and Aulëan and Primitve Quendian and all the other languages he was creating for his elves and his men. "The invention of languages is the foundation," he wrote in a letter to a friend. "The 'stories' were made rather to provide a world for the languages than the reverse. To me a name comes first and the story follows."[5] This frustrated Lewis, who believed that stories were our first and foremost means of making sense of our existence. It also inspired him: listening to Tolkien unfurl the innate logic of languages and then tether his insights into tales that involved characters like Carcharoth, the Wolf of Angband, Lewis felt his views slowly shifting. He had entered Oxford an avowed atheist, a materialist who believed only in what he could see and grasp and measure. Tolkien's penchant for creation—of worlds, of words—awoke in him a sneaking suspicion that maybe there was a Creator after all, some unspecified celestial spiritual life force that, ever so loosely and so gently, guided the affairs of humankind.

But it wasn't until the evening of September 19, 1931, that Lewis could put a name to his newfound faith. Late that evening, he, Tolkien, and their friend, the Shakespeare scholar Hugo Dyson, made their way past the ornate iron gates that led to Addison's Walk, a charming and narrow tree-lined trail by the River Cherwell. They were talking, as they often did, about mythology.

All myths, said Lewis, kicking off the conversation, were "lies breathed through silver," pretty but still untrue. This line, together with much of what transpired, was preserved because Tolkien immortalized the talk in a poem, "Mythopoeia,"[6] calling himself Philomythus, or lover of myths, and referring to Lewis as Misomythus, or the myth-hater. To the latter's provocative opening salvo, Tolkien responded by stating calmly that myths were absolutely true, reflecting, as they did, God's awesome powers of creation. Myths were nothing more than intelligible and digestible accounts of the infinite powers of the divine. And no myth was greater or truer, Tolkien continued, than Christ's life, death, and resurrection, all of which had really happened before transcending history and becoming a beautiful and inspiring tale. In heaven, Tolkien later summed up in his poem, we will all "renew / from mirrored truth the likeness of the True,"[7] seeing with our own eyes that what we thought was merely fiction was actually glorious fact.

He was just making this powerful point when something extraordinary happened. "A rush of wind," Lewis reported a few days later in a letter to his friend Arthur Greeves, "came so suddenly on the still, warm evening and sent so many leaves pattering down that we thought it was raining. We all held our breath, the other two appreciating the ecstasy of such a thing."[8]

Just over a week later, however, Lewis wrote Greeves another letter admitting that it wasn't just the other two who were moved by the ecstatic moment. "I have passed on from believing in God to definitely believing in Christ—in Christianity," he reflected. "I will try to explain this another time. My long night talk with Dyson and Tolkien had a good deal to do with it."[9]

By August of the following year, Lewis was already preaching what he'd just begun to practice: he wrote a fiery novel, *The Pilgrim's Regress*, an update of sorts to John Bunyan's 1678 Christian allegory. Lewis's hero, a young man named John, leaves his homeland of Puritania, meets a gaggle of characters who represent modern ideologies—it's not too hard to figure out that Mr. Neo-Angular and Mr. Humanist are Fascism and Marxism embodied—and struggles, only to be finally redeemed by Mother Kirk, the Christian faith in the flesh. It took him only two weeks to write, and it met with largely positive reviews. Lewis was now not only an ascendant author, but also a growingly important public Christian intellectual, which helped him climb up the university's social ranks. And his ascendancy was a mixed blessing for his mentor and friend, Tolkien. On the one hand, the older man enjoyed his protégé's growth and delighted to see him take on the world as a Christian thinker and writer. On the other hand, he found hastily dashed allegories to be an affront to his core idea of literature, with its slow world building and meticulous attention to linguistics.

Still, the two found each other's company pleasurable, and by 1933, they helped establish—or rather reestablish, as an original club bearing the same name had just gone belly-up—a literary salon called the Inklings. Every Tuesday, they'd meet for lunch at a pub called The Eagle and Child, known to its patrons as the Bird and Baby, and every Thursday they'd congregate chez Lewis after supper. Drinks would be served, and eventually, someone would produce some work in progress and read it out loud.

The work Tolkien sometimes shared was a departure from the heroic stuff with which he'd been toying. Gone were the brave Beren and the terrifying Morgoth, replaced with a small creature called Bilbo, a hobbit. It was, Lewis firmly believed, a story meant mainly for children, enjoyable but ultimately of questionable merit. "Whether it is really *good*," he wrote his friend Greeves, "is of course another question: still more, whether it will succeed with modern children."[10] Whatever doubt he had in private, however, Lewis kept to himself; in Tolkien's company, he was always warm and encouraging, even when urging his friend to focus less on the details and more on the storytelling. Eventually, Tolkien completed the manuscript and shared it with a student, who lent it to a friend, who passed it along to Stanley Unwin, the London publisher. Unwin gave it to his ten-year-old son, Rayner, who devoured it and delivered a glowing reader's report, dotted with superlatives like "terrific" and "rich" and "exiting," no less heartfelt for being misspelled. Unwin made Tolkien an offer, and the appearance of a contract—and a deadline—were just what the reluctant writer needed to get busy. The book was published on September 21, 1937.

Immediately, Lewis busied himself with singing Tolkien's praises in public. He penned unsigned reviews everywhere he had sway, from the London *Times* to *The Times Literary Supplement*, but Tolkien quickly surmised the identity of his secret admirer. "I must respect his opinion," he wrote to his publisher with his customary self-deprecation, "as I believed him to be the best living critic until he turned his attention to me, and no degree of friendship would make him say what he does not mean."[11]

And, for more than a decade, Lewis and Tolkien's friendship grew many degrees deeper and richer. In 1939, when the German blitz plunged Oxford into a defensive nighttime blackout, Lewis risked injury and stumbled in the dark to Tolkien's home to drink gin with a twist of lime and talk about the new project the author of *The Hobbit* was entertaining, a story about Bilbo's cousin, Frodo, and his quest to destroy an all-powerful ring in the fires of Mount Doom. Always the cheerleader, Lewis continued to encourage his friend to finish the book, devoting many hours to conversations about elves, hobbits, humans, and the languages they spoke.

Lewis was patient and kind, even though he sometimes found Tolkien's obsessions tedious. And Tolkien was grateful and sweet, even though he sometimes found Lewis's enthusiasm too unserious. They met with the other Inklings—the club's meetings, rivalries, and collaborations have filled several volumes—and reviewed each other's works both privately and publicly, before and after publication, and took walks and drank and felt grateful that they had someone with whom to share the undertaking that has come to define their lives, the forging of modern-day stories every bit as powerful as the old myths and every bit as likely to endure.

And then came Narnia.

By the time Lewis handed Tolkien the manuscript of what would become his most famous work, *The Lion, the Witch and the Wardrobe*, sometime early in 1949, their friendship was already showing signs of fatigue. Maybe it was the stress of the Second World War, or maybe it was Charles Williams, the charismatic Inkling who won Lewis over with his macabre fiction but left Tolkien cold. And yet, when Lewis shared his work with his still-best friend, he didn't anticipate rejection. After all, he'd always been there for Tolkien, even when the latter was spending days and days fretting over etymological and esoteric questions, like whether the plural of dwarf should be dwarfs, dwarves, or dwarrows. And he'd always praised Tolkien's writing, even when he wasn't particularly moved by it. So now that he had a passion project of his own, he expected similar indulgence.

None came. George Sayer, Lewis's friend and biographer, delivered the definitive account of what happened next. Lewis, he wrote, was "hurt, astonished, and discouraged when Tolkien said that he thought the book was almost worthless."[12] Like a professor correcting a sloppy student's term paper, Tolkien went on to demolish his friend's work. First, he noticed, and most troublesome, was the book's mythological incongruity: Why would the White Witch and Father Christmas and the fauns and Aslan and Mr. and Mrs. Beaver—all creatures who hail from disparate mythological traditions—occupy the same fantastic realm? Worse yet, even if Lewis chose to cram all these mismatched species into the same magical land, why not at least make sure that they behaved in ways that were true to their form? Why turn fauns, lustful and impulsive and sensual creatures according to all other mythological accounts, into kindly and friendly things who befriend children? And why write so quickly? Asked about Middle Earth, Tolkien could narrate the history of the past two millennia in his fictional universe; he'd spent years thinking about it. Did Lewis even know—or care—about the antiquity of Narnia?

This went on for a while, and it left Lewis brokenhearted and his friendship with Tolkien irreparably cracked. Lewis rushed home and almost immediately started work on the second book in the Narnia series, *Prince Caspian*. And Tolkien—spurred, maybe, by Lewis's speed—finally finished the first book of his *Lord of the Rings* trilogy, *The Fellowship of the Ring*. By the time it was published, in 1954, the two were no longer speaking.

Lewis passed away in 1963 after a series of health complications that included blood poisoning, a heart attack, and kidney failure. Tolkien did not attend the funeral. If he missed his friend or felt sad that he could no longer regale Lewis with hours and hours of conversation about literature and God and myth and ideas, he barely let on. But writing in 1965 to the head of the Tolkien Society of America—by then the *Lord of the Rings* books had made him a literary celebrity—he felt compelled to acknowledge Lewis's immense contribution to his life and success.

"The unpayable debt that I owe to him was not 'influence' as it is ordinarily understood, but sheer encouragement," he wrote. "He was for long my only audience. Only from him did I ever get the idea that my 'stuff' could be more than a private hobby. But for his interest and unceasing eagerness for more I should never have brought *The L. of the R.* to a conclusion."[3]

The friendship of Lewis and Tolkien, however ill fated, continues to attract so much attention—from critics and scholars and fans alike—not only because both men were titans, but also because of the passion with which they committed themselves to their joint pursuit. They believed in literature as an engine of faith, believed that by giving readers, especially young ones, grand myths to stir souls and soften hearts and steel spines, they could inch a bit closer to closing the gap between divine perfection and human fallibility. And even when they failed to be warm, or when they allowed their zeal for ideas to overcome their compassion for each other, they kept on accelerating each other, demanding of each other nothing less than utter dedication to their work.

In many ways, the history and the spirit of the Talmud are both made up of such unlikely and uneasy pairings. Once the Mishnah was redacted and its great author, Rebbi, was gone, the men entrusted with keeping the tradition alive were bereft and confused. Because the Mishnah rarely issued clear edicts, because it frequently did little more than record arguments, often very complex ones, and because the great teacher who had willed it into being was no longer around to explicate and adjudicate, the rabbis in the generation after Rebbi's passing were left wondering what, exactly, it was they were supposed to be doing. Was their job now merely to teach the Mishnah as it stood, with no deviations? That was hard, because, again, the Mishnah had a lot to say about almost everything with nothing definitive or decisive to say about almost anything. Yet, rabbis still had to sit in judgment and address everyday quarrels, from legal disputes to domestic discords. Even more vexing, the Mishnah itself, clear as it was about the problems it raised, was never designed to be the final word in the conversation. Rebbi himself knew that further commentary was needed, more analysis, a more detailed examination of the myriad issues under scrutiny. The Mishnah was only the beginning; it was now time to dive deeper. But how?

To answer this question, the rabbis doubled down on a profound insight that had served them for centuries, at least since the days of Hillel and Shammai: the best way to really understand something is to talk it through with someone you both respect and revile, admire and fear, need and resent. The Mishnah, as usual, put it best: the greatest way to go through life, it advised, was to follow this one simple principle: "acquire for thyself a companion."[14]

This peculiar word choice has sent scholars into paroxysms

for millennia. Why should one "acquire" a friend? Isn't friendship, an elected affinity, the polar opposite of anything transactional like an acquisition? Does the Mishnah propose that we go ahead and offer our friends cash payments to hang out with us? And wouldn't that pretty much guarantee a one-sided, toxic relationship?

The meaning of "acquire," the Talmud goes on to explain, is more complicated than that. First, the rabbis tell us, we should acknowledge that the true purpose of friendship isn't just to keep us company or allow us to feed our own solipsistic appetites by finding someone who shares our tastes, but rather to further tether us to our community and our traditions. A friend, the medieval Spanish rabbi Yonah Gerondi explained, needed to do three things: help you study Torah, make sure you keep the commandments, and give good advice when needed. He or she, in other words, should make you smarter, kinder, and more emotionally attuned. It's the sort of growth that is absolutely impossible to achieve alone, which is why the Talmud explicitly discourages any Torah scholar, no matter how brilliant, from studying by themselves. But it's also the sort of growth that can get very prickly. A friend may only teach you something new if you first acknowledge that there's much you still don't know and that your friend might, from time to time, prove smarter and wiser than you. A friend may only help you hold to higher standards if you're honest enough to admit that sometimes your behavior falls far short of ideal. And friendly advice, as sage as it may be, only means something when it lands on open ears and an open heart.

Having a friend, then, is an exercise in self-negation, a recommitment to first principles, an awkward and ongoing rebirth. It's work. We adore little children for forming fast friendships over the littlest details—We love the same cartoon! Let's be best friends forever!—but for adults things are infinitely more intricate. Adults, the Talmud tells us, must choose friends for the purpose of self-improvement, which means choosing exactly the people who are the *least* like us and the most likely to help us see the things in ourselves we are anxious to suppress and ignore.

Friendship, in other words, is a battlefield, and the story of how the Talmud came to be—how generations of rabbis took the Mishnah and argued it into something much more monumental and long-lasting—is, in large part, the story of frenemies arguing their world into existence. The Talmud gives us a radical reinterpretation of what it means to be a friend, one that more closely resembles Lewis and Tolkien's exhaustive, marathon conversations than, say, Goethe's doe-eyed view of friendship as a blazing union of two souls or Socrates's jaundice-eyed view of friendship as a near impossibility, derailed at every turn by the fact that humans are inherently unequal and teeming with self-interest and suspicion. The Talmud's prescription for a perfect friendship isn't the stuff of buddy comedies; more often than not, the recorded accounts we have are long on jagged disputations and very short on anything resembling affection and warmth. And yet, the model is worth studying, especially in times of rising rancor and ideological division, for the difficult but tenable path it offers out of rage and enmity. The Talmudic model of friendship is an exercise in keeping disagreements simmering and then using the heat they generate to power larger cultural, political, spiritual, and social enterprises, to build rather than consume. And it revolves around two pairs of mighty bickerers: Rav and Shmuel and Yochanan and Reish Lakish.

Before he died, Rebbi, every bit the monarch, left behind very clear instructions about which of his disciples should be elevated to which posts in the intricate web of sinecures he had at his disposal as Nasi. Rav, brilliant and faithful and beloved by Rebbi, was left unmentioned. The Talmud wonders why, with various sages opining that Rav, like Rabbi Meir before him, was likely just too smart for his own good, an eminence so learned that to give him a position of leadership would be too risky; he knew so much it was hard for mere mortals to follow his train of thought. Whatever the reason, the unrewarded Rav decided that the best balm for his wounded pride was to leave the Land of Israel and hightail it to Babylonia, where a large Jewish community had been thriving for centuries and where a man of his caliber would surely be warmly received.

It didn't go as planned.

Sitting by the Malka River, not far from Baghdad, the Talmud tells us, two of Babylonia's most esteemed rabbis, Karna and Shmuel—more about them in a moment—noticed that the water was rising and that it was murky. Immediately, they understood this omen to mean that a great sage was coming from the west, from the Land of Israel, and that he was suffering from terrible stomach pains. "Go sniff out his container," Shmuel told Karna, using a popular expression meaning figure out what he's all about, most pressingly whether or not he truly knew his Torah. Karna did as he was told: he walked about until he bumped into Rav and then pestered the newcomer with a series of complicated and increasingly explicit questions about Jewish law. Rav took it all in stride, until he didn't. Weary from his journey, no doubt, and annoyed by this sudden inquisition, he lost his patience and cursed at Karna. Then, to make matters worse, Karna took Rav to Shmuel's house, where the latter fed him barley bread and beer and fried fish and refused to let him use the bathroom.

Why? Some interpreters have argued that Shmuel, a physician, was simply trying to cure the newcomer of his intestinal agony; the meal, he had hoped, would eventually induce diarrhea, which would make Rav feel better. Other scholars were less charitable; the rabbis, they argued, were no saints, and the Talmud no hagiography. You can imagine that a young and ambitious and brilliant man like Shmuel didn't much care for the learned stranger marching into town and threatening to steal his spotlight and laurels. Whatever the reason for this guttural maneuver, Rav didn't take it too kindly, cursing Shmuel bitterly. It was the beginning of a beautiful friendship between two men who ended up accelerating the brilliance of each other precisely because they couldn't have been any more different.[15]

How different? The Talmud doesn't merely tell us; it wants us to see for ourselves. So it takes us back to Shmuel's childhood and gives us a peek into the education of a boy genius. One time, Shmuel's father—it says something about junior's greatness that senior is only ever referred to as Abuha D'Shmuel, or the Father of Shmuel—is quizzing his son about the laws concerning ritual slaughter. Imagine, father tells son, that someone brings an animal to the Temple, intending to sacrifice it, and imagine that the beast is standing with its front legs inside the Temple's court-yard and its hind legs outside. Can one still slaughter it? Simple, says the boy: the answer is no, because Leviticus 17:5 says clearly that people bringing offerings "may bring them to the Lord." This means bringing the whole animal, Shmuel argues, which, in turn, suggests that the beast may not be slaughtered unless all of it is inside the Temple.

The father is pleased, but the pop quiz is far from over. What if, he continues, the animal is somehow suspended in midair; may it be slaughtered then? Sure thing, says Shmuel; by the same logic, an animal suspended in midair is still the whole animal. That may be so, says the father, but another verse in Leviticus also teaches us that all ritual slaughter must take place with the animal laid on the side of the altar in the Temple, and an animal suspended in midair clearly doesn't meet these requirements. Therefore, no slaughter is permitted. The boy barely catches his breath, and the father strikes again: What, he demands, if the *priest* is somehow suspended in midair, but the animal is on the ground? Does the law permit sacrifice then? No, says Shmuel, now arguing that all interactions involving persons or animals suspended in midair aren't kosher. Wrong again, says his father: The Torah merely requires for the animal to be slaughtered on the side of the altar. It says nothing about the preferred location of the one who does the slaughtering. This goes on for a good, long while, with the father constructing increasingly ornate and improbable scenarios and young Shmuel getting them all wrong.[16]

Why bother telling us all this? Why should we care about the fumbling of an ancient child, especially as the questions posed to him, about levitating cows and such, border on the ludicrous? Like all Talmudic riddles, the answer to this one, too, is hiding in plain sight. What is Shmuel's father asking him to do? Not to recite settled laws or repeat the opinions of his elders. Instead, he wants the boy to become a critical thinker, the sort of scholar who can encounter any problem—even, or especially, one that is strange and vexing—and address it using nothing more than a firm understanding of the tradition and a strong command of logic and deduction. In other words, Shmuel's father wants to make sure his son is a fierce and free thinker.

Which, for those accustomed to seeing religious life as an exercise in submission to settled dogma, may sound perplexing. Why raise the boy to master dialectics? Why not escort him instead to a quiet room, teach him Torah from morning till night, and praise him for committing as much of it as he can to memory? What, in other words, is the real-life value of this method of education in a society that praises learnedness above all? The Talmud answers this question with another pair of stories about young Shmuel and his dad.

One day, goes the first, the boy Shmuel runs away from home. Knowing what we know about the circumstances of his home schooling, this shouldn't shock us; a child can withstand only so many hours of endless complicated riddles before rushing out to the street in search of distraction and relief. Desperate to make sure he's not discovered, Shmuel, a rich and privileged kid, escapes to the one place he knows his father would never think to look—the poorest part of town. There he stands perfectly still between two ramshackle huts and listens, fascinated by these voices, so vibrant and so different from the heady and demanding cadences of the schoolroom.

Then something strange occurs. "On which plates shall we eat today?" asks one of the poor people inside one of the huts. "The silver ones or those made of gold?"

Confused, Shmuel forgets all about his newfound, short-lived independence. He runs back home and tells his father what he's heard. The poor people inside weren't joking; how was it possible that they had enough money for such fancy dinnerware? The father is delighted. Some people are genuinely poor, he tells his son, and some pretend to be so that they may enjoy the considerable charitable resources rabbinic society dedicates to the less fortunate. Having now encountered a pair of con men, Shmuel's father tells his boy, wealthy swindlers who syphoned off sums and used them to buy luxury goods, you should be grateful: next time you come across someone asking you for a coin, be more discriminating and figure out if they really deserve it.[17]

It's a sour little tale to modern ears. Surely there were many genuinely distressed individuals huddling for warmth in the neighboring huts, and teaching the boy to be hardened in his charity seems intellectually correct but morally cold. Immediately, then, comes a second, and very different, story. This time, Shmuel's father gives the boy a few coins and instructs him to go out and give them to the poor. The boy does as he is told, but when he hits the poor part of town again, he sees a pauper feasting on meat and guzzling down wine. Perplexed, he again returns home to report what he's seen, and again, the father treats him to a lesson. But this time, the moral of the story is the opposite. The pauper's soul is bitter, says Shmuel's father, because he has expensive tastes and lacks the cash to indulge them. Go and give him more money so that he may experience a little bit of joy.[18]

Here, finally, we've all the pieces we need to put together Shmuel in full. His father's pedagogical method wasn't just preparation for a life of disembodied cerebral pursuits. It was training for a world rife with moral and emotional complexities and ambiguities. Sometimes people cheat, and you have no choice but to be strict with those who put on the appearance of suffering. Sometimes people hurt, and you have no choice but to be merciful to those who seem reckless. The laws of the Torah help, of course, but no codex, divine as it may be, could ever hold all the answers for the infinite intricacies of human interactions. To be a truly good person, you need to train your moral muscle, which means learning to look at each situation with great care and nuance and diving below the surface. If you learn how to do that with hypotheticals about levitating animals, you can soon apply the same skill in the streets of your town, seeing both the perfidy of the phony beggar and the real anguish of the pauper craving a steak.

His wisdom quickly made Shmuel famous. He was known as Arioch, which means both "the great" and "the lion," and his glory soon extended far beyond the Jewish community. He became friendly with Shapur I, the Sasanian king, interpreting the monarch's dream and predicting, correctly, that his Persian empire would soon humble Rome. The two were so close, the Talmud tells us, that Shmuel once delighted his royal buddy by juggling eight full glasses of wine without spilling a drop.[19] Their friendship was tested when the king killed twelve thousand rebellious Jews who sided with his enemies. Shmuel was saddened but not distraught. *Dina d'Malchuta Dina*, he said in one of his most famous rulings—"the law of the kingdom is the law."[20] No one had the right to break it and expect any special privileges or dispensations, and no religious, ethnic, or family ties were paramount to the loyalty one owed to the government, at least if the government wasn't despotic or murderous but bent on something approximating justice.

As Shmuel was being feted, however, Rav was being ignored, mocked, or some combination of both. One time, the Talmud tells us, he found himself in the study hall of Rav Sheila, a celebrated local sage in Babylonia. Having no idea who this stranger was, and feeling, perhaps, a bit of compassion for the older gentleman without any discernible friends or stature, Rav Sheila asked Rav to serve as his assistant, a lowly job that mainly entailed repeating Rav Sheila's lesson to the students in a clear and concise manner. Rav agreed, but mid-lesson Rav Sheila noticed that his new assistant was taking liberties, translating Hebrew words into Aramaic—the lingua franca of the day and the language most people in the region used in daily conversation—in a way that struck Rav Sheila as much too intricate. Why, he asked Rav, did you choose these specific words?

Rav replied with an insult. "A flute played for noblemen is music," he said, "but when played for weavers, they receive no pleasure from it, due to their lack of sophistication. Similarly, the interpretation I disseminated was accepted by Torah scholars greater than you. You, who lack their sophistication, cannot appreciate it."[21]

Mortified, Rav Sheila immediately realized the true identity of his aide. "Is this Master Rav?" he asked contritely. "Let the master rest and cease disseminating my lecture, as it is beneath your dignity to serve as my assistant." But Rav wouldn't hear of it. "People," he replied wearily, "say this aphorism: If you hired yourself to him, comb his wool. Once one agrees to perform a task, he should bear its less pleasing aspects and complete the job."[22]

Slowly, Rav made himself better known. Everywhere he went, his peers were impressed by his ability to recall reams and reams of rabbinic opinions and by his encyclopedic knowledge of the Mishnah. But they were also keenly aware that Rav, for all of his virtues, was the polar opposite of Shmuel. Whereas Shmuel championed logical dexterity and creative interpretation, Rav believed in faithful recollection. Now that the Mishnah existed, he argued, the primary task was learning it inside out, not engaging in thought experiments like the ones favored by Shmuel's dad.

Rav also disliked Shmuel's politics: the Persian kingdom, he believed, was good and well, but a Jew's ultimate fealty ought always to be to other Jews. One day, for example, a Jew walked into the house of study and told Rav that he intended to rat out his neighbor, a fellow Jew, to the Persian authorities, which would result in the neighbor's supply of straw being seized. "Do not show it and do not show it," Rav said, repeating himself twice to make sure he was heard. But the man wouldn't budge. "I will show it and I will show it," he replied. One of Rav's colleagues, Rav Kahana, was so disgusted by the man's insolent response that he leapt up, broke the man's neck, and killed him.

Rav thought things through for a moment. Then he spoke. The Persians coming for the Jewish man's straw would have likely killed him to seize the straw, he said, so Rav Kahana's act wasn't murder as much as it was a sort of justified defense. And because the Persians would now likely wish to execute Rav Kahana for his crime, he should escape to the Land of Israel and keep a very low profile for the next seven years.[23] So much for the law of the kingdom being the law.

How, then, was one community to contain two men united by their passion for Torah but divided by pretty much everything else? And how were they to accommodate each other? These were more than theoretical questions for Rav and Shmuel. For one thing, theirs was a small and tightly knit community, the kind that put everyone in close, daily proximity to everyone else. For another, they both realized that their shared mission, the task of passing down the Mishnah to future generations, required more than one flavor of scholarship. This realization came to them slowly, almost bitterly. The Talmud is sprinkled with references to one listening to the arguments of the other and then, begrudgingly, conceding that the point was good. Like Lewis and Tolkien, they argued endlessly about their divergent approaches, but also realized that each possessed a certain sort of genius that ought to be preserved and celebrated.

And so, they studied each other obsessively. One time, a few rabbis posed a question to Shmuel and his pal Karna about a relatively complicated case involving a minor who became betrothed without her father's consent. They recorded both rabbis' opinions and then ran to see Rav. But knowing that the older scholar was a stickler for repeating the opinions of others, they decided to trick him and reverse the opinions, reporting Karna's opinion as Shmuel's and Shmuel's ruling as Karna's. It didn't take Rav more than a minute to unearth the ruse. God forbid that Shmuel say such a thing, he bellowed. Having mentally cataloged all of Shmuel's interpretations and decisions, he was convinced, correctly, that Shmuel would never rule as reported.[24] Even as he resented Shmuel, he respected him immensely and took the time to understand his mind as well as he did his own. And Shmuel did exactly the same.

But getting to know each other didn't necessarily mean coming to like each other. And mutual affection was not, in Rav and Shmuel's world, the meaning of friendship. A friend was like a whetstone, there to apply maximum friction for ultimate sharpness. A friend poked you and forced you, sometimes rudely, to think harder, reason better, and be clearer. This was why Torah was studied in a *havruta*, a pairing of two people of equal intellectual capabilities yet very different sensibilities. The prevalent pedagogical method in Rav and Shmuel's time, it still is in ours. Visiting Yeshiva University recently, the conservative columnist— and non-Jew—George F. Will was shocked to enter the house of study and find nothing but cacophony, young students arguing loudly and appearing upset. "How does anyone get any thinking done amid all this shouting?" he reportedly asked.[25] Rav and Shmuel understood that the shouting was exactly the point: The shouting made you smarter and stronger. The shouting made sure you truly understood your stuff. And the shouting made you a truly good friend.

None of that, however, meant that this kind of friendship could necessarily sustain the sort of intimacy we moderns associate with our most rewarding relationships. Having a frenemy there to hold your feet to the fire might make you a better scholar, but it can also make you tired, as it eventually did Tolkien and Lewis. And Rav and Shmuel, to their immense credit, understood that well. Before too long, Rav realized that the town of Nahardea wasn't big enough for him and Shmuel. He had two choices: challenge Shmuel and become the community's uncontested spiritual leader, or leave. The first option was costly, mainly because it would require prioritizing resentment and ambition over mutual admiration and shared concerns. The second seemed easier. Rav picked up and left.

Eventually, he found his way to the town of Sura and started a school of his own. There he focused mainly on teaching the Mishnah verbatim. No analysis was required or encouraged; instead, students were expected to familiarize themselves with the intricate teachings of their predecessors and commit these teachings to memory. Which, while not as thrilling as Shmuel's brainy acrobatics, was every bit as necessary to guaranteeing that the sacred codex survived. Distance made the heart grow fonder. Rav and Shmuel grew closer the farther apart they were. With each finally ensconced in his own community, free to teach in his own chosen way, their arguments could continue to inspire rather than throttle. They made their friendship work.

Which, alas, could not be said for Yochanan and Reish Lakish, the Talmud's star-crossed friends whose mercurial bond led to a tragic end and a warning about letting your passions carry the day.

Yochanan was marked as a superstar even before he was born. His pregnant mother, the Talmud recounts, was fasting on Yom Kippur, the Jewish Day of Atonement, when she walked by an eatery and smelled something delicious. She was famished and craved a bite, and her hunger made her feel woozy. A wealthy woman, she went to confer with Rebbi: Was she allowed to break her fast? Sure, said the great rabbi. Jewish law encouraged pregnant women to do whatever was necessary to protect themselves and their unborn babies, even if that meant not properly observing the holiest day of the year. But before you go ahead and eat, Rebbi added, let me try one more thing. And with that, he leaned over and whispered in the woman's ear. "Today is Yom Kippur," he said ever so softly, and immediately the woman's hunger subsided. Your child heard me, Rebbi told the woman; he understood that today was a holy day of fasting, and stopped demanding to be fed. He will be a great scholar and a righteous man.

Yochanan's mother, sadly, died in childbirth, and his father perished shortly after, which meant that Yochanan, like so many epic heroes, was an orphan. This pleased him in an interesting way. He was glad to have neither father nor mother, he told one of his teachers, as the commandment to honor thy parents was one of the most difficult to obey. Now that his parents were dead he was exempt from even trying. He sold most of the real estate he inherited to dedicate himself exclusively to his studies. It made perfect mathematical sense, he said to a colleague; it took God six days to create the world and forty days to deliver the Torah to Moses, which meant that if you wanted to maximize your returns, investing in Torah was the better bet.[26] This brand of logic and piety, no surprises there, mightily impressed Rebbi. He invited Yochanan to his house of study, although, given his extremely young age, he asked Yochanan to stand way in the back, in the seventeenth row.

Yochanan's brain was one thing; his body was another. He was handsome—rotund, tradition tells us, which, back then, was the ideal shape, with smooth alabaster skin and shiny hair—and he knew it. Frequently, he would go and sit by the ritual bathhouses where Jewish women were required to bathe immediately after their periods. He did this, he told his friends, so that the ladies might gaze upon his great beauty and then go home, make love to their husbands, and conceive sons as beautiful as him. This struck his friends as a bit weird; aren't you, they asked, even the least afraid of the evil eye? Not at all, replied Yochanan with a smile. "I descend from the seed of Joseph," he roared, leaving his friends to guess whether he was reporting an accurate genealogy or merely putting on airs, "over whom the evil eye has no dominion."[27]

His friends were soon swayed, and as much talk was devoted to Yochanan's physical features as to his astounding brilliance. His penis, the Talmud records his friends noting, was "the size of a jug of five *kavs*,"[28]—about a gallon and a half— meaning extraordinarily large. "One who wishes to see something resembling the beauty of Rabbi Yochanan," the Talmud concludes definitively, "should bring a new, shiny silver goblet from the smithy and fill it with red pomegranate seeds and place a diadem of red roses upon the lip of the goblet, and position it between the sunlight and shade. That luster is a semblance of Rabbi Yochanan's beauty."[29]

Yochanan's infatuation with aesthetics—he is on record as saying that "I alone remain of the beautiful people of Jerusalem"[30]—carried over to his wardrobe, too. The first Talmudic rabbi to devise a comprehensive theory of fashion, Yochanan believed passionately that Torah scholars, being the most exalted of all men, had better dress the part. Patched shoes were verboten, even if you were only running errands in the marketplace. Were you seen with a stain from fatty meat on your cloak? You should, according to Yochanan, be sentenced to death, as you were giving people the impression that those who study Torah were unclean and uncareful in their ways.[31] Similarly, like a Jordan Peterson before his time, Yochanan believed that a gentleman must always make his bed: there should, he taught, be "nothing except sandals beneath it during the summer, and shoes beneath it during the rainy season."[32] A cluttered bedroom was a sign of a cluttered mind. Since being a great Torah scholar meant being highly attuned to minute details, one had to begin training by paying very close attention to the intricacies of one's bed, clothes, and personal hygiene.

And a cluttered mind was a luxury a rabbi couldn't afford, especially not in Yochanan's time, a period of great upheaval. In 235 CE, with Yochanan already a man in full, the Roman emperor Severus Alexander was having lunch in his tent with his mother and his troops when a German servant walked in and issued a bloodcurdling cry. Before Alexander could understand what was going on, his troops rose and stabbed him and his mother to death. Thus began the unimprovably named period of Military Anarchy, also known as the Crisis of the Third Century, fifty years of barbarian invasions, peasant uprisings, political instability, natural disasters, and a string of unworthy brutes seizing power in succession. This chaos was much felt in the Roman-controlled Land of Israel. Anytime a new emperor rose to power, for example, he would immediately levy new taxes to fatten his coffers, which gave rise to mad inflation, tax evasion, and an economy on the brink of collapse. Yochanan and his friends were called on to pass wise laws that both appeased their Roman masters and protected their Jewish brethren, a gargantuan task that took a man of Yochanan's caliber to pull off.

He accomplished it not only by being sensitive and sensible—permitting, for example, working the land during the year of *shemitah*, during which Jews are commanded to let the land rest, in order to afford paying taxes to Rome—but also by taking the Mishnah and codifying it into a coherent book of rules and laws. In his house of study, he and his students pored over Rebbi's masterwork. Whenever they found a disagreement, they weighed the merits of the two opposing scholars and judged which of them ought to decide the argument. And wherever a discussion in the Mishnah suggested the correct way of behaving in a given situation, Rabbi Yochanan quickly codified it as the halacha, the law. It was a mighty intellectual, emotional, and political project, and, increasingly, Yochanan realized he couldn't do it alone. He had many teachers and many friends, but none to match his splendor. He was well aware that he was an almost mystical and mythical figure, and his *havruta*, therefore, would need to be someone just as magical. Yochanan found him under the most incredible circumstances. One day, he was bathing in the Jordan River when a man approached from afar. The stranger, seeing Yochanan's radiant beauty and blinded by the glitter of the sun on the surface of the water, believed Yochanan was a naked woman and so quickly took off his clothes and jumped right into the river with malevolent intentions.

Who was that stranger? Depends on who you ask. The Talmud was so uncomfortable with the likely circumstances of his childhood that alternative theories quickly sprang forth, suggesting that the man, Shimon ben Lakish, better known as Reish Lakish, was a great Torah scholar gone rogue. But by the time he met Yochanan in the river, Reish Lakish was a gladiator, a highway robber, and, according to Rashi, the leader of a brood of canni-bals.[33] He was large and fierce looking, muscular and hairy, the very opposite, in other words, of the refined-looking Yochanan. And when this mountain of a man swam to his prey and discovered that the figure he'd lusted after wasn't a helpless maiden but a dude, he was not so much disappointed as surprised. "You are so beautiful, you really ought to have been a woman!" Reish Lakish said. Yochanan, not missing a beat, shot right back. "And you," he said to the bulky stranger, "you are so strong, you really should've been a Torah scholar."

The two got to talking. The marauder, Yochanan soon learned, was much smarter than his appearance suggested. And the rabbi, Reish Lakish quickly realized, was much more charming than one might have expected from a man who spent his days doing nothing but reading and arguing about books. And so, sensing an opportunity, Yochanan made Reish Lakish an offer he couldn't refuse: "If you return to the pursuit of Torah," he said, "I will give you my sister in marriage, who is more beautiful than I am."[34] Reish Lakish agreed on the spot, yet when he tried to jump out of the river and get dressed he was shocked to discover that all of his physical strength had abandoned him. He was instantly and miraculously transformed from a man of great physical strength to a man of unparalleled intellectual and spiritual might.

Or, more accurately, *almost* unparalleled. Yochanan taught his new brother-in-law the Torah and the Mishnah, and Reish Lakish took his studies so seriously that he would recite each lesson forty times before entering the study hall to hear the next one. Not an hour went by, the Talmud tells us, which did not find Reish Lakish nose-deep in a book; even as he lay sick, he asked to be put on his stomach so that he could continue to read as he convalesced. And while his brawn might have dissipated that day at the river, his courage never waned. Often, we're told, he stuck to his proverbial guns, insisting that his interpretation of the Torah was correct even when he risked running afoul of older, more celebrated scholars.

His attitude impressed Yochanan, and soon Reish Lakish became, if not precisely Yochanan's equal in intellect, then not too far off from it. Helping his friend bring order into the financial tumult of the time, he was instrumental in developing the idea of the *umdana*, a halachic tool for judging a person's behavior in the absence of any evidence. Because many people in those days struggled to get by, and because many had to rely on loans just to make it through the year, disputes often arose about whether or not money that was owed was ever paid back. Receipts and witnesses weren't always the norm, and accusations often got testy, with each side swearing the other was lying. How to judge? The wise Reish Lakish jumped into this fray.

"If a lender set a time for another to repay the loan that he had extended to him," he explained, "and when the debt came due the borrower said to the lender: I already repaid you within the time, he is not deemed credible, as people do not ordinarily repay their debts before they are due."[35] This kind of logic—based, no doubt, on Reish Lakish's intimate knowledge, as a former bandit, of people's worst instincts—helped set up better rules, requiring proofs for loans, for example, and helping rabbis judge disputes more fairly.

Having someone nearly as great as he was by his side made Yochanan deliriously happy. A proud man, he nevertheless understood that if you wanted to keep your *havruta* in fighting shape, you had no choice but to sometimes get as well as you gave. The Talmud regales us with a slew of disputes between the two, each artful and intricate and fiery. One time, for example, Yochanan's relatives came to him for advice. Their father, they said, had a young wife, and he lavished such luxuries on her that they were afraid he'd squander his entire fortune just keeping her happy. What to do?

Simple, said Yochanan: tell dad to set aside a certain portion of his land specifically for his wife's sustenance, and if she accepts the deal, it means she has relinquished her right to any other part of the property. Yochanan's relatives appreciated the advice and followed it, but when their father finally passed away, they came before Reish Lakish and were shocked to hear a starkly different judgment. When the father was alive, Reish Lakish said, he provided for his wife at a very high level, and she was now accustomed to living the good life. You may not deprive her of it, he said, no matter what arrangements you had previously made.

"But Rabbi Yochanan did not say so," the aggrieved relatives cried out. This annoyed Reish Lakish. "Go and give her all she requires," he hissed, adding that if they refused, he would treat them so harshly that they would forget all about Yochanan's original ruling. The relatives, of course, then ran to Yochanan to complain, but he just smiled. "What can I do?" he said. "I cannot impose my opinion, as a man equal to me disagrees with me."[36]

What followed was a master class showing the two giants at work. What, the Talmud asked, did the husband mean by that additional plot of land? Did he present it as an add-on to the wife's already ample resources, in which case he'd done nothing but inflate her allowance? Or was he very clear that the newly designated plot of land was now the wife's sole source of income, in which case she may take only it but nothing more? The case, Yochanan admitted, wasn't sufficiently clear, which meant that Reish Lakish was right to rule in the woman's favor, as, whenever there's confusion, compassion should always carry the day.

Together, Yochanan and Reish Lakish continued to turn the Mishnah's teachings into legal precedents. They continued to argue, sometimes bitterly, with Yochanan usually triumphant and Reish Lakish usually subdued. But unlike Rav and Shmuel, they weren't separated by many miles and many years of age and two very different styles. They were peers, like Lewis and Tolkien, occupying the same space at the same time, close to each other in mind and in heart. They were Torah scholars, which meant that they were primarily interested in seeing their disagreements shape Jewish law. But they were also human, which meant that they ran the risk of eventually succumbing to their baser instincts, letting jealousy and acrimony seep in and take the place of camaraderie and shared purpose. And as is befitting two such larger-than-life figures, their final act was just as dramatic as their first.

Yochanan and Reish Lakish and their friends, the Talmud narrates, were sitting in the house of study one day and debating what made a weapon—a sword, a knife, or a dagger—susceptible to ritual impurity. The halacha teaches that metal vessels can become impure only from the moment their manufacturing is complete; what, they then asked, did that mean when it came to blades? When, in other words, was a blade considered fully manufactured and done?

Yochanan, who knew very little about weapons, opined that a sword was fully a sword from the moment it was placed in the furnace for forging. Reish Lakish snickered in response. The moment you put any metal in the furnace, he said, is the moment it grows softest, so that it may be further molded. It's actually the least swordlike when it's in the fire; only when you scour a sword in water after removing it from the furnace does it cool down, harden, and become the weapon we know and need.

Livid at hearing his friend deliver such a concise and definitive refutation, Yochanan lost his cool. "A bandit knows about his banditry," he said cruelly. Reish Lakish could have responded by reminding Yochanan, calmly and respectfully, that Judaism absolutely forbade reminding a repentant person of his former misdeeds. Instead, he opted for a more emotional retort.

"What benefit did you provide me by bringing me close to Torah?" he asked. "There, among the bandits, they called me: Leader of the bandits, and here, too, they call me: Leader of the bandits." What have I gained for all my labor if I'm still being treated as a villain?

"I provided benefit to you," Yochanan replied imperiously, too proud to see his friend hurting. "I brought you close to God, under the wings of the Divine Presence."

This was too much for Reish Lakish to take. He stormed out of the house of study and ran home, where he promptly fell ill.

His life, he felt, had been in vain. He dedicated his years to study only to now be denigrated as a lowly thief. He devoted his love to his friend, only to now be put down in a merciless way. He was ready to die.

Seeing this, Reish Lakish's wife, Yochanan's sister, ran to her brother and begged him to pray for Reish Lakish's recovery. Do so, she said, for the sake of my children; I don't want them to grow up without a father.

But Yochanan's brilliance, his ego, his insecurity—all pushed him too far. He no longer cared for the Talmudic principle of friendship, which encouraged combat but forbade destruction. He wanted to assert his supremacy, and he did so in the only manner he knew how—by citing a verse of Torah.

"Leave your fatherless children," he said to his sister, quoting Jeremiah 49:11, "I will rear them." The sister, shocked by Yochanan's unfeeling arrogance, continued to beg, telling her brother that if her children were of no concern to him, perhaps he would pray for Reish Lakish's well-being so that she herself was not rendered a widow. Yochanan merely quoted the rest of the verse: "And let your widows trust in Me." The sister returned home, heartbroken. A few days later, Reish Lakish died.

The news sent Rabbi Yochanan into a fit of madness. All at once, he realized what he had done. He had succumbed to arrogance and fear, choosing his own pride over the difficult and challenging but ultimately life-giving friendship he had enjoyed with Reish Lakish. Now his friend was dead, and there was nothing he could do to bring him back. And so, Yochanan walked all over town howling in grief, no longer the handsome and magisterial master but instead a broken man wild with suffering.

Seeing him, the other rabbis were at a loss. Someone had to try to comfort Yochanan, they decided, but who? Their teacher, they knew, was a devilishly clever man, a thinker and an orator unlike any other, and now grief had made him unhinged. Anyone attempting to reason with him, therefore, could very well be assaulted, verbally or otherwise. After much deliberation, they decided that a young man named Elazar ben Pedat should go. "He is clever," they said, "and will be able to serve as a substitute for Reish Lakish."

With a heavy heart, poor ben Pedat paid Yochanan a visit. He let the older man talk, and anytime he did, ben Pedat tried to please him by saying, "There is a ruling which is taught that supports your opinion." What Yochanan needed in his dark hour, ben Pedat assumed, was the comfort that comes from validation, affirmation, and support.

That only made Yochanan angrier.

"Are you comparable to the son of Lakish?" he said sharply, referring to his late friend. "In my discussions with the son of Lakish, when I would state a matter, he would raise twenty-four difficulties against me in an attempt to disprove my claim, and I would answer him with twenty-four answers, and the halacha by itself would become broadened and clarified. And yet you say to me: There is a ruling which is taught that supports your opinion. Do I not know that what I say is good? Being rebutted by Reish Lakish served a purpose. Your bringing proof to my statements does not."

And with that, Yochanan stood up, tore his clothes, and started weeping and shouting: "Where are you, son of Lakish? Where are you, son of Lakish?" He had finally taken leave of his senses and had gone irreparably insane. Ben Pedat returned to the house of study and reported all that he saw to his colleagues. There was no choice now, they agreed, but to hope that Rabbi Yochanan merited a quick and painless deliverance. They prayed for God to have mercy on his soul, and immediately Rabbi Yochanan died.[37]

Could it have gone any differently? Could Yochanan and Reish Lakish have emulated Rav and Shmuel, deciding to separate before acrimony ensued? Or were they always destined, like Tolkien and Lewis, to have their contentious friendship end in one awkward chat followed by an unhappy ending? The Talmud doesn't say. But the story of these two tragic friends continues to occupy an oversized place in the hearts and minds of students to this day, not in spite of but because of its complications. Yochanan and Reish Lakish tried to be friends in the ideal Talmudic way, and their failure takes nothing away from the nobility of their efforts.

Reish Lakish held a mirror in front of Yochanan, showing him his own coldness and arrogance. Yochanan responded by proving to Reish Lakish that for all of his piety and brilliance, he was still a work in progress. Rav reminded Shmuel that when it came to the Mishnah, he had much to learn. Shmuel forced Rav to acknowledge that his own intellectual and interpretative abilities were lacking. Tolkien urged Lewis to pay more attention to the intricate structures of mythology, and Lewis responded by reminding his friend that telling moving stories and being kind to your friends were just as important, if not more, as fretting about linguistics. And throughout all of this emotional turbulence—all the insults and name-calling, all the small torments and big fights—these men remained close, bound by their commitment to the larger cause of distilling their culture into something stronger and purer.

You may say that none of the above were truly friendships, or at least not as we understand the term today. Was there real warmth between Rav and Shmuel? Doubtful. Did Tolkien truly care for Lewis, not only as a brilliant reader and promoter but as an intimate? Maybe, and maybe not. And there's little to suggest that Yochanan went to any lengths to rush to Reish Lakish's aid or support him in any way. But when it comes to the way we think about friendships, we could use some course correction. We could use a gentle nudge away from our expectation of mutual affection and toward something less feeling but more generative. Rav and Shmuel and Yochanan and Reish Lakish taught us, and Tolkien and Lewis agreed, that there's another path in friendship. They believed that two friends owe each other little more than to make each other sharper in the service of a cause bigger and more meaningful than both. It may not have been an idea that produced very content people, but it did help produce very sharp ones.

Now that they'd learned how to sharpen each other by engaging in endless bouts of intellectual sparring, and now that they had a set of solid rules in the Mishnah, it was time for the rabbis to meet their final and, arguably, most daunting challenge, the challenge of figuring out how to tell their story to generations not yet born.

CHAPTER SEVEN

The Stories We Tell

or

How to Find Your Voice

ALL ALDRICH HAZEN AMES, known to his friends as Rick, ever wanted was to be in theater. His father lectured at the local Wisconsin State College–River Falls, and his mother taught high school English, and nothing about small-town American life struck Ames as particularly promising. There was a moment, soon after his eleventh birthday, when life became thrilling. His father had somehow secured a job with a new federal bureaucracy, the Central Intelligence Agency, and was shipped along with his family to Southeast Asia. But that was short-lived, because Carleton Ames was an alcoholic, and his superiors soon noted that a man like him had no business being a spy. He was promptly returned to Virginia, to a dreary desk job and a suburban life that struck his oldest son as stifling.[1]

Ames wasn't the only kid in class whose father worked "for the government"—McLean, Virginia, was a company town. To stand out, and to make something interesting of his life, the young teenager joined the drama club and flourished both onstage and off, enjoying the manual labor involved in building elaborate sets. In the summertime, to earn some pocket change, he was grateful for a part-time gig with the Agency, preparing classified documents for storage. He graduated high school in 1959 and entered the University of Chicago. He told his mom he was studying history and foreign cultures, but most of his time was spent at this theater or that, and by the middle of his sophomore year, he dropped out and took a job as an assistant technical director with a local drama company.

Backstage life suited Ames just fine. It was fascinating, he thought, to see the play unfurl from the other side of the curtain, to be the one controlling the levers and lights that made the theatrics on display cohere. But the life of a stagehand wasn't the one his middle-class parents had wished on their bright and affable boy, and they pressured him to find a more promising and stable career. Ames returned to the Washington, D.C., area and took the only job he could easily find, doing exactly what he'd done as a summer intern.

Back at CIA headquarters packing up boxes of files, Ames realized that if he wanted to move up from the basement, he had to turn things around. He registered at George Washington University, finally finishing that history degree, and took his work at the Agency seriously enough to merit admission into a junior training program, where he did fine. Sure, there were a few instances of public intoxication and excessive inebriation, but Ames's superiors didn't think much of it. Besides, he had just gotten married to Nancy, a young woman he met in the program, and a life of service, they thought, would mellow him out.

He was shipped to Ankara, Turkey, where he quickly proved to be a much better operative than his father. The major threat to American interests in the country at the time was the Marxist guerilla group known as the Revolutionary Youth, which set fire to the American ambassador's car and violently pushed a few of the sailors of the Sixth Fleet into the sea. The CIA set him to finding out who was in the secretive and paranoid student-led group. But how? The lessons he'd learned in Chicago proved priceless: Whenever some big drama unfurled, Ames knew, the key to getting the inside track on it was to walk a fine line. A good backstage guy knows very well that he's not star material; he neither seeks nor accepts the limelight, because doing so would put him in direct and immediate competition with the actors he's there to serve. But he can't afford to be too reticent, either, as folks in the dramatic arts don't wish to be surrounded by unfeeling technocrats who don't particularly care for the magic onstage. A good backstage guy, then, weaves together the dullness of the craft—all those carefully timed levers and lights—with just enough flair to be trusted and embraced. And Ames was a very, very good backstage guy: soon, one of his newfound student friends told him that his roommate, a charismatic law student named Deniz Gezmis, looked like he was up to no good. Ames poked around and learned that Gezmis was the founding leader of the People's Liberation Army of Turkey and widely considered the local version of Che Guevara. Based in part on Ames's work, Gezmis was arrested, tried, and hanged.

Overjoyed, Ames's superiors decided he was ready for the big time, which meant hunting down Soviet spies. Before too long, he was sent to New York City and entrusted with cultivating and handling some of the Agency's prime informers. He was so good at his job that the suits at Langley didn't much mind that he drank way too much or that he was prone to sloppy mistakes, like leaving top-secret documents on the subway. The Soviet stool pigeons trusted him, talked to him, and delivered the right information at the right clip, and Ames wrote it all down faithfully and passed it along. From Manhattan it was onward to Mexico City, where he met and fell in love with Maria, a cultural attaché at the Colombian Embassy. He divorced Nancy, married Maria, and soon found himself back stateside, his debts mounting. Nancy was entitled to alimony, and Maria spent hundreds of dollars every month on long-distance calls to her family in Colombia, assuaging her loneliness with the occasional shopping spree. Ames needed money, a lot of it, and quickly. And there was only one way he knew to get it.

At the time, his job was figuring out which of the Soviet Embassy's employees might consider crossing the line, which meant that he was routinely in touch with the enemy. In one of these clandestine encounters, Ames made the Soviets an offer they couldn't refuse: give him cash payments for information.

He crafted his communications like a good play. At first, he delivered dribs and drabs, useless information that, when analyzed, taught the Soviets little except the fact that their new American friend was in a position to tell them much more interesting things. He started having lunch each week with Sergey Dmitriyevich Chuvakhin, the Soviet Embassy's First Secretary, receiving between $20,000 and $50,000 in an envelope each time. The payments vastly expedited the pace of Ames's stories. He knew what his audience wanted, and knew, too, that he had to deliver. He could no longer be a stagehand. He was now forced to be the hero of the story, an actor standing in the limelight, everything he'd always sought to avoid. And so, each week, like a secret Scheherazade, he told another tale of another spy.

Soon, Ames's superiors started noticing that their best informants were disappearing at an alarming rate. Gennady Varenik, code name GTFITNESS, a Russian correspondent in East Berlin who furnished the CIA with the names of 170 Soviet agents, was suddenly summoned to Moscow, tried for treason, and summarily executed. Dmitri Polyakov, code name BOURBON, a Soviet major general who had provided Henry Kissinger with the insights he needed to make Nixon's trip to China possible, was captured and shot. Others soon followed.

At first, the CIA thought it was just bad luck. Then, when assets kept going dark, the Agency investigated the possibility of a code being broken and looked for wiretaps in its offices. No one wanted to believe that the world's greatest spy agency could be betrayed by one of its own. But when one informant after another ended up with a bullet in the head, Langley finally started searching for a mole.

Reviewing the evidence on hand objectively, you might wonder why it took the Agency as long as it did to find out the truth about Ames. Had they merely driven by his home, they would have learned that a midlevel staffer earning $60,000 a year was living in a sprawling $540,000 home in Arlington, paid for in full and in cash. Or they might have noticed that he drove a brand-new Jag to the office every day, or that he was now wearing not his usual droopy, cheap suits but fine couture, or that he had invested in dental procedures to make his teeth, yellowed by nicotine, white again. But even had these facts been recorded, they might not have raised any eyebrows. The CIA at the time was still very much a clubhouse for adventurous upper-crust men who, like the Princeton-educated Donald Wilber, served as presidents of rare rug collecting clubs and received doctorates in architectural history and wrote charming treatises on antiquity when not orchestrating regime change halfway across the world. Reckless spending was hardly out of the ordinary, and the money, Ames told his colleagues, came from his new wife's rich parents.

It was a good story because, like all the best stories, it contained multitudes. Ames wasn't merely covering his tracks—that would have been easy enough to do, considering he had offshore bank accounts and could have easily squirreled away the money without anyone noticing. Instead, he was hiding in plain sight, courtesy of a cover story that was sufficiently layered and imperfect and unresolved as to feel absolutely authentic. Even as he was struggling to adjust to his role as an actor rather than an observer, he knew his colleagues' vices well—the drinking, the splurging, the adventurous streaks that sometimes led to missteps—and played out his life in ways he knew they'd understand. And he was such a competent storyteller, fully embodying his fictions, that he effortlessly aced two lie detector tests, buying himself more time.

Eventually, though, the Agency sobered up. It took nearly a

decade and a host of false starts and accusations, but when the mole-hunting team decided to use all of its resources to look into Ames's life—including combing through his trash and bugging his car—they soon discovered that he was their guy.

On President's Day of 1994, Ames's boss, Dave Edgers, called him early in the morning. He apologized for troubling Ames on a federal holiday, but said he'd love it if the two could meet briefly at the office to discuss some pressing matter before an upcoming work trip. Ames left the house shortly thereafter. A cigarette hanging from his mouth, he got into his Jaguar and made a right on North Quebec Street. Before he could make a left at the next intersection, he was approached by FBI agents and arrested. He admitted everything in court. Before being sentenced to life without the possibility of parole, he told investigators that becoming the most significant Soviet spy America had ever seen was surprisingly easy; all he had to do, he said, was disappear into his story.

The rabbis who redacted the Talmud would agree.

Their names were Ravina and Rav Ashi, and they both lived in Babylonia in the fifth century. They were the last of the Amoraim, the sages—including Shmuel, Yochanan, and Reish Lakish—who spent two centuries parsing the Mishnah, affixing their commentaries and interpretations and raising a torrent of questions so thick that it eventually became the Gemara.

What do we know about these magisterial compilers? The man who compiled the Mishnah, after all, the great Rebbi, is accessible to us in all his splendor. We know of his ailments and friendships, his rulings and misgivings, his observations and apprehensions. He is available to us like a character in a great classical novel, as if Balzac himself had turned his attention to Jewish antiquity and given us a man as glorious as he is flawed. We understand his mission, too: The oral teachings that Jews believe were passed down by God to Moses and from him onward to each successive generation were in danger of being forgotten, and so Rebbi codified them and wrote them down. Few mysteries there. But hear someone these days tell you that they're studying the Talmud, and it's very likely that what they're actually doing is turning their attention to the Gemara, which cites the Mishnah briefly before proceeding on its own investigations. What can be said, then, of the men who shaped the Gemara?

A story comes readily to mind. One day, the Talmud tells us, the Angel of Death appeared to Rav Ashi in the marketplace. Understanding that it was his time to depart this earthly plane, Rav Ashi was nonetheless unbowed. They say, he sweetly cooed to the Grim Reaper, that anyone who ascends to heaven with his knowledge of the Torah strong and intact is richly rewarded; won't you be a dear and give me thirty more days so that I might review my studies and go out strong?

Not even the Angel of Death could refuse such a reasonable request from such a prominent man, who had been by then the aged leader of the Babylonian Jewish community for more than six decades. But on the thirtieth day, the Reaper, no fool, appeared again to complete the transaction. This time, Rav Ashi was less sweet. Say, he poked at the Angel, why are you in such a hurry to take me anyway? What gives?

Simple, said the Angel of Death: "The foot of Rav Huna bar Natan is pushing you, as he is ready to succeed you as the leader of the generation, and one sovereignty does not overlap with its counterpart, even by one hairsbreadth. Therefore, you cannot live any longer."[2] And with that, Rav Ashi died.

It hardly takes a Talmudic scholar to realize that little about the story adds up. Why would the Angel of Death enter into negotiations with a mere mortal in the first place? And why would the angel then reveal themself to be not the omnipotent and terrible harvester of souls but rather a foreman of sorts for the affairs of humans, only removing one rabbi so that the next may succeed him in due order? And, most startlingly, how can the Talmud, redacted by Rav Ashi, contain a story about the death of . . . Rav Ashi?

This final conundrum in particular has haunted scholars for

centuries, and they produced answers that were far from decisive. Who was Rav Ashi's father? Who were his teachers? And who, exactly, recorded the story of his death if he was allegedly, according to widely accepted tradition, the final editor of the Talmud? Similar questions arose about his friend and student Ravina, who is mentioned 902 times in the Talmud and yet leaves so few biographical details behind that researchers now believe there were anywhere from three to five rabbis named Ravina, living generations apart and melding somehow into a single composite character.[3]

For hundreds of years, the rabbis recorded lineages and opinions with obsessive meticulousness; yet when their project, the task of committing the oral law to writing in perpetuity, came to an end, they took a radically different approach. Why? Because they were worldly men who realized that they were pawns in a large global game that they had no power to control. For one thing, they were subject to the whims of a long and rapidly changing succession of kings. For another, they were rarely guaranteed the obedience of their own followers. Erecting a rigid legal framework and demanding fealty, therefore, wouldn't work; neither would hoping that each generation produced as many brilliant and capable minds as the previous one. Instead, their best bet was to do what all people trying to survive in a highly ambiguous and tenuous and ever-shifting reality do: tell stories that were equal parts background and foreground, rich and layered, and make them inviting to anyone who would listen, suspend disbelief, and join in.

But stories, the rabbis understood very well, were powerful and combustible things. Stories could drive men to abandon reason, defy reality, and go mad. They could deceive entire nations, and easily turn, as they had for Ames, into a scoundrel's retreat. How to keep their stories from souring into something selfish or solipsistic or cruel? How to make sure devious and inventive men—Ames, again, comes to mind—wouldn't seize the story and use it to further their own treasonous ends? The rabbis had known their share of heretics, men like the cursed Acher, who had taken all they'd learned and used it to betray their people. And so they were adamant about crafting a style of storytelling that was steeped in kindness. They would assert their authority while at the very same time admitting that they were powerless before the primal urges that drove human beings to appease their appetites at any cost. And they would lay down the law while at the same time acknowledging that laws alone carried very little weight for the human species. They would recognize all the myriad forces converging to tear their way of life apart, yet they would will their way to survival simply by telling a better, more propulsive story than the grim one that unfolded around them.

To make that possible, Ravina and Rav Ashi had to do more than merely convey the laws as they were understood—the way the Mishnah had—or record reams of arguments, as generations of Amoraim before them had done. They needed to invent a brand-new genre. The late Rabbi Adin Steinsaltz, who translated the Talmud into modern-day English and is considered one of its greatest students, explained this idea movingly. "Rav Ashi," he wrote, "wanted to preserve in the Talmud not the Halachic ruling or this or that topic but rather movement itself—inside a book that can no longer move or renew. Not as an engineer building a house but as an artist trying to bring a sculpture to life, Rav Ashi sought to do something seemingly impossible—preserve the movement and the flexibility, the questions without answers and the inquisitive spirit tackling problems—inside a format that's written, edited, and defined."[4] And the first step toward that format required shattering the barriers between legal code and tall tale.

For centuries, students of the Talmud had assumed that their beloved book was really two works inconveniently crammed into one. One half of it was halacha, or Jewish law, hundreds and hundreds of pages of discussions of impossibly intricate machinations, requirements, and punitive measures. If you can conceive of a real-life question pertaining to the commandments of the Torah, it's almost certain that the Talmud devotes a few lengthy passages to discussing it in depth, emerging, if not with an answer, then at least with a thorough understanding of the issue to allow rabbinic courts to pass judgment. On the other hand, the Talmud's other half was devoted to Aggadah, a word literally meaning "legend" or "story" and used to refer to anything that isn't a clear analysis of legal principles. Naturally, bickering camps soon emerged, one arguing that teaching the law alone is the purpose of the Talmud and that all those silly fairy tales—rabbis haggling with the Angel of Death! Flatulent prostitutes!—were merely a distraction from the intellectual work of trying to understand God's words. The other held that too much legalese made minds wither and that no lesson was taught better than the one conveyed by means of a lively yarn. Some rabbis even attempted to excise their least favorite elements from the Talmud, publishing, for example, volumes consisting solely of halacha or others compiling nothing but the Talmud's stories. But as scholars have recently and increasingly come to believe, it was precisely the tethering of these two elements that was Rav Ashi and Ravina's brilliant insight. They understood that laws without stories were abstractions and that stories without laws were distractions. To make real and lasting sense, they needed to come together.

Here, for example, is the Talmud in Tractate Yoma, devoted to Yom Kippur, the Day of Atonement, which is the holiest day of the Jewish calendar. On this day, we're told, we are required to repent before God and man. The former is all merciful and forgiving; the latter, however, can truly be a handful. Merely saying "sorry" isn't enough. How, then, ought we to go about the delicate business of asking someone we wronged for forgiveness?

Simple, says the Talmud, drawing proof, as ever, from the Bible. First, understand that there are two ways you can wrong friends: you might have wronged them by failing to pay them back money you owed, in which case you should repay your debt right away, or you might have wronged them by speaking to or about them unkindly, in which case you should send messengers their way to beg them to accept your upcoming apology. And why send messengers first? The Talmud offers a ready answer: Because the people you've wronged are likely mad at you, and seeing you at their doorstep may cause them to lose their cool. Better, then, to first dispatch emissaries to prepare them for the upcoming apology, which increases the chances of the apology being accepted.

And if it isn't? The Talmud offers laws for this occasion, too. "Rabbi Yosei bar Hanina," it instructs us, "said: Anyone who asks forgiveness of his friend should not ask more than three times, as it is stated: 'Please, please forgive the transgression of your brothers and their sin, for they did evil to you. And now, please forgive' (Genesis 50:17). The verse uses the word please three times, which shows that one need not ask more than three times, after which the insulted friend must be appeased and forgive." And if said friend fails to do so, he is no longer entitled to an apology. In fact, the Talmud concludes, it is now he who is in the wrong and must apologize.

So far, so good! Anyone curious about the laws of saying sorry may simply turn to the Talmud and receive clear and comprehensive instruction, providing not only laws but also their reasoning. Just as Joseph's brothers in Genesis apologized three times for the nasty business of throwing their sibling down a pit and selling him into slavery, so, too, must anyone seeking forgiveness apologize thrice and no more. Hallelujah. But then the Talmud takes an unexpected turn.

Rabbi Yirmeya, it tells us without skipping a beat, once insulted his colleague, Rabbi Abba. Feeling bad about the whole affair, Yirmeya sat in front of Abba's house, waiting for the right moment to ask his pal for forgiveness. Just then, however, Abba's maid emptied Rabbi Abba's bedchamber the way folks did back then—by pouring it out the window, straight onto Rabbi Yirmeya's head. "They have made me into a trash heap," the stunned and soiled rabbi said to himself, but then a smile came to his face as he remembered Psalms 113:7 and that bit about God "who lifts up the needy out of the trash heap." Being humiliated, he realized, was a sign of redemption to come. And, indeed, Rabbi Abba, witnessing this smelly mistake, ran out, greeted his friend, and apologized to him with another verse: "Go, humble yourself and urge your neighbor."[5]

Did we really need this quirky little tale? The law itself, after all, is clear enough, and a dash of slapstick—the tried-and-true poop joke—seems to add little to the proceedings. But the story, as a number of scholars have noted, is precisely what makes the law come alive. "The self-humiliation of the wrongdoer in his act of apology almost forces the victim to accept the apology," wrote Yeshiva University's Richard Hidary in his analysis of the tale. "This is the psychological mechanism that is behind the legal principle noted above—that one who refuses to be pacified even after three apologies incurs the guilt upon himself."[6] The French Jewish philosopher Emmanuel Levinas took things a step further. The story, he observed, isn't just adjacent to the legal discussion; it is its engine of moral growth, its beating heart, its essence. "Strict justice," Levinas observed, "even if flanked by disinterested goodness and humility, is not sufficient to make a Jew. Justice itself must already be mixed with goodness."[7] And that's precisely what a great story is: a mix of justice and goodness, of law and human example, of that which is true regardless of circumstances and that which lives only in the moment, precious and fleeting and impossible to replicate.

Coming after five generations of Amoraim diligently studying the Mishnah, Ravina and Rav Ashi knew that for these discussions to withstand the test of time, they would have to commit them to paper in a way that melted together law and legend. Their insight remains surprisingly startling and fresh; this precise mixture, Harvard law scholar Martha Minow recently argued, is just the course corrective that our own exhausted legal system needs. "Stories," she wrote nearly sixteen hundred years after Rav Ashi and Ravina's passing, "are weak against the imperializing modes of analysis that seek general and universal application. But their very weakness is a virtue to be emulated. A story also invites more stories, stories that challenge the first one, or embellish it, or recast it. This, too, is a virtue to be copied. And stories at the moment seem better able to evoke realms of meaning, remembrance, commitment, and human agency than some other method of human explanation. All this might change if theorizing picks up some of the themes of stories, but, then again, it might not."[8]

But weaving together legalistic discussions with rousing stories is one thing; making the two cohere into a singular work is another. How could Rav Ashi and Ravina make sure that readers understood that the Talmud wasn't a reference book only to be consulted in case of emergency, but rather a living instruction, a rich and strange work that required absolute immersion? To answer this question, we must make the acquaintance of the Talmud's greatest hero, as omnipresent as it is unsung—the *stam*.

Hebrew for "plain voice," the *stam* is the nearly invisible narration that ties the Talmud's parts together, the superglue that binds so many disparate elements into one unparalleled text that reads much more like a postmodern stream of consciousness than a document painstakingly pasted together eons ago over centuries. Before it is analyzed, discussed, and explained, it has to be experienced. Here we go.

At one point in the Talmud's Tractate Sanhedrin, Rav Yehuda recounts a story told to him by his teacher, Rav. Once upon a time, the tale goes, "a certain man . . . set his eyes upon a certain woman and passion rose in his heart, to the point that he became deathly ill." Concerned, the rabbis brought the man to see the finest doctors available to ask what might be done to save the man's life. No doubt about it, said the doctors: the only cure is for the gentleman to have sex with the lady he so desires.

"Let him die," replied the rabbis, "and she may not engage in sexual intercourse with him."

The doctors were not surprised. Judaism, they knew, did not permit casual carnal encounters. Nor did it consider women's bodies the property of men to use and abuse at their pleasure. Naturally, then, sex was out of the question. Still, a man was on the brink of death, and so the doctors proposed a compromise: let the woman come and stand naked before the fading patient.

"Let him die," replied the rabbis, "and she may not stand naked before him."

The doctors were flustered. Eager to prescribe some course of treatment, they offered one more diminished alternative: let the woman at least stand behind a fence in a secluded area and talk to the man for a brief while, so that he should have a few fleeting moments of pleasure in her company.

"Let him die," replied the rabbis, "and she may not converse with him behind a fence."

Then, without taking any time to explore this strange and loaded scene, we get a sharp transition to another conversation by two rabbis who lived about a century later, Rabbi Ya'akov bar Idi and Rabbi Shmuel bar Nahmani. The woman in question, said the former, was a married woman. Not so, said the latter, she was single. Why is that distinction significant? Here the Talmud stops functioning as a faithful recorder of rabbinic disputes and slips into its *stam* voice to explain: "According to the one who says that she was a married woman, the matter is properly understood." No difficulty there! The rabbis in the story prescribed death over even the merest intimation of impropriety because the Torah strictly and severely prohibits intimacy of any sort between men and women who aren't married. "But," the *stam* continues, "according to the one who says that she was unmarried, what is the reason for all this opposition? Why did the Sages say that the man must be allowed to die, rather than have the woman do as was requested?"

The question itself matters much more than the answer. First and foremost, it's a criticism, and a not-so-subtle one, at that, of the rabbis in the story. Clearly, their statements—let him die, let him die, let him die, repeated three times to great emotional and literary effect—are problematic. Any sensible person can understand, and admire, their adamant refusal to force a woman into nonconsensual sex; let him die lest she be raped. Amen. But as the doctors' proposals grow milder and milder, the rabbis' obdurate stance, expressed in the exact same words and the exact same stentorian tone, grows increasingly bizarre. Do they really think it's best to let a man die rather than ask a woman to speak to him from behind the safety and seclusion of a fence? And if not, could they not have, at the very least, chosen different, softer words, if only to make us understand that they, too, realize there's a difference between intercourse and conversation?

We needn't, however, raise any of these objections. The *stam* raises them for us, just as committed to questioning the opinions of the rabbis as it is to reporting them verbatim. "The *stam*," wrote Northwestern University's Barry Wimpfheimer, an insightful Talmudic scholar, "is a different author than one with which contemporary readers are familiar." On every page of the Talmud, "one encounters the *stam* as a writer who is also a reader. The *stam* interprets the early materials by introducing them, interpreting them, and commenting upon them."[9]

But to what end? The answer becomes clearer as the story continues to unfurl. True to form, the Talmud begins to address the question by providing two more rabbinic opinions. Even if the woman in question was unmarried, says Rav Pappa, she shouldn't be seen cavorting with the lovesick gent, as doing so would bring shame to her family. That's not the reason, Rav Aha butts in; the real reason is much simpler. If the woman, unmarried and available as she may be, followed the doctors' advice and got cozy with the man who so desperately desired her, it might loosen her moral restraint. If we want people to remain pious, we can't create precedents that permit them to test the boundaries of propriety.

Stop there, and what you've got is a perfectly serviceable running commentary, an explanation that doubtless satisfies anyone deeply interested in the legal reasoning of the rabbis—a very small readership, that—but no one else in particular. Once again, hallelujah, the *stam* rides to the rescue.

"But if the woman was unmarried," the Talmud continues in its anonymous *stam* voice, "let the man marry her." The same idea probably occurred to any unschooled reader trying to make sense of the issue at hand. What's the problem? She's single, he's lusting after her, and if she's so inclined, they should just tie the knot and have all the permissible, sanctioned sex they want.

Again, this little question, easy to mistake for a throwaway line, is deceptively deeper than it seems. Why, the *stam* is asking, is this even a problem? Why waste so much space on a hypothetical—complete with stipulations, speculations, and complications—that a reasonable, commonsensical person can address in a straightforward and rather obvious manner? All you have to do, after all, is figure out if these two adults are available, and if they are and are consenting, let them marry and let us hear from them no more. Why waste another minute studying this conundrum?

The *stam* asks, and the *stam* answers, now subtly shifting poses again, from curious reader to wise interpreter. Marrying his inamorata would do little to cure the poor schlub, it says. After all, Rabbi Yitzhak taught us the following: "Since the day the Temple was destroyed, sexual pleasure was taken away from those who engage in permitted intercourse and given to transgressors, as it is stated: 'Stolen waters are sweet, and bread eaten in secret is pleasant' (Proverbs 9:17). Therefore, the man could have been cured only by engaging in illicit sexual interaction."[10]

We are now miles away from where we started. Let us track the course of the story: First, the Talmud delivered an anecdote—a certain man yearning for a certain woman and growing deathly ill as a result—followed by a brief exchange between the doctors and the rabbis. The former devise possible palliative alternatives; the latter reject them on a legal basis. Two commentators then step in to clarify the case, noting, rightly, that we lacked crucial information, since we would adjudicate differently for a married woman than we would for one who was unattached. The Talmud then dismisses one scenario, that of the married woman, as an open-and-shut case and proceeds to summon two additional commentators to provide additional legalistic reasoning to illuminate the other scenario, that of the unmarried woman. And then, just when we think there's nothing more that could possibly be said about this strange tale, the *stam* shows up and takes us right back to the beginning, reexamining the entire premise of the discussion by offering a simple solution that appears to override all rabbinic explanation. And yet, before we've recovered comes the coup de grâce, an opinion, backed by a biblical verse, that, in our fallen world, sexual pleasure is now tragically tethered to illicit desire. Marriage won't help here, the *stam* tells us, because what the lovesick man is really after is the titillating thrill of the forbidden. Make the woman of his dreams his lawful wedded wife, and she'll lose all of her dangerous allure.

At this point, Wimpfheimer notes, it's clear that the story isn't about the forlorn man anymore; it's about the rabbis. "Faced with anxiety about their own marginalization," he wrote, "rabbis could either attempt to assert power or explain its absence."[11] Instead, they chose a third option: write *both* into one dazzling story that uses the mixture of law and legend as a springboard into the deepest philosophical waters imaginable. To read Rabbi Yitzhak's exhortation is to stop in one's tracks and consider morality and mortality. It is to ask if there's any point to law at all, given the beastly nature of our desires and the ever-waning pull of religion in our lives. It is to admit that all earthly authority is limited, and it is to find both comfort and dread in this reckoning. It is, in short, to enter the centuries-old rabbinic debate not as a reader but as a fellow interpreter at first and then, very soon thereafter, as a writer. That's the magic of the *stam*; it is the literary equivalent of a deliberately featureless space—like an airport or a doctor's office waiting room—which makes everyone and no one feel at home. It is, by design, transient, insisting that we use it merely as a point of departure, never a destination. The *stam* isn't here to orate or educate; it's here to agitate, to keep us moving along on our intellectual and moral pursuits.

Where to? Emmanuel Levinas offers an inspiring answer, which might as well serve as the epithet for the entire Talmud: toward the realization that we all "belong—or must belong—to the elite," or the wisest and most diligent and most well-read. The Talmud, Levinas continued, teaches us that "morality begins in us and not in institutions which are not always able to protect it. It demands that human honor know how to exist without a flag." And Jews, having suffered millennia of inhuman cruelty from the Greeks to the Germans, understand very well the idea that remaining moral under the most trying circumstances is truly a superpower. Being truly moral, Levinas wrote, means "finding within oneself the source of one's moral certainties. He knows that only a hedge of roses separates him from his own fall."[12]

But how to maintain this superpower? How to avoid the temptation that swept another master storyteller, Aldrich Ames? Here, Ravina and Rav Ashi had the toughest insight of them all: By disappearing. By fading into the *stam*. By declaring that generations of rabbinic prominence have come to an end and that the story now belongs to everyone interested in it. By doing so, they allowed their successors to continue and to tweak the Talmud—hence the story about Rav Ashi's death, inserted by colleagues who survived him. But, more importantly, they allowed us all to join them on an equal footing. And when we do, we, too, are reminded to read and write our life stories just as the Talmud teaches us: not as heroic epics—those always end in downfall—but as complicated collaborations between people and ideas and emotions, complementary but never complete. Life stories never end, not even in death. Nor do they cohere into a single, shining moral. They merely instruct, gently but surely, guiding us, although none are quite like us, along the same path so many have walked down before.

EPILOGUE

LIKE SO many others before me, I only came to the Talmud when things started falling apart.

Descending from a long line of rabbis, I'd seen the book before, but it was not, I was convinced, for me. I wasn't an observant Jew and so had no use for ancient edicts and obscure arguments about levirate marriages and goring oxen. I was a middle-of-the-road liberal with a healthy skepticism of everything and anything that felt too zealous or too sweeping. And being a creature of contemporary pop culture, I was much more at home with Rambo than with the Rambam. Let the bearded believers pore over their tomes, I thought, and let me cherish the great cornucopia of other cultures, from Achilles to Batman.

And then came one fateful week, early in November 2016. I was a few days shy of my fortieth birthday, and I was in good shape and feeling optimistic about the future. On Saturday, I had written a note to Leonard Cohen, who I had the pleasure of getting to know while writing a short biography of him, my favorite artist. I told him that I'd be running in the New York City marathon the following day and that while his songs weren't exactly what you'd call workout music, when you're trying to cross long and harrowing distances, you might as well summon a hallelujah or two. He responded like a kindly grandfather, urging me not to be a hero and to stop if it hurt too much. He consoled me with a promise that we would meet again soon, maybe even in a few weeks' time. He signed his note in Hebrew: *hazak hazak ve'nithazek*, we are strong and we shall get stronger.

I was thinking about this cheerful mantra the next day, running through the streets of Brooklyn, cheered on by so many kind neighbors who'd come out to show their love and support. Dominican grandmothers, Haitian dads with their boys on their shoulders, young Hasidic men in their black hats and coats, Chinese girls clapping enthusiastically—the borough was a promise of America coming together, a gorgeous mosaic of ethnicities and beliefs and sensibilities. I ran fast, high on hope and endorphins. And then, somewhere on the Kosciuszko Bridge connecting Brooklyn and Queens, I heard something snap.

Three seconds later, a wave of pain propelled me to the railing, where I stopped and vomited more intensely than I ever had before in my life. I wobbled over to a nearby infirmary tent and was informed by a bored-looking young medic that I'd probably torn something or strained something or hurt myself somehow. It was common at my age, he said, making me feel like a relic. Then he pointed me toward a nearby van that would drive me wherever I wanted to go.

I looked at the van, and then at the man. I thought of Leonard. I muttered a brief "no thank you," and before either he or I had the chance to grow wise, I ran out and down the street. "Ran" may be a misnomer—the pain was awful, and all I could manage for the remaining 12 miles or so that separated me from the finish line was a hoppy sort of hobbling, the sort you see baby birds attempting when they've just hatched and are learning to walk. I completed the race more than seven hours after starting it, physically shattered but emotionally strong. It was going to be a good year.

That was Sunday. The following Tuesday, the nation witnessed one of the strangest elections in its history, and with it chaos and rancor and fear. Wednesday was my birthday, passed largely in a daze, trying to make sense of what felt like a stark new reality scrubbed of the joy and promise I'd felt while running through the streets of New York. On Thursday, sensing my despair, my wife took me out to dinner at a favorite Italian restaurant. The martini hadn't even touched my lips when I received a text message informing me that Leonard had died.

It was all downhill from there.

Ideological inflammations on all sides left me feeling, for the first time in my adult life, politically homeless. To suggest that there might be well-meaning if misguided folks on the other side of any combustible political question became anathema. It was tribal time, and I refused to join a team, even as several of my nearest and dearest issued heartbreaking ultimatums that I'd lose their friendship.

My body must have picked up on my heartbreak, because it, too, was cracking in strange ways. A walk through a park in the Bronx ended with a tick bite, undiscovered for months. Intense fevers surged, leaving me—a six-foot-five "gentleman of noble proportions," as Leonard would lovingly say—quivering under five or six blankets for hours each day. I lost 145 pounds, along with the ability to consume more than rudimentary amounts of food. Then came COVID, and the turmoil seemed total and complete. Institutions, relationships, expectations, health—all I had ever taken for granted now seemed in flux, all that was solid melting into air. Despairing over the state of the world struck me as counterproductive, and medicating myself with alcohol or Netflix or rage seemed like a losing bet. I needed something to reorient me. I needed—quoting Leonard again—"a manual for living with defeat."[1] I needed some guide to help me help myself.

It came, as real relief always does, almost without notice. A news story reported that more than ninety thousand people packed New Jersey's MetLife stadium to celebrate *Siyum HaShas*, the culmination of a seven-and-a-half-year cycle of reading one page of Talmud every day. In attendance were Orthodox Jews, secular Jews, non-Jews, women, men, the young and old, bound by curiosity and dedication. I was always the bookish sort, and something about this sight—a football stadium crammed with fans of a *book*—struck me as preternaturally hopeful. I was still a little uneasy about the Talmud—Wasn't it notoriously hard? Wasn't it exclusively for the faithful?—but I was also in pain. I needed answers, inspiration, a blueprint, a clue—anything to help me navigate through the turmoil I was feeling. I leaped in, purchased forty-two hefty volumes, and got to work.

To say that this book represents the culmination of my efforts would make the rabbis laugh. Among the many beauties of the Talmud is the fact that you never really finish it. Each tractate concludes with a promise, recited out loud, that we shall return and reread it just as it, too, shall return and revisit us. This isn't just a bit of hokey spirituality. A famous story tells of a boastful student who, eager to impress his rabbi, reported that he'd been through the entire Talmud three times. "And how many times," the wise rabbi retorted, "has the Talmud been through you?"

Letting the Talmud go through me, I learned, first and foremost, how to live in my body. It was a relationship I'd resisted for most of my life: perpetually overweight, nerdy and tragically unskilled at sports, I treated my body as the cumbersome and almost comically inept container for my brain, the true star of the show. I only exercised out of a sense of duty and thought of my corporeal form as the lowly purveyor of earthly pleasures, fun but not fundamental to my mental growth. The thing I called myself lived in my head and my heart and my soul, not my stomach and arms and thighs.

Hillel helped me change all that. I was sitting with my friend Josh Wolk, who practices the Feldenkrais Method of exercise and who has been central in helping me overcome my bodily ailments. When I complained that my shoulder felt frozen and stiff, Josh said, quick, tell me the first things that come to your mind when you hear the word "shoulder." Easy, I replied: shoulder the burden, shoulder the responsibility, a shoulder to lean on. . . . I hardly needed to continue. The prognosis was obvious: Years of working hard and thinking I was obliged to say yes to anything and everything anyone asked of me had taken a toll, and because mind and body are one, that toll now manifested itself in the form of an aching limb. The solution wasn't treating one organ in isolation; the solution was rethinking the way I lived my life and letting my body, not my mind, take the first step on that complicated journey. Just as Hillel knew that a body that couldn't poop also couldn't pray, and just as he'd propelled this insight into a way of being in the world that curbed anger, pride, and physical phenomena we sometimes mistakenly elevate into emotional prominence, I was now learning how to be embodied. In the Talmud, with its intricate discussions of expectorations and ejaculations, I found a guide, as funny and bawdy as it is profound, to thinking my way out of thinking too much, learning to prioritize experience and movement over analysis and abstraction.

But starting to become bodily present was just the first step. Next came a bigger and harder realization: that the work we had to do to repair this fractured place was entirely on us, and that it was, by design, not a mission any one person could ever complete on their own. If you're looking for a silver lining in these years of chaos and rancor, consider this: We now know, beyond a shadow of a doubt, that the cavalry ain't coming. We know that our elected officials, our pundits, our philanthropists, our self-appointed intellectual and moral betters can't save us from sliding further and deeper into discontent. Only we can redeem us, and we can do it by working together in ways that shun the stentorian tones of absolute truths and that seek instead, like Rabbi Yehoshua did, to see each other's humanity, each other's flaws, each other's suffering.

To connect to others in this way, however, we first need to find our true selves, buried under the rubble of other people's expectations, inner and outer societal pressures, temptations and anxieties. For this, we can ask for no better guide than Rabbi Akiva, who knew that it was never too late to become who you were always meant to be and that, once you became that radiant person, there was no better way of showing it than working hard and staying humble. When every technology and reward system at our disposal is urging us to turn ourselves into brands, neatly packaged and easily commoditized, Akiva is here with a reminder that the real work of self-discovery is much more arduous than anything that happens on Instagram or, for that matter, on the therapist's couch. Constructing a self, the Talmud teaches us, isn't a solipsistic undertaking or an invitation to snuggle tightly in our own preoccupations and concerns. Instead, it's a much more difficult—and social—task of constantly asking ourselves what really matters in life and then realizing that the path that leads us to these virtues is one that, by definition, never ends.

Nor, for that matter, might it be traveled alone. Love—reprising Leonard again and for the last time—is our only "engine of survival," and in the Talmud we find a primer on love like no other. In Bruriah and Meir's marriage we've a radically different model than the one hailed by modernity: not, as our contemporary publications would have it, a relationship that empowers two strong and accomplished individuals, but a communion in which two strong and accomplished individuals are transformed by virtue of shared values and self-sacrifice into a sum that's much greater than its parts. Talmudic love isn't a battlefield; it's an altar where sacrifices are offered and language transcends from the mundane to the holy.

And yet, even with a loving spouse by your side, it's hard to know how to bring order into the world. These days, the old definitions—left and right, religious and secular, to name but two of the usual suspects—hardly apply. We gleefully challenge every category, even those, like gender, previously considered relatively solid, because we sense, correctly, that the times they are a-changin' and the old terms no longer apply. We can ask for no better Sherpa than Rebbi when we undertake the Sisyphean task of trying to bring order into something—life—which, by definition, resists it. When too many around us try to lure us in with simple and steely and foolproof ways of approaching the task of living—from thunderous political beliefs to can't-fail diets to get-rich-quick schemes—the Talmud gives us a systematic way of thinking about the world that embraces our drawbacks and weaknesses, distilling them first into introspection and then into cohesion.

Armed with clarity, we're free to fight for what we believe, but the fight, we discover very quickly, is a very public one. Whether it's in our children's school or our workplace, in our city or our state or our nation, we're going to need friends. Friendship, the Talmud teaches us, should never be a celebration of confirming each other's biases while lulling each other into complacency. Friendship can be jagged, often unpleasant, but is one of the few human endeavors dedicated to real growth. Rav and Shmuel, Yochanan and Reish Lakish—these difficult men remind us to seek out friends who sharpen us and force us to confront our worst fears and confront our vulnerabilities and grow. If our goal is rebuilding—our communities, our relationships, ourselves—we can accept no other kind of companion.

When we've done all this work—of figuring out our bodies, our communities, and ourselves, of attaching ourselves to lovers and friends and methods for ordering the world around us—we've one more order of business left: figuring out the story of our lives. Jews have survived for millennia by telling themselves a more compelling story than the grim one forced on them by others. When persecuted, Jews retorted with the words that still conclude each Passover seder: "Next year in Jerusalem," an expression of eternal hope. Jews found meaning and a future in a story of survival. They did so, as Ravina and Rav Ashi teach us, by erasing all traces of an omniscient narrator and creating instead a tale that's pure flow, inviting all readers to participate as coauthors and interpreters in the making of its meaning. Because life, these sages understood, isn't a sprint. It isn't even a marathon. It's a relay race, and the best we could hope for is passing the torch to someone who needs its light and its warmth as badly as we do.

These insights and others I gleaned by studying the Talmud haven't made me an entirely new person. They didn't make me richer or handsomer, didn't drive me to lose 10 pounds or bench-press 50 more. They delivered no ready-made answers to the thorniest political questions of the day and no clear instructions on how to be a better husband, father, or son. But they did change my life, showing me the great strength that can be rooted in weakness, the wisdom that begins to bloom only when you acknowledge how little you know for certain, and the joy that washes over you once you admit just how lonely and afraid you feel. The rabbis I wrote about—and the many others I didn't— aren't just characters in a book or historical figures. They're my *havruta*, my study partners, there for a great argument whenever I'm so inclined. And when I get frustrated by their obsessive attention to the minutiae, they remind me, with a smile and a poke, that God and humans alike are in the details, that big conversations about big ideas so often gel into oppositions and harden into hate but that little inquiries about particulars help us really understand not only the world but also each other. And real understanding, the Talmud reminds us in every line of every page, is about asking questions, not expecting answers.

An old Hasidic tale captures this idea neatly. Once upon a time, it goes, a small shtetl was rocked by very big news: A celebrated rabbi was due to arrive soon, and when he did, he would pose a Talmudic question to the town's students. The one who answered it would receive not only a small fortune in gold coins, but also the rabbi's daughter in marriage.

Naturally, then, by the time the wise old man rode into town, the local folks were thrilled, welcoming him with signs and cheers, lined up by the side of the road in their finery. The rabbi proceeded slowly atop his big, black horse, stroking his long, white beard until he arrived at the dead center of the shtetl. There he stopped and asked his question.

As the townsfolk listened, their faces drooped. The question was a beast, an intricate problem requiring intimate knowledge of just about every category of Jewish law. It was a more difficult riddle than anyone present that day had ever heard, and a few people, despairing, shuffled off before the rabbi was even done speaking. But when he finished asking his question, the old eminence smiled mischievously and told the townsfolk that he'd be staying precisely three days and that anyone who wished to take a stab at an answer should come meet him at the local inn.

The following morning, the rabbi was swarmed by a hundred young men. These weren't the shtetl's best and brightest, merely guys who figured they might as well take a shot at the holy grail. The rabbi listened to their proposed solutions with patience and kindness, but none got it right. The rabbi hugged each one, thanked them all for coming, and sent them all home. The next day, only fifty people showed up. These were smarter cats, students who had spent the previous day cramming in the library and were now equipped with reams of notes. Passionately, they bombarded the rabbi with their theories, all of which were erudite and some of which were brilliant. None, alas, was right. And so, on day three, the rabbi awoke to find but ten men awaiting him. These were the town's elite, the sharpest and most learned, geniuses who'd been up for forty-eight hours straight reading, revising, and grappling with the rabbi's tough question. Each had several leather-bound volumes tucked under his arm, and each was sure that his was the correct answer. The rabbi listened as these brilliant men explained their ideas, each more inventive and impressive than the last. But again, not a single one of them hit the mark.

The following morning, the rabbi woke up early, mounted his horse, and began riding. This time, no one was lined up by the roadside to see him off. The town was silent, stung by its collective failure to rise to the challenge. Just as the rabbi was nearing the edge of town, however, he heard a voice shouting, "Wait!"

Turning around, the rabbi saw a young man running toward him. He was not one of the students who'd attempted answering the question on the three previous days.

"If you're here to take a shot at the question, you're too late," the rabbi said, somewhat haughtily. "You had your chance already. Please return to your home."

The young man was now standing right by the rabbi's horse. "That's not why I'm here," he said, still breathless. "I'm here because I really want to hear the answer."

The rabbi's eyes filled with tears. He jumped off his horse and gave the young man a big, warm hug.

"You, my son," he said. "You are the answer."

And whenever you study the Talmud—which is to say, whenever you engage in trying to connect to others, to yourself, to something higher, to all things lower, to asking questions because asking questions brings clarity, to resisting absolutes because only young children and zealots and machines think in binaries, to connecting to the basic and elemental empathy that reminds us that we're all in this together, just walking each other home—the answer, too, is you.

ACKNOWLEDGMENTS

THOSE WHO attempt to study Torah on their own, Rabbi Yosei bar Hanina instructs us in the Talmud's Tractate Taanit, end up growing foolish, because the task of unlocking the mysteries that matter most isn't for any one person to attempt on their own. As I reflect on the men and the women who did their best to instruct me, I'd like first of all to say that any of my failures to comprehend are mine alone and not a testament to their wisdom and their patience.

First among these great teachers is Rabbi Dovid Bashevkin, who answered my meandering call one cold Thursday afternoon and agreed, on faith, to guide me on a seven year journey of reading the Talmud, one page a day. Even now, many pages and many days later, I remain awed by his fierce mind, his enormous heart, and his ability to find invitations to human dignity and grace in even the seemingly most exacting of phrases. His gift—of faith, of erudition, of empathy—is one I will never be able to repay, but take great pleasure in trying nonetheless.

My dear friend Rabbi Dr. Stuart Halpern continues to inspire me with his passion for learning and his keen insights, seeing the magic of creation even in the most mundane of corners. His constant encouragement and indefatigable organization prompted me, when the spirit was strong but the flesh spongy, to muster the strength I needed, follow his example, and work tirelessly at keeping Judaism's eternal conversation alive. He was also kind enough to read early iterations of this book, and, with superhuman attention to detail, save me from stumbling needlessly.

Stu also introduced me to Yeshiva University, the Hogwarts of the Jewish People, where I met a host of impossibly erudite and endlessly generous people who showed me not only how to study the questions that mattered most but also how to teach them to others. YU's president, Rabbi Dr. Ari Berman, taught me how to force the torrents of modernity into conversation with tradition for the mutual benefit of both, and how to do so with the humility and the insight needed to bring even the most reluctant of learners into the fold. Rabbi Meir Soloveichik continues to dazzle me with his brilliance, his erudition, and his humor, and Dr. Neil Rogachevsky is the best guide I or anyone could've asked for on the journey into the intricacies of Jewish history and thought. Dr. Erica Brown showed me that a working soul is a soul we can bring to work or anywhere else we choose to go, even to those pursuits we don't usually think of as particularly elevated or illuminating. Rabbi Yitzchok Radner put me through Talmud bootcamp, and lovingly but sternly insisted that I come to the Talmud on its own terms and in its own language, Aramaic. And Dr. Shaina Trapedo educated me by showing me the deep Jewish roots not only of Shakespeare but also of much of our most cherished literature. At YU, I've also had the pleasure of getting to know, and of learning from, bright students who delighted me with their curiosity and their commitment. Many are inspiring, but two, Baruch-Lev Kelman and Benjamin Gottesman, stand out.

I'm also indebted to my dear friend Rabbi Dr. Ari Lamm for teaching me so much and for showing me that the spirit of the Talmud is alive everywhere from rap lyrics to must-see TV. Rabbi Motti Seligson remains an important source for renewable spiritual energy, reminding me never to despair, and Rabbi Mordechai Lightstone inspires me with his insistence that the greatest thing a person could be in this world is a lamplighter, lighting the way for others. I am also immensely indebted to my friend Bernard-Henri Lévy, for his ability to see what is broken in our world, his courage to act out to heal it, and his generosity to invite others along for this journey of rebirth. I'm also deeply grateful to Emily Hamilton, for putting her considerable brilliance and boundless energy always in the service of good.

I've had the profound honor of calling W. W. Norton my literary Beit Midrash for years now, but every turn at the hands of the great Amy Cherry is always a distinct pleasure. She is the best rabbi any author could wish for—unrelenting and brilliant and empathic, and always for the sake of heaven, or, at least, for the sake of a book with far fewer adjectives than I would've liked. Also at Norton is Huneeya Siddiqui, who helped enormously to shepherd this book into existence, for which I am grateful. And, as always, my agent and dear friend Anne Edelstein brought her keen mind and her radiant soul into this project, seeing profundities and possibilities where I saw only frustrations and sharpening me as any great rabbi would.

Fourteen years ago, I was fortunate to join in on an adventure of a lifetime, when my dear friend Alana Newhouse called to say she was starting a new magazine and invited me to come on board. That plucky publication, *Tablet*, grew up to be the finest magazine in America, and it is an immense privilege—professionally, personally, emotionally, intellectually, and spiritually—to work with people I love so much and admire so deeply. Each of them deserves an epic poem of their own, but for now, let their names suffice: David Samuels, my great friend, who accelerates me with his brilliance and his warmth; Stephanie Butnick, my partner in podcasting who is every bit as canny and strategic as I am prone to musing; Tanya Singer, who brought sweet order and vision into the whirlwind that is thinking and talking about big ideas; Josh Kross, producer extraordinaire, who captured the voices I heard in my head and made them sound so good on tape; Mark Oppenheimer, Quinn Waller, Darone Ruskay, Robert Scaramuccia, Courtney Hazelett, and Elie Bleier—all are podcasting's best and brightest. I am also greatly indebted to the wise and wonderful Wayne Hoffman, *Tablet*'s executive editor; to Jeremy Stern,

Tablet's deputy editor; to Jacob Siegel, Park MacDougald, Armin Rosen, Sean Cooper, Clayton Fox, Maggie MacFarland Phillips, Noam Blum, Ani Wilcenski, Gabriel Sanders, Matthew Fishbane, Isaac de Castro, Samantha Hacker, Jordana La Rosa, and the inimitable Menachem Butler, whose mind, heart, and hard drive are three of the Jewish people's greatest treasure troves.

If the Talmud is anything, it is very much a conversation between those of us alive today and the sages who no longer walk this earth yet are here for a good argument and a life-changing lesson whenever we open the book. There are so many departed teachers at whose feet I sit still and who I wish I could pepper with questions, but three in particular stand out. Rabbi Adin Even-Israel Steinsaltz, whose unparalleled mind produced the translation and elucidation that made the Talmud accessible to me and to millions of others; Rabbi Lord Jonathan Sacks, who breathed a new spirit of joy, discovery, and transcendence into the ancient teachings of the rabbis; and my own great-great grandfather, Rabbi Yosef Chaim Sonnenfeld, who was as loving and as kind to his fellow Jews as he was fierce and uncompromising in his dedication to studying the words of God. May their merit shield us.

My late grandmother, Rivkah Leah Greller, the daughter of a long line of distinguished Talmudic scholars, would've been delighted to see her grandson taking to the family business. To my mother, Iris Mindlin, for her faith and support, I am deeply thankful. And finally, as ever, to my beloved wife, Lisa Ann Sandell, and to my children, Lily and Hudson: You are my greatest comfort, my wildest joy, my wisest teachers, my engines of enchantment, my everything. My love for you could not be described even if the heavens were parchment, and the forests quills, and if all the seas were ink.

NOTES

INTRODUCTION

1. Babylonian Talmud (BT), Avoda Zarah 17a.
2. Jerusalem Talmud (JT), Sotah 8:3.
3. Pirkei Avot 5.
4. Jonathan Rosen, *The Talmud and the Internet: A Journey between Worlds* (New York: Macmillan, 2000), 6.
5. The question of God's pronouns is a complicated one. Some aspects of the Almighty, like the *shekhinah*, or Divine Presence, are feminine, and a number of references suggest that God is both masculine and feminine and is therefore better understood by using the contemporary pronouns they/them. Some scholars have even argued that the Creator is more of an experience than an entity, therefore transcending pronouns altogether. But for the most part, the Hebrew Bible refers to God repeatedly, consistently, and deliberately as He, a distinction I will replicate in this book without rejecting the objections of those who would prefer to make other choices.
6. Tosafot s.v. *"Ad She-anu Mivakshim Alekha Rahamim."*
7. Rabbi Aharon Lewin, *Ha-derash Ve-HaIyun, Bereishit* (Biłgoraj, Poland: 1928), 119–122.
8. Rabbi Yisroel Shapira, *Binat Yisroel* (Warsaw: 1938), 158–159.
9. Quoted in Shloime Schwartz, "Rabbi Elazar Ben Dordaya: The Master of Teshuvah," in *The Lehrhaus*, August 16, 2021, https://thelehrhaus.com/scholarship/rabbi-elazar-ben-dordaya-the-master-of-teshuvah/.
10. Rabbi Aharon Leib Shteinman, *Yimaleh Pi Tehilatekha*, Volume 1 (Bnei Brak, Israel: 2003), 143.
11. Rosen, *The Talmud and the Internet*, 14.
12. As the modern state of Israel wasn't established until 1948, and as the geographic area where many of this book's protagonists lived was known by many names throughout the centuries, I will refer to it

as most of the rabbis I describe had, as *Eretz Yisrael*, or the Land of Israel.

13. BT Shabbat 112b.
14. BT Avoda Zarah 10b.
15. Mishnah Brachot 1.
16. Avraham Walfish, "Literary Considerations in the Redaction of the Mishnah and Their Meaning," *Netuim* 1 (1994): 38–39.
17. Yakov Nagen, *The Soul of the Mishnah* (New York: Koren Publishers, 2021), 32.
18. BT Brachot 35b.
19. Deuteronomy 11:14.
20. BT Brachot 35b.
21. Jean M. Twenge, "Have Smart Phones Destroyed a Generation?" *The Atlantic*, September 2017, https://www.theatlantic.com/magazine/archive/2017/09/has-the-smartphone-destroyed-a-generation/534198/.
22. Anne Case and Angus, "Rising Morbidity and Mortality in Midlife among White Non-Hispanic Americans in the 21st Century," *Proceedings of the National Academy of Sciences of the USA* 112, no. 49 (2015): 15078–15083, https://www.pnas.org/doi/10.1073/pnas.1518393112.
23. BT Shabbat 31a.

CHAPTER ONE: OUR BODIES, OUR SELVES

1. Jean Nidtech, *The Story of Weight Watchers* (New York: W/W Twentyfirst Corp., 1970), 33.
2. Nidtech, *The Story of Weight Watchers*, 36.
3. Nidtech, *The Story of Weight Watchers*, 81.
4. Nidtech, *The Story of Weight Watchers*, 83.
5. Plato, *Phaedrus*, 250c.
6. Aristotle, *History of Animals*, Book VI, part 15.
7. Louis MacNeice, *Autumn Journal* (London: Faber & Faber, 2001), Kindle location 508.
8. Plato, *Republic*, Book I, 353d.
9. Edith Hall, *Aristotle's Way: How Ancient Wisdom Can Change Your Life* (New York: Penguin, 2020), 25–26.
10. Flavius Josephus, *Against Apion*, Book One, Chapter 22.
11. Josephus, *Against Apion*, Book One, Chapter 22.
12. Herman Gollancz, *Translations from Hebrew and Aramaic* (London, 1908), 117. Quoted in Marvin J. Heller, "Sefer ha-Tappu'ah, The Book of the Apple: Aristotle Expresses an Interest in Jewish Concepts," *Hakirah*, 32 (Fall 2022): 273–286.
13. Babylonian Talmud (BT) Yoma 69a.

14. Tosefta Nazir 4:7.
15. BT Yoma 35b.
16. BT Yoma 35b.
17. Avot DeRabi Natan, Nusach Bet, 30.
18. Vayikra Rabbah 34.
19. Binyamin Lau, *Chachamim*, Vol. 1 (Jerusalem: The Jewish Agency for Israel, 2006), 183.
20. BT Beitzah 16a.
21. BT Beitzah 16a.
22. BT Shabbat 31a.
23. Pirkei Avot 2:4.
24. Jerusalem Talmud (JT), Sanhedrin 22a.

CHAPTER TWO: ALL TOGETHER NOW

1. John C. Esposito, *Fire in the Grove: The Cocoanut Grove Tragedy and Its Aftermath* (New York: Da Capo Press, 2006), Kindle location 326.
2. Esposito, *Fire in the Grove*, location 36.
3. Cited in John C. Nemiah, *Foundations of Psychopathology* (Oxford: Oxford University Press, 1966), 152.
4. Erich Lindemann, "Grief and Grief Management: Some Reflections," *Journal of Pastoral Care* 30, no. 3 (September 1976): 198. Quoted in Eva K. Rosenfeld, "The Fire That Changed the Way We Think about Grief," *Harvard Crimson*, November 29, 2018, https://www.thecrimson .com/article/2018/11/29/erich-lindemann-cocoanut-grove-fire-grief/.
5. Lindemann, "Grief and Grief Management," 198.
6. Jonathan Rosen, *The Talmud and the Internet: A Journey between Worlds* (New York: Macmillan, 2000), 54.
7. Babylonian Talmud (BT), Gittin 55b.
8. BT Sukkah 28a.
9. BT Gittin 56b.
10. BT Gittin 56b.
11. Avot deRabbi Natan, 4, 5.
12. Elie Wiesel, *One Generation After* (New York: Knopf, 2011), 194.
13. Wiesel, *One Generation After*, 194.
14. BT Bava Batra 60b.
15. BT Bava Batra 60b.
16. Avot deRabbi Natan, Nusach Alef, 6.
17. BT Shabbat 153a.
18. Pirkei Avot 2:8.
19. BT Bava Metzia 59b.
20. BT Bava Metzia 59b.

21. BT Sanhedrin 68a.
22. BT Sanhedrin 68a.
23. Deuteronomy 30:11–14.
24. Walt Whitman, "Song of Myself," in *Walt Whitman: Poetry and Prose* (New York: Library of America, 1982), 203.

CHAPTER THREE: HOLDING OUT FOR A HERO

1. Erich Auerbach, *Dante: Poet of the Secular World* (New York: New York Review of Books, 2007), 44.
2. Quoted in Arthur Krystal, "The Book of Books," *New Yorker*, December 9, 2013.
3. Kader Konuk, *East West Mimesis: Auerbach in Turkey* (Stanford: Stanford University Press, 2010), 133.
4. Erich Auerbach, *Mimesis* (Princeton, NJ: Princeton University Press, 1953), 3.
5. Auerbach, *Mimesis*, 12.
6. Auerbach, *Mimesis*, 13.
7. Babylonian Talmud (BT), Pesachim 49b.
8. BT Ketubot 62b.
9. BT Nedarim 50a.
10. Proverbs 12:10.
11. Avot deRabbi Natan, 6.
12. Avot deRabbi Natan, 6.
13. Exodus 8:15.
14. Exodus 14:31.
15. Barry Holtz, *Rabbi Akiva* (New Haven, CT: Yale University Press, 2017), 108.
16. BT Menachot 29b.
17. Mishnaha, Rosh Hashanah 2:9.
18. In Holtz, *Rabbi Akiva*, p. 111.
19. BT Semachot 4:34.
20. BT Berakhot 27b.
21. Jerusalem Talmud (JT), Berakhot 4:1:34.
22. Sifre Devarim.
23. Søren Kierkegaard, *Works of Love* (Princeton, NJ: Princeton University Press, 1949), 37.
24. BT Yevamot 16a.
25. Song of Songs Rabbah 1:27.
26. BT Chagigah 15b.
27. W. H. Auden, "The Christian Tragic Hero," *New York Times Book Review*, December 16, 1945, 1.

28. Numbers 24:17.
29. BT Yevamot 62b.
30. BT Berakhot 60b.
31. BT Berakhot 61b.
32. BT Berakhot 61b.

CHAPTER FOUR: ROMANCE IN THE DARK

1. Billie Holiday, *Lady Sings the Blues* (New York: Crown, 2006), 7.
2. Holiday, *Lady Sings the Blues*, 9.
3. John Chilton, *The Song of Hawk: The Life and Recordings of Coleman Hawkins* (Ann Arbor: University of Michigan Press, 1993), 2.
4. Leonard Feather, *The Book of Jazz* (New York: Bonanza Books, 1965), 90.
5. Tom Vitale, "Lester Young: 'The Prez' Still Rules at 100," NPR's *Morning Edition*, August 27, 2009, https://www.npr.org/2009/08/27/112255870/lester-young-the-prez-still-rules-at-100.
6. James Maycock, "Billie Holiday and Lester Young: The Intimate Friendship between Lady Day and Prez," *The Guardian*, April 8, 2015, https://www.theguardian.com/music/2015/apr/08/billie-holiday-and-lester-young-friendship-between-lady-day-and-prez.
7. Holiday, *Lady Sings the Blues*, 146.
8. Babylonian Talmud (BT), Bava Kamma 38a.
9. BT Yevamot 63b.
10. Daniel Boyarin, *Carnal Israel: Reading Sex in Talmudic Culture* (Berkeley: University of California Press, 1993), 134.
11. BT Avoda Zara 18a.
12. BT Gittin 56a.
13. BT Eruvin 13b.
14. Jerusalem Talmud (JT), Moed Kattan 3:5.
15. JT Sotah 1:4.
16. BT Berakhot 10a.
17. Plato, *Laws* 5, 731d.
18. Isaiah 54:1.
19. BT Berakhot 10a.
20. BT Eruvin 53b.
21. BT Berakhot 62a.
22. BT Nedarim 20a.
23. BT Yoma 66b.
24. BT Nedarim 20b.
25. Pirkei Avot 1:5.
26. Tosefta Kelim 141:4.

27. BT Pesachim 62b.
28. BT Eruvin 54a.
29. Job 1:21.
30. Midrash Mishlei 31:2.
31. Leonard Cohen, "The Future," in *The Future*, Columbia Records, 1992.
32. BT Avoda Zara 18b.
33. BT Avoda Zara 18a-b.
34. Eitam Henkin, *Studies in Halakha and Rabbinic History* (Jerusalem: Koren, 2022), 127.

CHAPTER FIVE: EVERYTHING IN ORDER

1. Wayne A. Wiegand, *Irrepressible Reformer: A Biography of Melvil Dewey* (Chicago: ALA Editions, 1996), 7.
2. Joseph Cundall, *On Ornamental Art* (London: Society of the Arts, 1848), 14.
3. BT, Tractate Gittin, 59a.
4. BT, Tractate Kiddushin, 72b.
5. JT Maasrot 3:1.
6. Exodus 20:8.
7. Deuteronomy 5:12.
8. BT Shabbat 33b.
9. BT Bava Metzia 84b.
10. JT Shabbat 10:5.
11. BT Eruvin 86a.
12. BT Nedarim 50b.
13. BT Chulin 7b.
14. BT Berakhot 16a.
15. BT Bava Metzia 85a.
16. JT Kilayim 9:3.
17. Plato, *Phaedrus*.
18. Genesis 1:26.
19. Genesis 2:7.
20. Exodus 21:7.
21. Deuteronomy 25:6.
22. For more on this, see David S. Katz, *The Jews in the History of England, 1485–1850* (Oxford: Clarendon Press, 1997).
23. Quoted in Shalom Carmy, "Don't Stop Hoping for Redemption: Religious Optimism and the Meaning of Life," *Tradition* 39, no. 3 (2006): 1–6.
24. Carmy, "Don't Stop Hoping for Redemption," 1–6.

25. Christopher Lasch, *The True and Only Heaven: Progress and Its Critics* (New York: W. W. Norton, 1991), 80–81.
26. Carmy, "Don't Stop Hoping for Redemption," 1–6.
27. Dovid Bashevkin, "Family Ties," *Tablet*, July 7, 2022, tabletmag.com/sections/belief/articles/family-ties-tractate-yevamot.
28. Bashevkin, "Family Ties."
29. Isaiah 57:2.
30. BT Ketubot 104a.

CHAPTER SIX: THANK YOU FOR BEING A FRIEND

1. C. S. Lewis, *The Four Loves* (London: Geoffrey Bles, 1960), 126.
2. C. S. Lewis, *All My Road Before Me: The Diary of C. S. Lewis, 1922–1927* (New York: HarperOne, 2017), 524.
3. Quoted in Philip Zaleski and Carol Zaleski, *The Fellowship: The Literary Lives of the Inklings* (New York: Farrar, Straus and Giroux, 2015), 177.
4. Zaleski and Zaleski, *The Fellowship*, 177.
5. J. R. R. Tolkien, *The Letters of J. R. R. Tolkien*, ed. Humphrey Carpenter (Boston: Houghton Mifflin, 2013), 219–220.
6. Available at https://home.agh.edu.pl/~evermind/jrrtolkien/mythopoeia.htm.
7. Available at https://home.agh.edu.pl/~evermind/jrrtolkien/mythopoeia.htm.
8. C. S. Lewis, *The Collected Letters of C. S. Lewis, Volume I: Family Letter, 1905–1931*, ed. Walter Hooper (New York: HarperCollins, 2000), 969–970.
9. Lewis, *The Collected Letters*, 973.
10. C. S. Lewis, *The Collected Letters of C. S. Lewis, Volume II: Books, Broadcasts, and the War*, ed. Walter Hooper (New York: HarperCollins, 2004), 96.
11. Tolkien, *Letters*, 23.
12. George Sayer, *Jack: A Life of C. S. Lewis* (Wheaton, IL: Crossway, 2005), 312.
13. Tolkien, *Letters*, 361.
14. Pirkei Avot 1:6.
15. BT Shabbat 108a.
16. BT Zevachim 26a.
17. JT Pe'ah 8:8.
18. JT Pe'ah 8:8.
19. BT Sukkah 53a.
20. BT Bava Batra 55a.

21. BT Yoma 20b.
22. BT Yoma 20b.
23. BT Bava Kama 117a.
24. BT Kiddushin 44b.
25. Stuart Halpern, "The Fast for the Furious," *Tablet*, September 21, 2020, https://www.tabletmag.com/sections/belief/articles/fast-for-furious -tzom-gedaliah.
26. Midrash Shir HaShirim Rabbah, 8:7.
27. BT Brachot 20a.
28. BT Bava Metzia 84a.
29. BT Bava Metzia 84a.
30. BT Bava Metzia 84a.
31. BT Shabbat 114a.
32. BT Bava Batra 58a.
33. BT Shabbat 10a.
34. BT Bava Metzia 84a.
35. BT Bava Batra 5a.
36. BT Ketubot 54b.
37. BT Bava Metzia 84a.

CHAPTER SEVEN: THE STORIES WE TELL

1. The portrait of Ames is drawn largely from *An Assessment of the Aldrich H. Ames Espionage Case and Its Implications for U.S. Intelligence: Report Prepared by the Staff of the Select Committee on Intelligence, United States Senate* [84-046] (Washington: U. S. Government Printing Office, 1994), as well as from Tim Weiner, David Johnston, and Neil A. Lewis, *Betrayal: The Story of Aldrich Ames, an American Spy* (New York: Random House, 1995).
2. Babylonian Talmud (BT), Moed Katan 28a.
3. Avinoam Cohen, *Ravina and the Sages of His Generation* (Tel Aviv: Bar-Ilan University Press, 2001), 23.
4. Adin Steinsaltz, *Personalities in the Talmud* (Tel Aviv: Ministry of Defense Publishing, 1987), 82. Translation mine.
5. Proverbs 6:3.
6. Richard Hidary, "Make Yourself Available to Forgive," in *High Holidays Reader* (New York: Tebah, 2009), 38–44.
7. Emanuel Levinas, *Nine Talmudic Readings*, trans. Annette Aronowicz (Bloomington: Indiana University Press, 2019), 39.
8. Martha Minow, "Stories in Law," in *Law's Stories*, ed. Peter Brooks and Paul D. Gewirtz (New Haven, CT: Yale University Press, 1996), 36.

9. Barry Scott Wimpfheimer, *Narrating the Law: A Poetics of Talmudic Legal Stories* (Philadelphia: University of Pennsylvania Press, 2011), 50.

10. BT Sanhedrin, 75a.

11. Wimpfheimer, *Narrating the Law*, 60.

12. Levinas, *Nine Talmudic Readings*, 116.

EPILOGUE

1. Leonard Cohen, "Going Home," in *Old Ideas*, Columbia Records, 2012.

INDEX